Performing Kinship

PERFORMING KINSHIP

Narrative, Gender, and

the Intimacies of Power

in the Andes

Krista E. Van Vleet

UNIVERSITY OF TEXAS PRESS   AUSTIN

Requests for permission to reproduce
material from this work should be sent to:
    Permissions
    University of Texas Press
    P.O. Box 7819
    Austin, TX 78713-7819
    www.utexas.edu/utpress/about/
        bpermission.html

⊗ The paper used in this book meets the
minimum requirements of ANSI/NISO
Z39.48-1992 (R1997) (Permanence of
Paper).

Library of Congress Cataloging-in-
Publication Data

Van Vleet, Krista E., 1965–
Performing kinship : narrative, gender, and
the intimacies of power in the Andes / by
Krista E. Van Vleet. — 1st ed.
p. cm.
Includes bibliographical references and
index.
ISBN 978-0-292-71707-7 (cl. : alk. paper)
ISBN 978-0-292-71708-4 (pbk. : alk. paper)
1. Quechua women—Bolivia—Social
conditions. 2. Kinship—Bolivia. 3. Oral
tradition—Bolivia. 4. Bolivia—Social
conditions—1982– I. Title.
F2230.2.K4V368 2008
305.48'8983230984—dc22
                            2007030971

For Lawrence

CONTENTS

ACKNOWLEDGMENTS

WHILE RESEARCHING AND writing this book, I have relied upon the generous support of many institutions and individuals. Over the course of many years, I have been fortunate to receive fellowships to fund both field research in Bolivia and writing in the United States. My original fieldwork in Bolivia was funded by a Fulbright-Hays Dissertation Research Abroad Fellowship and a Horace H. Rackham Thesis Grant. At the University of Michigan, I wrote the initial analysis as a doctoral dissertation supported by the Institute for Research on Women and Gender, the Horace H. Rackham School of Graduate Studies, and the Department of Anthropology. I also received a generous predoctoral fellowship from the Andrew W. Mellon Foundation. Bowdoin College has supported my research and writing through a Kenan Fellowship, various awards from the Faculty Research and Travel Fund, and a generous sabbatical leave. A Richard Carley Hunt Postdoctoral Fellowship from the Wenner-Gren Foundation for Anthropological Research provided crucial support during the revision process. I gratefully acknowledge each of these institutions.

Several people have challenged and inspired me from the time I initially conceived of the project through moments of uncertainty and creative revisioning to the final stages of editing. Bruce Mannheim has provided critical advice and encouragement since I began the research for this project more than a decade ago. The influence of his scholarship is evident in the pages of this book. I have also benefited from the incisive scholarship and the generous mentoring of Tom Fricke, Jennifer Robertson, and Sabine MacCormack. Thanks to my fellow graduate students at the University of Michigan for stimulating discussions inside and outside the classroom. I am greatly appreciative of each of my colleagues in the Department of Sociology and Anthropology at Bowdoin College, who offered advice and encouragement at critical moments. Anne Henshaw patiently answered my questions about maps, and Bob Gardner painstakingly prepared the index. Special thanks to Nancy Riley, who read the entire manuscript and has been generous with her time and energy in so many ways.

In addition to the individuals named above, many other people have also read parts of this book. I have also benefited from the perspectives of Denise Arnold, Rossana Barragán, Susan Bell, Coralynn Davis, Lelia DeAndrade, Sara Dickey, Carolyn Greenhouse, Julie Hastings, Oren Kosansky, Diane Lakein, Charlene Makely, Matt Tomlinson, Gina Ulysse, Gary Urton, Mary Weismantel, and Katherine Zirbel. I have presented parts of this book at various conferences, where the comments of Robert Albro, Andrew Canessa, Daniel Goldstein, Janet Hart, David Nugent, Susan Paulson, and Maria Tapias have provided me with valuable insights. My understandings of narrative and of kinship and gender have been enhanced by lively discussions in two interdisciplinary and intercollegial study groups, the Narrative Study Group in Cambridge, Massachusetts, under the mentorship of Elliot Mishler, and the Colby-Bates-Bowdoin Working Group on Gender and Family. Katherine Dauge-Roth was a wonderful writing partner on a writing retreat in 2004, and a decade earlier Susanna Loeb enabled me to attend a conference on kinship in the Andes. I thank them both for their friendship and collegiality. I was fortunate to receive wonderfully thoughtful commentaries on an earlier draft of this book from Marcia Stephenson and an anonymous reviewer at the University of Texas Press. I am grateful for the keen editorial eyes of Leslie Tingle and Kathy Lewis. Theresa May has offered kind words and wisdom throughout the publication process. All shortcomings, of course, are my own responsibility.

Several people have helped make my trips to Bolivia memorable and enjoyable as well as productive. I first want to thank Luis Morató Peña and Primitivo Nina Llanos, who have taught me much about the Quechua language. Marianela Méndez has helped me transcribe tapes and has patiently refreshed my memory of Quechua on my research trips since 2001. Special thanks go to Antero Klemola and Martha Tango for welcoming me into their home whenever I arrive in Sucre. Verónica Cereceda and the late Gabriel Martínez initially suggested that I conduct research around the provincial town of Pocoata, Bolivia. Gary Urton encouraged me along that path at a crucial juncture during my initial dissertation fieldwork. Thanks also to Freddy and Angélica Chavez and their family, Desiderio and Dionysia Cocha, Ginger Hamby and Helmut Rogg, Ann Lindemann, Kathy Plume, Ermelinda Ramírez, Herminia Ríos de Ibañez and family, Caroline Stem, Mamerto and Cristina Torres, and Vicki and Paul Wilabeek-LeMaire, who offered friendship and comfort in Sucre and La Paz. I will always be grateful to Melanie Gunn for accompanying my daughter and me to Bolivia in 2003. Melanie helped Isabel cope with an unfamiliar language and culture and proved to be a fabulous travel companion as well as a great friend.

I am also thankful for my family, who have supported my intellectual endeavors over the years and—just as important—have also been there for me in so many other ways: Mark and Lisa Klein, David and Claudia Kovacs, Diane Kovacs, Dr. Ernest and Rhonda Kovacs, Peter and Gail Schneider, Jim and Carmella Van Vleet, Matthew Van Vleet, and David and Amanda Van Vleet. Each of them has made this book about relatedness more meaningful to me.

Lyle and Marian Van Vleet, my parents, deserve a very special thank-you for raising me and for teaching me how to build foundations under my dreams.

Although I cannot name them individually, I have incurred many debts among the people of Sullk'ata. This book could not have been written without their generosity. In particular, the women of the community that I have called Kallpa were patient teachers, friends, comadres, and neighbors.

Finally, a heartfelt thank-you to Lawrence Kovacs, my husband, and to Isabel and Sophia, our daughters, who ground me and inspire me every day.

AUTHOR'S NOTE: Portions of Chapter 2 appeared in "Partial Theories: On Gossip, Envy and Ethnography in the Andes," *Ethnography* 4(4) (2003): 491–519. Chapter 4 includes material previously published in Bruce Mannheim and Krista Van Vleet, "The Dialogics of Southern Quechua Narrative," *American Anthropologist* 100(2) (1998): 326–346. An earlier version of Chapter 7 was previously published as "The Intimacies of Power: Rethinking Violence and Kinship in the Andes," *American Ethnologist* 29(3) (2002): 567–601. All are used with permission, which is gratefully acknowledged. Unless otherwise noted, all photographs and all translations are by the author.

ALTHOUGH I HAVE written this book in English, three other languages appear on its pages. The research for this book was conducted primarily in Bolivian Quechua. It was originally the language used by the Inca to administer their far-flung territories in the Andean region, but millions of people still speak Quechua today. I use many Quechua terms throughout the text and have relied on several Quechua dictionaries and grammar books (Cusihuamán 1976; Herrero and Sánchez de Lozada 1983; Lara 1991; and Morató and Morató 1993). All Quechua words and phrases are italicized at first use but are otherwise unmarked. Spanish terms are italicized at first use and indicated by the abbreviation "Sp." The indigenous language Aymara appears in a few instances, indicated by the abbreviation "Ay."

For many place names, I follow the customary spelling rather than proper orthography. For example I spell the name of the provincial town Pocoata as it appears in most maps and documents. The Quechua spelling of the word would be Pukwata. Personal names follow the Spanish spelling in most cases. Except where indicated otherwise, the stress in Quechua words is always placed on the penultimate syllable. The Quechua plural -kuna indicates a collection of several similar things and is not strictly equivalent to the English plural. In most cases, however, I have pluralized Quechua words by using the English plural –*s*. In a few instances both singular and plural are indicated by one word (e.g., *arku*). When a word is drawn from Spanish I use the Spanish plural –*s*.

The Quechua language was first written in the context of Spanish colonialism, which has influenced its orthography. One controversial aspect has been whether Quechua should be written with three vowels or with five (as in Spanish). In most cases, I have followed the system of using three vowels: /a/ like the *a* in "all," /i/ like the *i* in "hit," and /u/ like the *oo* in "hoot." I have limited my use of /e/ and /o/ (which are variants of /i/ and /u/, respectively) to unassimilated Spanish words.

Quechua speakers recognize several consonant sounds. English speakers use some of these sounds but do not recognize them as indicating different meanings. For example, the *t* in "tan" is aspirated (carries a breath behind it), in contrast to the *t* in "hit," which is unaspirated. Quechua speakers would recognize these as two distinct consonants: the aspirated consonant is /th/ as in *thanta* (old, ragged) and the unaspirated consonant is /t/ as in *tanta* (together). In addition, some consonants in Quechua use a voiceless glottal stop, in which the flow of air in the throat is stopped momentarily. This is indicated by an apostrophe: /t'/ as in *t'anta* (bread). English *ch*, *k*, *p*, *q*, and *t* all have these three variants in Quechua. Some consonants are similar to those in English (for example, /m/ as in "man") or in Spanish (for example, /ll/ as in *llama*). Finally, certain sounds appear only in words derived from Spanish: /d/ like the *d* in "dog," /f/ like the *f* in "fun," /g/ like the *g* in "great," and /v/ like the *v* in "vet."

ONE

Introduction

Relative Intimacies, Storied Lives

Relatedness in Sullk'ata

PEOPLE WHO LIVE in the rural Andean highlands of Sullk'ata, Bolivia, establish "relatedness"—that is, bonds of belonging and affiliation—through their interactions with each other. They create and maintain relatedness through habitual everyday activities such as eating together, sharing work, and sleeping under the same roof. Sullk'atas also navigate their relationships with each other through more intensely emotional performances and occasionally violent interactions—and stories about them. A woman wonders how the child she helped raise has forgotten that she is also his mother. Elderly couples sorrow for children who have migrated to cities and are "no longer Sullk'atas." People gossip about brothers whose envy for each other causes harm to befall them. Married adults—men and women—tell folktales about young lovers who run away together only to meet with dire consequences. Women—alternately angry, matter-of-fact, or resigned—recount the physical and emotional pain of being hit by a loved one, a husband, or a mother-in-law. In these everyday performances and narratives, Sullk'atas create social relationships, navigate inequalities of power, and negotiate the meanings of the expected and the extraordinary events of their lives.

In this book I develop critical perspectives on the cultural construction of social relationships that take kinship as their core but not as their boundary. I illuminate relatedness through a double focus. An ethnographically grounded discussion of the intimacies and hierarchies of kinship and gender among Quechua speakers who live in the rural region of Sullk'ata, Bolivia, is the heart of the book. My own negotiation of relationships with Sullk'atas is a secondary but analytically significant nexus of reflection. By highlighting the everyday talk and practices of Sullk'atas, and especially the telling and retelling of stories, I show how relatedness is a mutual production among people, including the ethnographer and her informants. People interpret meanings and relationships *in process.* Thus this book underscores the local details of events and interactions and demonstrates the collaboration and conflict through which relatedness emerges.

Rather than being based on some essential biological relationship or on static social structures, relatedness emerges among individuals who have differing life experiences and move within and between communities that are marginal to but not isolated from national discourses or global processes. Even in small rural communities, people express and enact a complex heterogeneity of identities and ideals, material needs and political concerns, dreams and lived experiences. Tracing these differences among women, as well as between men and women, brings to light significant webs of social, economic, political, and emotional support and tension.

Retelling a Story of Violence

The ways in which Sullk'atas evoke and perform their connections and disconnections with each other in domains including but not limited to kinship were brought forcefully into my awareness one day near the end of June 1996. I had been living in a Sullk'ata community for a year and a half, conducting ethnographic field research, hearing people's stories, and participating in their daily lives as much as I could. I had just returned from the city of Sucre after saying good-bye to friends, for I was soon to return to the United States. Dusty and stiff after eight hours on a bus with shock absorbers and seat springs that had long since deteriorated, I shouldered my backpack for the walk to Kallpa. Though she was far ahead, I recognized Claudina, a middle-aged woman from Kallpa. Her brilliant turquoise *pollera* (the full skirt typical of native Andean women) stood out against the multiple shades of brown of the landscape: low adobe buildings, already plowed fields, and rounded mountains too dry and high to support trees. A patchwork of green laced with the purple and white flowers of potato plants had brightened the landscape during the short rainy season from December to March, but the harvest had already begun. The grazing areas and *chakra*s (planted fields) that stretched out from either side of the road were fading to the dun of winter. I caught up with Claudina easily. I had not lost my habit of walking quickly, even after a year and a half of living in this rural region of the Bolivian Andes. Claudina and I greeted one another and climbed together, resting for a short while at the top of the pass, where we could see the steep yet rounded mountains rising as a wall behind the community of Kinsa Kallpa. "Where have you come from?" Claudina asked me. I told her that I had just come from Sucre.

Descending from the pass, I wondered aloud, "Has my comadre Ilena returned from Cochabamba yet?" I did not want to leave Kallpa without saying good-bye to Ilena. Claudina's reply surprised me. She said: "She's already gone again. That woman is angry." I prodded her to tell me more. I had been living in Ilena's household for over a year and had become close to her and her family. "Ilena's husband hit her," Claudina informed me. "Ilena has gone to see a judge in Pocoata to ask that someone be arrested." Although I had heard of violent incidents between other community members (brothers; sisters-in-law, mothers-in-law, and daughters-in-law; as well as spouses), I had never seen any evidence of violence between Ilena and Marcelino.

Concerned by Claudina's news, in Ilena's absence I tried to find out more about what had happened. One woman told me that a lot of talk about Ilena had been circulating in the community during the week I had been gone. The week before my own trip to Sucre, Ilena had gone to the city of Cochabamba to visit her oldest children. She left her husband, Marcelino, in charge of their two youngest children, twelve and ten years old. Ilena's visit lasted longer than expected. Even before I left for Sucre, people began asking Marcelino about Ilena's whereabouts. One woman told me that on the night before Ilena finally arrived home a man named Julio had been prodding Ilena's husband, asking, "Where is your wife? Where is your wife?" The two men were drunk; they had been pouring libations and drinking at a funeral. When Ilena returned home the next morning, Marcelino scolded her, accusing her of infidelity. Claudina suggested that Marcelino might have said to Ilena, "Where have you been! Are we going to separate now?" Another woman said that perhaps Marcelino had asked Ilena, "Why would Julio ask me, 'Where is your wife?' Maybe you are walking with him now!"

I assumed that Ilena had gone to the judge in Pocoata to ask that her husband be arrested. A law against domestic violence had been signed in December 1995 by President Gonzalo Sánchez de Lozada. Supported and promoted by international development organizations such as United Nations Children's

Fund (UNICEF), the law had received much media attention. The commercial that aired most often on Sullk'ata radios began with a woman crying and a man yelling in the background. A male voiceover then said, "I have seen many women come to my medical clinic like this. Now, with the Law against Familial Violence, women are protected." Ilena knew about the law, for we had heard the commercials together many times as we sat preparing dinner.

When I finally had the chance to talk with Ilena late in the afternoon the next day, I realized that I was mistaken. Ilena had not gone to the judge to complain about her husband's violence. More subdued than usual but with no apparent bruises or cuts, Ilena explained that her husband had hit her because of the envy and gossip of other people in the community. First, she told me, she went to the godmother of her marriage (*madrina de matrimonio*, Sp.) to ask for advice.[1] Her godmother, who lived in the town of Pocoata, encouraged her to see the judge. The judge told Ilena that other people should not be gossiping about her: "They should not be talking about you, they have no reason." Ilena added: "But they talk and talk, and then when Marcelino is drunk he hits me. He hits me then because of their talk about me. The señoras talk a lot, don't they? It's because of envy [*envidia*, Sp.]." Ilena told me that people envied her because she earned money by selling corn beer and because three of her children were at the university in Cochabamba. I suspected that she was envied for other reasons as well, including my presence in her household. Although envy is understood by Sullk'atas to cause physical and metaphysical damage to the envied person, the harm cannot be easily tracked back to any particular individual.

I did not have long to contemplate Ilena's analysis of the situation. The provincial judge arrived in Kallpa the following day. He had walked for more than two hours along the unpaved road in his black dress shoes in order to reach the community. On his back he carried a manual typewriter wrapped in a colorful machine-made carrying cloth. The church bells rang to announce a meeting, and community members gathered on top of the low rise just beyond the barren central plaza. The judge introduced the purpose of his visit without much preamble, speaking about the problem involving three community members: Marcelino, Ilena, and Julio. He allowed each of them in turn to state his or her view of what had happened. Then the judge reprimanded the community members for "not living like brothers and sisters" and told Julio that he must publicly apologize for his malicious talk. Julio complied, going first to Marcelino and Ilena and then around the circle of gathered community members, bending down to shake hands, clasp elbows, and kiss each person in a highly formalized gesture of respect. Julio said that he had been drunk and could not remember exactly what he had said to Marcelino that night.[2]

The judge set up his typewriter on a chair that someone had carried out from the primary school. Outside in the wind he typed a document, an "Act of Contrition," using carbon paper in triplicate. Those present at the meeting had discussed the judge's suggestion that a fine be levied on people who talk maliciously about others in the community. Few wanted to contribute to the conversation. While the judge typed, most of the community members who had come to the meeting wandered away, silently walking down the hill back to their homes, ignoring the judge's calls to wait. Only a few remained to sign the document or mark their thumbprint upon the page. In the agreement, which he read to those still assembled, the judge had written that there should be no more talking about each other within the community. If someone maligned another person, whether drunk or not, in the presence of witnesses, then a fine of 1,000 bolivianos (at that time roughly US$250) could be levied, an exorbitant amount of money for most people of the community.

A few days after the community meeting, I traveled again, saddened by leaving behind the friends that I had made in Sullk'ata and burdened with unanswered questions about the events of my last week. As it turned out, I would not be able to make a return trip to Kallpa until five years later, in August 2001. By then Ilena and her husband had migrated from the community to the city of Cochabamba so that the entire family could live together while the remainder of their children attended high school.

This incident allows no simple interpretation, yet it may serve as a touchstone for exploring the intimacies and hierarchies of relatedness and examining the construction of reality through everyday interactions. Drawn from my informal conversations with Sullk'atas, my observation and tape-recording of the community meeting, and my fieldnotes on the events of that week, the story that I have pieced together is not simply a tale of gendered violence in which a man abuses a woman or of the power hierarchy within a marriage. The series of events also indicates a woman's active attempts to contest public opinion. In claiming to be envied and to be harmed by that envy, Ilena endeavors to maintain a particular kind of relationship with her husband. She also negotiates other relationships as well, consolidating associations and coping with antagonisms, through her interactions with her godmother, the judge, the resident anthropologist, her children, and other Sullk'ata women. Although it shows the ways in which state authorities intervene in the intimate lives of individuals, the story also reflects the ways in which Ilena's "private" business circulated in gossip. Long before I inscribed Sullk'atas' interactions in my fieldnotes or in the pages of this book, stories of this incident were told and retold. Balanced in part on the recognition of certain categorical relationships, these events also indicate how relationships e performed and constituted by individuals. In this situation, and in far more mundane circumstances, the talk and actions of Ilena and other Sullk'atas produce affective, social, political, and economic bonds.

This story and other stories threaded throughout the book illuminate the notion that relationships (between husbands and wives; brothers and sisters; parents and children; neighbors, strangers, and compadres; gringos and native Andeans) are subject to individual idiosyncrasies, local and national discourses, and the contingencies of events. These stories also serve to open windows onto broader issues. How do we understand the ways in which violence emerges among family members in spite of ideals of closeness, sociality, and conviviality? What might stories, and the act of telling stories, reveal to us about everyday life and social relationships? How do we represent others, recognizing both the structured configurations and the contingencies of their lives? In the pages that follow, I situate this storied example by briefly describing two broad theoretical and methodological currents—one based on gender, kinship, and power and the other on narrative and dialogism—and by discussing the context and methodology of my research in Sullk'ata.

Gender, Kinship, and Power

More than two decades ago, anthropologist Michelle Rosaldo (1980b:408–409) challenged scholars to examine not only the intricacies of kinship relationships but the hierarchies as well. Noting that "few analysts probe the various *contents* of familial bonds or ask how varying relationships within the home might influence relationships outside it," she urged us to acknowledge the ways in which our ideas about families are so commonsensical that the specific affective, social, political, and economic parameters of other people and places are lost in our assumptions.

> [T]hat people elsewhere do not view domestic groupings as the close familial groups we know, that warmth and altruism are rarely the unique prerogatives of close coresident kin—in short, that we cannot presume to know just what, in any case, it means to be a parent, sibling, spouse or child—are things too rarely probed because we start by thinking that we know just what the answers are. (Rosaldo 1980b:408–409)

Since the turn of the twentieth century, anthropologists had done much to demonstrate that kinship structures varied widely across cultures. But by the 1970s Rosaldo and other feminist anthropologists were criticizing the ways in

which anthropological analyses tied women to a "domestic sphere" or a specific "biological nature" (reproductive role or hormonal constitution) in their
analyses of kinship. Drawing on her ethnographic work among the Ilongot of
the Philippines and her engagement with feminist theory, Rosaldo argued for
a further rethinking of the affective, social, and political bonds that link people
together.

Integrating Gender and Kinship

Feminist anthropologists had already begun to question universal categories
and the naturalness of particular relationships when they debated both the universality and the origins of women's subordination to men in the 1970s.[3]

In a foundational work, Jane Collier and Sylvia Yanagisako (1987) integrated
this attention to the cultural construction of gender with an attention to kinship. They first highlighted North American conceptions of gender by question-
ing "whether the *particular* biological difference in reproductive function that
our culture defines as the basis of difference between males and females . . . is
used by other societies to constitute the cultural categories of male and female"
(Yanagisako and Collier 1987:48; my emphasis). They then criticized the parallel
relationship between sexual reproduction and kinship—namely, the assumption
that sexual reproduction is the universal biological base of kinship. In doing
so, they recognized that gender and kinship might be unified into one field of
analysis.

Collier and Yanagisako drew on the earlier work of David Schneider (1968,
1972, 1984), who famously argued that the category of kinship should be dis-
carded. Based on a symbolic analysis of North American kinship, Schneider
(1968) demonstrated that "kinship" as an analytical category was grounded in
European and North American concerns, specifically the notion reflected in the
phrase "blood is thicker than water." Kinship analysis as practiced by anthropologists thus obscured rather than illuminated locally significant categories and
relationships.[4] Not satisfied with a symbolic analysis, Collier and Yanagisako integrated attention to gender and power. Their argument has been productive,
leading to studies examining the variety of ways in which people in different social contexts and historical moments understand reproduction and addressing
socially significant relationships based upon different arrays of "natural facts."

Like other scholars I have found gender to be crucial to making sense of
Sullk'ata kinship. "Gender" here refers not simply to women. It is an analytic
category in which the differences, and the power asymmetries, between men
and women are *denaturalized*—located in particular historical moments, social

institutions, cultural meanings, and political economies.[5] In the 1980s scholars and activists also pointed out that identity and inequality are experienced along multiple trajectories simultaneously. Consequently, gender cannot be experientially or analytically isolated from other aspects of power, such as race or sexuality.[6] In other words, it is necessary to examine the "differences among women" as well as the differences between women and men to understand gender. Age, affinity (or in-law relationships), race, and class are among the important categories that mutually reinforce or constrain gender in Sullk'ata. Although gender is not always the most salient nexus of power, and rarely stands alone, gender is rarely absent from everyday social life.

Attention to power relationships has been integrally linked to gender analysis and thus to the new kinship studies.[7] One of the ways in which scholars have traced hierarchies has been to explore how kinship and gender, as well as other domains such as race, are normalized (e.g., Yanagisako and Delany 1995). The "naturalness" of certain categories or identities or actions seems to emerge from an individual's personal experience, obscuring the ways in which these are also structured and always entail relations of domination and subordination, as Michel Foucault (1972, 1978) has demonstrated. Practice theories (e.g., Bourdieu 1977; Certeau 1984; Williams 1961, 1977) have also enhanced understandings of both the habitual dispositions that shape people's actions and the dynamic processes through which social actors produce, reinforce, and reshape cultures and cultural domains by their words and actions. The perceived naturalness, everydayness, and common sense of a domain or discourse reflect its hegemony, its lived domination. At the same time, hegemony is never complete (Williams 1977:110–113; see also Abu-Lughod 1990; Ahearn 2001a). Human beings are born into an already ongoing social and historical context, into a world of relationships and interactions. Analyzing the complexities of "relatedness" (Carsten 2000) thus requires understanding the ways in which relationships of power are differently constituted and contested in the everyday lives of individuals.

Affinity, Affect, and Violence

As is evident from the story about Ilena, in Sullk'ata one important locus of power is the relationship between affines or in-laws.[8] In Sullk'ata people must marry and have children to be considered adults. As in other societies, the social, economic, and political centrality of marriage reinforces a compulsory heterosexuality (Rubin 1975). Scholars of the Andean region have explored the symbolic ideals of gender opposition and complementarity (Allen 2002; Harris 1978, 1981; Isbell 1978) as well as the hierarchies that characterize the relationship between spouses (Harris 1978, 1994; Harvey 1994). Married couples do not operate in a vacuum, however, and women may also navigate relations of hierarchy and ambiguity with other women, especially their mothers-in-law and sisters-in-law, as much as with their husbands.

Marriage produces both affective bonds and arenas of contestation that are crucial to understanding the daily burdens and benefits of relatedness more generally. As much as a married couple is viewed as a unit, referred to as *qusawarmi* (husband-wife), marriage also embeds Sullk'atas in a broad network of relationships. Married couples traditionally live together in the household of the husband's parents for the initial two to five years of marriage. A daughter-in-law often works for her mother-in-law long after she has a household and family of her own to maintain. Once married, both men and women accumulate relationships of *compadrazgo* (spiritual kinship, Sp.), through the birth and baptisms, graduations, and marriages of their own and others' children. Both men and women develop arrays of labor exchange relationships crucial to the subsistence economy. As Evelyn Blackwood (2000:13) notes, the negotiation of social identities and relationships is also an expression of power that takes place in a multiplicity of ordinary daily practices.

Women and men, young and old, put energy and effort into maintaining relationships and treasure their families and friends. The physical violence that I mention in this Introduction and discuss more thoroughly in Chapter 6 occurs infrequently in Sullk'ata and is also, of course, part of a broader pattern of domestic violence that occurs among individuals of virtually all social classes, ethnicities, genders, sexual orientations, and ages. Integrating consideration of ambiguities and antagonisms into a discussion of relatedness, however, disrupts the tendency to reduce the strategic interactions and practices of individuals to static structures or biological givens (cf. Peletz 2001).

For many North Americans, the "obvious" aspect of kinship—that families are composed of individuals with bonds of genetic inheritance—is overlaid with an assumption of intimacy or conviviality. Family members are assumed to have some essential bond, some deep-seated connection of feeling.[9] During the early part of the twentieth century, the analysis of the sociality of everyday life or affective relations between kin was elided by an emphasis on the formal interrelationships of groups.[10] Since then anthropologists have recognized the ambivalences and attachments in kinship relationships and practices and have shown how gender and other trajectories of power influence kinship. Few anthropologists, however, have explored just *how* the affective aspects of relatedness emerge between people in the process of their interactions.

Relatedness in Dialogue

My close attention to tracing the intimacies and the hierarchies of social and affective relationships is coupled with an emphasis on developing an analytical framework that takes account of how kinship is *lived* among people with diverse experiences of identity and inequality, within and between households and communities that can no longer be viewed as isolated from global processes and transnational discourses. I focus in particular on the embodied, linguistic and social activity of telling stories. As human beings, we engage in face-to-face interaction in our everyday lives. In the small rural communities of Sullk'ata, narrative and everyday talk more generally are especially significant to affective, social, and political economic relationships. Relatedness is produced through the joint or dialogical interactions among people.

In emphasizing the dialogical production of relatedness, I follow an approach to culture and language that draws on the work of Mikhail Bakhtin (1981). The term "dialogical" refers, most basically, to dialogue or talk between two people. Bakhtin (1981) developed the notion of dialogism to describe the form of the novel and challenge the assumption that a word has simply one meaning intended by the author. Words bear the traces of those who have used them in the past and can never be completely appropriated as one's own. Although originally referencing a relationship between author and reader, the concept of dialogism has been used increasingly in the social sciences to recognize the multiple meanings and interpretations, and social relationships and subjectivities, that emerge between people in their talk and actions.[11] Not only do participants interpret and evaluate each other's words and actions in the course of an event, but no single individual may control the meanings and relationships that transpire.

Throughout this book I bring to the forefront the creative ways in which people (speakers and hearers, informants and anthropologists) locate themselves in stories and relationships. Narratives are important because of the social interactions through which they materialize and the social relationships and affective bonds that they produce as much as for the information they contain. People tell stories in order to socialize and spread news as well as to make sense of those more troubling or problematic events of their lives. In Sullk'ata, stories circulate within a community and move beyond the community, as people evaluate each other's words and actions, local historical events (such as the passage of a law against domestic violence or the arrival of an anthropologist), and even broader discourses of progress and modernization. Yet narratives have been little explored in relation to the sociality of everyday life and the constitution of relatedness in the Andean region.

Drawing on folktales and personal narratives that were primarily told in conversations and interviews and on observations of daily practices and ritual events, I analyze the ways in which social relationships are established by examining multiple levels of dialogue within these texts.[12] First, at a formal level, narratives may be dialogical because individuals depend upon other participants in the conversation—other interlocutors—to contribute to and shape what is said. In the Bolivian Andes, for example, two or more people may jointly tell a narrative in conversation as they add to, contradict, question, and elaborate upon each other's words. Often the recounting of events and interpretations that occurs in everyday interaction is formally dialogical and thus far more open-ended and embedded in the context of a particular situation than a western traditional notion of a narrative would assume (e.g., Mannheim and Van Vleet 1998; Ochs and Capps 2001). A narrator may not have an interpretation or overarching plotline already developed when she introduces a character or event. Interlocutors, rather than listening silently to a seamless story of linear chronology or causality, may add their own details or ask questions as well as give back-channel responses such as "yes" and "and then . . ." to keep a story going or change its course. Interlocutors may also remain silent about other conversations, concurrent events, or their own interpretations.

Second, as people tell stories, they also include the words, voices, and styles of others—some present and others not. Thus I also analyze the embedded dialogue in texts. Narratives, whether formally solicited and recorded on tape or spontaneously told in gossip, are dialogical because they contain the words of others as direct and indirect quotations. Embedded or reported speech is ubiquitous in the narratives of Sullk'atas as well as those of many other societies (e.g., Irvine 1996). Moreover, narratives are also dialogical at a third level, because people draw on and refer to other texts—conversations, ritual events, stories, personal histories—to make sense of an interaction as it is in process and even days or years after the event. I explicitly analyze the intertextual dialogue of Sullk'ata narratives by elaborating upon some of the coexisting texts relevant to a particular event. Intertextuality is also an implicit aspect of my analysis, as I draw on additional texts (only some of which are included here) to make sense of Sullk'ata stories, events, and relationships.

Meanings of linguistic and social interactions are also closely linked to the particular situations in which those interactions take place. People interpret narratives in terms of their own experiences, the histories of interaction of various interlocutors, and the context in which a story is told. These aspects of social relationship and narrative engagement are significant to the ways in which relatedness and conflict are played out and interpreted in Sullk'ata. By tracing multiple and overlapping layers of dialogue in texts and highlighting how everyday practices and talk occur in specific circumstances, I demonstrate how relatedness is a mutual production among people and how multiple interpretations of relationships, and stories, emerge and are negotiated in particular situations.

Beyond the domains of written narrative and spoken dialogue, the term "dialogism" also encompasses the complex and layered configurations of talk and action in the (physical or imagined) presence of multiple others. A dialogical perspective on narrative thus has implications for understanding cultural arenas more generally. As Bruce Mannheim and Dennis Tedlock (1995:8) point out, "the task becomes one of identifying the social conditions of the emergence of linguistic and cultural forms, of their distribution among speakers, and of subjectivity itself as an embodied constellation of voices." Identities and relationships are not so much located in the intentions of individual actors as emergent in the practices among actors, which no individual may completely control (see also Hirsch 1998). Not located within an individual or lodged in static structures, relatedness emerges *in between* embodied individuals in joint performances that act upon the situation at hand but that may not directly reference "relatedness" at all.

The Ethnographic Context

My discussion of relatedness is situated in an apparently out-of-the-way place that is nevertheless integrated into national and global political economies. The region of Sullk'ata encompasses eight small and widely dispersed communities, including Kallpa, the community of fifty families where I lived for the majority of my twenty months of field research in the region. The communities and territory that make up Sullk'ata are located between 11,000 and 13,000 feet above sea level in the northern part of the Department of Potosí, in the Province of Chayanta. Chayanta is one of the poorest provinces in Bolivia, which is, in turn, one of the poorest nations of Latin America. Bolivia has a long history of colonial and postcolonial economic extraction, political unrest, and entrenched social stratification.

Living at elevations too high to support trees and too dry to support ample vegetation, Sullk'atas depend upon herding sheep and llamas and planting a variety of crops for their subsistence. Yet they are not isolated peasants. Most Sullk'ata families depend on wage labor as well as subsistence agriculture for their survival.[13] Much migration is seasonal, with married men typically traveling to the city or to lowland agricultural regions after their own fields have been planted. Unmarried men and women also migrate to cities to go to school, serve

Sullk'ata is located in the Province of Chayanta (highlighted in gray), Department of Potosí, Bolivia. The region is approximately two days' bus travel from the city of Cochabamba. Landlocked within South America, Bolivia is about three times the size of Montana. (Map compiled by Anne Henshaw.)

their year of mandatory military service, work as domestic servants or day laborers, or just visit family and friends.

The day-to-day demands of locating water and pasture for animals, feeding children, plowing fields with oxen or hand-held tools, harvesting and storing crops, and maintaining relationships of reciprocity with supernatural forces ab-

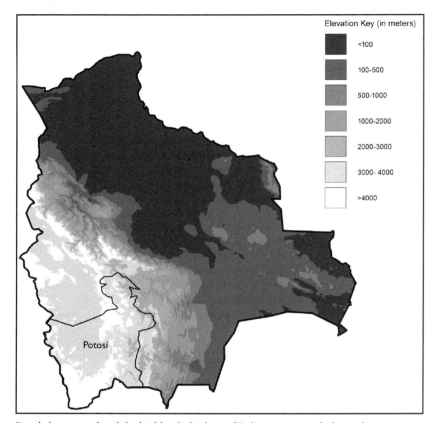

People have populated the highland *altiplano* of Bolivia, a vast arid plateau between the two mountain ranges of the Cordillera Occidental and the Cordillera Oriental, for centuries. Primarily relying on subsistence agriculture and herding for survival, native Andeans, including Sullk'atas, have also migrated seasonally to semitropical valley and eastern lowland regions of the country for argriculture, trade, and employment. (Map compiled by Karin van Schaardenburg.)

sorb the time, energy, and thoughts of most Sullk'atas. During most of the year, brown is the predominate color of the Sullk'ata landscape. The adobe houses grouped around the hard-packed earth of a central plaza reflect the muted colors of the rounded mountains of Kinsa Kallpa, Aramani, and Wayna Kachi. August is the coldest and driest month, when fields are turned over in preparation for the plowing and planting that occurs in September and October. In spite of the altitude and the scarcity of water, Sullk'atas plant many varieties of potatoes as well as other tubers such as *oka* and *papa lisa* and grains such as wheat, quinoa, and barley on the steep slopes of the mountains that undulate throughout the territory. Those individuals with lands at lower elevations also plant corn, fava beans, and peas, plowing the flatter fields with teams of oxen rather than with the hand-held tools necessary at higher elevations. In the short rainy season from December to March, the sides of the mountains rising behind the community are brightened by the pale fluorescent green of wheat fields, the dark green of potato plants laced with purple and white flowers, and the emerald green of young corn plants.

This transformation of the earth's aspect by the new growth is more than a beautiful sign of the change of seasons. It reflects a much broader set of cosmological and material relationships through which Sullk'atas understand their world and navigate their everyday relationships. The earth is animate, gendered, and sacred.[14] Pacha Mama (Earth Mother) nurtures the plants, animals, and human beings. The potatoes growing within Pacha Mama, and on individual plots of land that are sometimes called *wirjines* (little virgins) or *mamitas* (little mothers), sustain human beings. The springs of water that flow down the mountains as creeks and rivers are female forces as well. In contrast, mountains (*urqus*) are male forces that control hail and thunder, produce wealth, and dominate the landscape through which people traverse, daily and seasonally, as they plant potatoes, herd sheep and llamas, and travel to work in cities. The larger mountains are older and more powerful. The gendering of the cosmos, which extends from the land to the sun and moon, from the constellations to the underworld, intertwines Andean Catholics' conceptions of sacred time and place with the regeneration of life—the birth of lambs, the flowering of plants, and the reproduction of households and communities.

Everyday life in Sullk'ata is also permeated with efforts to maintain relationships of reciprocity between human and supernatural beings. Sullk'atas constantly remember the forces of the land through their *ch'alla*s or libations. An integral aspect of all Catholic fiestas and rituals as well as certain activities such as planting, weaving, and harvesting, ch'allas feed the Earth Mother and mountains so that Sullk'atas may themselves be fed. Making libations also reinforces relationships of sociality among human beings.

Additionally, Sullk'atas create relationships of reciprocity through exchanges of labor and products between individuals. In *ayni,* the most fundamental form of reciprocity, an individual performs a service with the expectation that the service will be reciprocated in kind. As Mannheim (1991b:90) argues, ayni is at once a "comprehensive principle governing the conduct of social life" and "an assumption about how the world is organized." During certain times of the year, especially planting season, labor is in high demand. Individuals develop networks of labor exchange so that they may access the labor of people who are not their kin. Mar-

Some planted fields (*chakras*) are divided by stone walls, but most are marked less obviously. (Photo by Lawrence Kovacs)

ried couples do not exchange labor as a unit. Instead, all labor exchange follows a gender division of labor, with women exchanging labor with other women and men exchanging labor with other men. For Sullk'atas, giving in ayni—whether working in a neighbor's field, feeding the supernatural forces, or helping to build a road—establishes a moral obligation for the labor to be returned.

Peoples' lives are shaped by the broader context of the Bolivian state even though the consumer bustle of cities, national debates over bilingual education, and the political protests of coca growers may at times seem to be a world away. For example, most Sullk'atas speak the Quechua language in their daily interactions. Quechua, the administrative language of the Inca, was systematically spread through the Andean region during the colonial period at the expense of many local indigenous languages as the Spanish attempted to subdue and missionize the diverse ethnic groups of the region (Mannheim 1992). In Sullk'ata and the Province of Chayanta more generally, the shift from the indigenous language Aymara to Quechua has been more recent, taking place in the last several generations (Howard-Malverde 1995). A few of the elderly grandfathers and grandmothers speak Aymara as well as Quechua. Several Sullk'atas also speak some Spanish, which they have learned by attending public school,[15] working in Bolivian cities, and serving in the military.

Most Sullk'atas are also Catholics, missionized in the seventeenth century by the Spanish. Their everyday lives and ritual events are tied to the annual ritual cycle of the Catholic Church. Both Catholic and evangelical Protestant missionaries are still active in the region. Catholic nuns and priests recognize Sullk'atas as Catholics and work to reeducate them about the proper beliefs and practices of the religion. The nuns teach in the local public high school, lead classes on baptism and marriage, and operate a clinic in the region.

The neoliberal reforms of the late twentieth century, including the closing of mines in the highlands and the privatization of national industries, as well as the increase in the coca and cocaine trade, have also created specific political economic conditions that have had an impact on familial relationships in

Sucre is a colonial city that has expanded in recent years as a result of migration. (Photo by Lawrence Kovacs)

Sullk'ata. By the mid-1990s, for example, young single women were migrating in increasing numbers to urban regions of Bolivia to work as domestic servants. Young women often found work more easily than did single or married men. Although most women returned to the rural region to marry, in recent years some young wives have refused to live with and work for their in-laws, reconfiguring expected residency patterns and strong moral and material obligations to the older generation.

Other young couples have drastically reduced the amount of time they live with the husband's parents by buying building materials, household items, and land with money earned by both partners prior to marriage rather than relying on exchanges of labor to build a house. Once a young couple establishes a separate household, the daughter-in-law is less entangled in kinship and labor obligations to her in-laws. Because daily habitual interactions are crucial to maintaining kinship relationships (see Chapter 2), refusing to live with in-laws removes daughters-in-law from one significant affective and social context through which they are made into kin.

Sullk'atas draw upon layers of personal experience, local and national discourses, and the relations of power and privilege that these entail, as they negotiate the practices and meanings of relatedness. In particular, discourses of relatedness among Sullk'atas are sometimes intertwined with national discourses of "progress" and modernization. Men who have worked in the city may mobilize discourses of being more advanced (*avansado,* Sp.) than their wives, sometimes using their earnings to buy new shoes for themselves rather than gifts for their families. Women also mobilize these discourses as well. Daughters-in-law may criticize the "backwardness" of their mothers-in-law and recount stories of a "more civilized" life in the city in order to contest their own subordination to older women affines. Mothers-in-law sometimes resort to physical violence in an attempt to reinstate their authority over daughters-in-law. Although Sullk'atas would not admit to envying another person, a person who claims to be envied implicitly draws attention to his or her access to commodities and relationships beyond the subsistence sphere. Thus Sullk'atas collude with and contest national discourses and relationships of inequality as they actively construct relatedness.

Ethnography and Reflexivity

A Methodological Interlude

The question of how to go about making sense of the relationships of those who have very different understandings of the world is not new to the discipline of anthropology. I have approached the problem of how to understand the emergence of relatedness in everyday life among Sullk'atas by gathering information related to three different methodological frames. First, I have explored the everyday habitual practices in which Sullk'atas are engaged. These practices contribute to an aesthetics or sensibility of relatedness (e.g., Bourdieu 1977; Desjarlais 1992) even though people may not explicitly talk about kinship. Second, I have also examined performed or narrated interactions in which the intimacies and hierarchies of relatedness are explicitly negotiated. Finally, I have collected information on local historical events and national discourses that shaped Sullk'ata social interactions and relationships. Integrating these three sets of information has allowed me to recognize configurations of relationships and practices that are significant to Sullk'atas and to link the meanings of talk and actions to specific situations.

In order to collect information in each of these arenas, I used several different methods.

1. PARTICIPANT OBSERVATION

I learned a tremendous amount about Sullk'atas' lives as well as their desires and concerns and their understandings of the world by living in the region for an extended period. Daily practices are imbued with meaning for Sullk'atas: the food one eats, the water one drinks, the people with whom one works all have material, social, political, and spiritual impact upon one's body and network of relationships. I became integrated into the community through the accumulation of my daily interactions with people and by entering into relationships of compadrazgo. In addition, in spite of the local politics of living with a family, I chose to do so in order to acquire an intimate understanding of relationships within and between households, refine my Quechua language skills more rapidly, and ease the strain of loneliness that living without friends and family created. After about three months of living alone in the community of Kallpa, I was invited to live with Ilena's family.

Whenever possible, I spent extended periods among women and their children, spouses, and in-laws. I also paid close attention to tracing people's networks of labor exchange and compadrazgo relationships. I participated in daily activities such as planting and harvesting, preparing food, and making corn beer as well as in the annual cycle of community and regional festivals, work projects, and life course events. Finally, I accumulated information about the broader sociohistorical context of Bolivia as well as locally relevant historical events and histories of relationships among people in Sullk'ata. I gained day-to-day information from radio broadcasts and discussions with community members. I also observed Catholic marriage classes taught to Sullk'atas.

2. CONVERSATIONAL NARRATIVES

In order to understand more explicit negotiation of relatedness, I recorded instances of talk and embodied interaction both on audiotape and in writing. Initially, I formally solicited narratives with the help of an assistant. As I became increasingly integrated into Sullk'ata social life, I realized that narratives more often arose spontaneously in conversations. I tape-recorded several hours of naturally occurring conversations with the permission of Sullk'atas (see the analyses of these conversational narratives in Chapters 4 and 5). I also participated in endless hours of unrecorded informal conversation and gossip (Van Vleet 2003b).

3. FIELDNOTES

I took extensive fieldnotes in order to document everyday interactions and practices, ritual events, instances of emotional expression, and historical events. I also took notes on the contexts of interviews, naturally occurring conversations, and narratives. When Sullk'atas did not want to be tape-recorded during an interview, I took notes during the conversation and immediately afterward. I integrate some of the fieldnotes into the following chapters.

4. OPEN-ENDED INTERVIEWS

I conducted open-ended interviews on marriage with three generations of married couples. These interviews focused on memories of the events leading up to marriage, wedding rituals, and relationships among affines. I primarily interviewed women and men individually. Four interviews were conducted with the help of an assistant; during these interviews both the husband and wife were present, but the husband was the primary participant. I have determined generational boundaries through attention to local events such as the initiation of marriage classes by the Catholic Church, generational terms employed by Sullk'atas, and historical research in the archives of the local Catholic diocese and the regional archbishopric based on marriage records for the nineteenth and twentieth centuries. The relatively small numbers of informants for the interviews (twenty-eight) allowed me to collect rich contextual data and detailed descriptions of individual experiences.

Reflections on Fieldwork

I quite explicitly concentrated my research on the ethnographic details of people's lives in the rural communities of Sullk'ata. In spite of their long history of engagements with "external" social, cultural, and political economic institu-

tions, Sullk'ata conceptions of the world—and of relatedness more specifically—
may be quite opaque to outsiders. Of the twenty-three months of fieldwork for
this project (from December 1994 to July 1996; in March 2001; in August 2001;
and from January to March 2003), I spent about twenty months in Sullk'ata and
the remainder of the time in the cities of Sucre and Cochabamba. Thus I include
discussion of the national social and political economic context and its impact
on local relations, but this alone cannot illuminate the lives of Sullk'atas. I nevertheless challenge the image of a timeless rural native Andean, "lo andino" (Starn
1991, 1994; see also Salman and Zoomers 2003), by accentuating the complex
heterogeneity of relationships among people, even in small rural enclaves; tracing the ways in which everyday talk is embedded in local historical events; and
considering the contradictory ways in which power, identity, and intimacy are
intertwined.

Wherever the ultimate location(s) of fieldwork may be, ethnographic research takes place among particularly positioned people, in specific situations,
and during certain historical moments. Of course, people continue creating and
revising their lives long after the anthropologist has gone; but it is just as important that people have certain relationships with each other and experiences
of the world *before* an anthropologist arrives. Like other anthropologists, I was
drawn into already ongoing histories of relationships among interlocutors and
became part of other people's "scripts" or frameworks for making sense of interactions (Behar 1995; DeBernardi 1995; Mannheim and Tedlock 1995). Anthropologists are also constrained by the contingencies of situations and may
have very different understandings of what is going on than their interlocutors
do. Especially in the initial months in an unfamiliar community, ethnographers
often depend upon different assumptions about and ability to negotiate the verbal and nonverbal cues of interaction, a shallower history of relationships, and
a variable array of social knowledges (Mannheim and Tedlock 1995:14). During
the course of ethnographic fieldwork, I constantly reinterpreted and reevaluated
my understandings of people's talk and actions and of events more generally.
At the same time, my informants—friends, collaborators, acquaintances, interlocutors—made their own interpretations of me, drew on previous knowledges,
revised and challenged each other, and stayed silent.

My understanding of Sullk'ata relatedness has developed over the course of
several years, through the depth of my relationships with a core of people and
the diversity of social interactions, observations, and events in which I have been
engaged. A final aspect of my research that bears mentioning here is that most of
my day-to-day interactions in the community of Kallpa and more generally in
Sullk'ata took place among married women. There is no rule explicitly prohibit-

ing a woman from being in the presence of men, whether kin or stranger. Nevertheless, men and women often operate quite independently of each other. To a certain extent, this corresponds with the division of labor by gender. Women have primary responsibility for herding sheep, cooking, caring for children, washing clothes, and maintaining the household. Men, when they are not working in the city, have primary responsibility for the agricultural fields and tending oxen. Although they eat and sleep together and often work side by side in their fields, women and men gravitate toward separate spheres of relationships.

Women also say that they simply prefer the company of women. Early in the course of fieldwork, because of the questions I was interested in pursuing and as a strategy for becoming integrated into the community, I chose to follow local gender conventions and spend most of my time with women. Indeed, much of my understanding of the conflict and contradiction as well as the camaraderie in Sullk'ata relationships is refracted through informal conversations with Sullk'ata women. Some became my friends or ritual kin; others were simply my neighbors or acquaintances; many were linked to each other by kinship or ritual kinship ties.

Ethnography and Dialogue

In this ethnography I represent Sullk'ata relatedness, both the communality and the conflict, through retellings of stories. I begin with my own rendering of the story about Ilena, but I also draw readers into other stories interwoven throughout this book. Through the retelling of stories, none of them completely mine, I explore the interrelationships of narrative, relatedness, and violence among Sullk'atas. I present these stories, and my interpretations, to demonstrate that husbands and wives, brothers and sisters, parents and children, strangers and compadres, gringos and native Andeans are not simply categories but rather actors in dynamic relationships negotiated on a daily basis.

In the process I also hope to give readers a sense of the dialogical process of ethnography. Thus I inscribe Sullk'atas' words and actions into this text. I represent the voices of others through transcriptions and translations of tape-recorded interviews and conversations and through entries from my fieldnotes included as quotations or citations embedded in a larger text. The extended quotations demonstrate the ways in which an ethnographer and her interlocutors mutually create the conditions for the form and content of ethnography and allow for a process of reinterpretation and revision. The ethnography is thus dialogical in the sense that it is permeated by multiple voices.

At the same time, I am the one who has chosen whose voices to include and whose to exclude. Even before determining the form and content of this book, I made decisions about what questions to ask, how to transcribe and translate the words of my Quechua-speaking collaborators, and how to represent the spoken words and actions of people as printed texts. Quechua does not have an extensive tradition of written literature—its traditional texts are spoken words, woven textiles, music, and theatrical performances (e.g., Howard-Malverde 1997). But the problem is even more general: inscribing people's words and actions into fieldnotes, audiotapes, or published texts freezes them in time. As philosopher Paul Ricoeur (1981:198) has noted, "In living speech, the instance of discourse has the character of a fleeting event. The event appears and disappears. This is why there is a problem of fixation of inscription. What we want to fix is what disappears."

Thus transcriptions and translations are not neutral; they are always already interpretations. The written transcriptions themselves can be extremely important in conveying meaning, and I used a variety of forms with the recognition that different facets of meaning or aspects of social action and interaction are highlighted or obscured in different forms (Hymes 1980; Irvine 1996; Ochs 1979; Tedlock 1983). Throughout this ethnography, words in quotation marks are drawn from taped recordings or from notes written during the conversation. Because the Quechua texts are significant pieces of evidence that only some readers will be equipped to read, I have included Quechua excerpts in Appendix A and Appendix B but have discussed translation of words and phrases throughout the book. I do this advisedly: as Walter Benjamin (1992:79) notes, "Fidelity in the translation of individual words can almost never fully reproduce the meaning they have in the original." In general, I have tried to render the words of Sullk'atas as faithfully as possible and wherever possible have included longer stretches of speech. I do not present these as perfect translations but as vehicles to carry readers toward meanings that are significant for Sullk'atas.

In the pages of my ethnographic text, I also initiate a discussion of the ways in which people position and reposition themselves in their interactions. By analyzing the relationships between the anthropologist and her interlocutors, rather than leaving them as subtexts, I bring ethnographic interactions into the field of analysis. Although I have given the community in which I lived and the individuals with whom I worked pseudonyms to protect them from any potential harm or embarrassment, I have not created composites of individuals or fictional events. I also represent myself as "an other," as having occupied and occupying different positionalities and remembering events and conversations in particular ways.

In taking this approach I may reinforce the "I was there" claim to authority that literary critic James Clifford (1983) rightly points out to be one of the major tropes of ethnography. However, the "clues" (Ginzburg 1989) that we draw on as interlocutors in the process of interactions impinge on what questions we can ask as ethnographers. The relationship between what a person tells an anthropologist and the situation in which that telling takes place is crucial to the meanings that emerge. Writing from a "situated position" (Haraway 1991) may thus refer to those interactional clues as much as to a reflexive rendering of the gender, racial, ethnic, and sexual categories that a researcher may fit into.[16] The conversation between sisters overheard, pages of fieldnotes written under the gaze of children, the conditions of interviewing married couples, and even the books read by lantern-light may be seen as positioning the ethnographer and contributing to the sentimental and epistemological layerings of evidence.

My representation of Sullk'ata relatedness is from this perspective partial, in both senses of the term. Interpretations are shaped by individuals' experiences, their relationships with each other, and the more general social and historical context. Even within a small community, people voice different understandings of the same events. And I have been able to include the words of only a few Sullk'atas in these pages. In writing about Sullk'ata and representing relatedness in a text, the very processes of navigating relationships that transpire in everyday life may also fade to the background. In highlighting the complex ways in which people narrate stories, collude with and contest multiple hierarchies, and claim identities, however, I hope that I have also illuminated Sullk'atas' active participation in the construction of social reality and affective social relations.

Mapping a Terrain of Inquiry

This ethnography is presented in two sections. In the first three chapters I introduce the theoretical stance from which I explore relatedness and the ethnographic context of Sullk'ata. The remaining chapters examine the narratives and practices through which Sullk'atas navigate relationships, both sociable and hierarchical.

In Chapter 2, "Sullk'ata Contexts: Reflections on Identities and Localities," I describe local practices of social and economic exchange that characterize Sullk'ata and broader social and political economic relationships in Bolivia. As I give voice to Sullk'ata perceptions of a clear distinction between the countryside and the city, I also demonstrate the ways in which Sullk'atas navigate national and even transnational discourses and relationships. In Chapter 3, "Circulation of Care: A Primer on Sullk'ata Relatedness," I explore the ways in which Sullk'atas naturalize the intimacies and hierarchies of kinship relationships. By juxtaposing the relationship of parents and children with the relationship of brothers, I show how relatedness is understood and enacted through a paradigm of ayni or reciprocity rather than genetics or "blood." These chapters provide a broad theoretical and ethnographic background for the social, cultural, and political economic issues that I discuss in the following chapters.

In Chapter 4, "Narrating Sorrow, Performing Relatedness: A Story Told in Conversation," I analyze the conventional contexts and expression of sorrow as an arena for the performance of kinship. Drawing on a narrative told in conversation, I show how Sullk'atas may produce relatedness with participants in the speech event as well as characters in the story. In Chapter 5, "Storied Silences: Adolescent Desires, Gendered Agency, and the Practice of Stealing Women," I analyze a series of "intertexts" about the practices of marriage initiation. *Warmi suway* (stealing a woman or wife) is considered by many Sullk'atas to be both customary and "uncivilized." Drawing on folk stories told in conversation as well as interviews, informal conversations, and fieldnotes, I trace the multiple meanings that emerge in spite of the silences around the event.

Chapter 6, "Reframing the Married Couple: Affect and Exchange in Three Parts," describes the ways in which discourses of companionate marriage, consumption, and debt shape relationships between spouses. Through the juxtaposition of narrative accounts of different generations of married couples and observed interactions during wedding fiestas and Catholic wedding classes, I explore the ways in which Sullk'atas reconfigure national (and transnational) discourses of progress in terms of relatedness.

In Chapter 7, "'Now My Daughter Is Alone': Violence and the Ambiguities of Affinity," I use publicly circulating stories of the often ambiguous and sometimes physically violent relations among women and their in-laws to illuminate the articulation of broader social, economic, and political relations of power. The chapter complicates understandings of relatedness by bringing attention to conflict as well as camaraderie among women and understandings of violence by disrupting the distinction between the domestic and public realms.

Sullk'atas negotiate intimacies and hierarchies of relatedness through narrative performances and through the habitual practices of their everyday lives. In Chapter 8, "Conclusion: Reflections on the Dialogical Production of Relatedness," I argue for an approach to ethnography that integrates narrative analysis with ethnographic detail. By tracing the ways in which people's words and actions are situated in a particular moment of time and place and tied to broader social and historical contexts, I show how relatedness in Sullk'ata is lived and emergent in everyday performances of individuals. From this perspective, relatedness is not solely about the genealogical relationships between people but about the practices of connection—and disconnection—through which people maintain and contest the emotional, social, political, and material parameters of their daily lives. An approach that integrates attention to talk and actions, language and practice, enables anthropologists to understand more fully both the social parameters of specific narrative events and the broader discursive frameworks that they illuminate.

Sullk'ata Contexts

Reflections on Identities and Localities

Prelude: To Walk Calmly in the City

EULOGIO LEFT KALLPA, where he was born and raised, to live in the city of Sucre in the dry, cold month of August 1995. His wife had died, shortly after giving birth to their second daughter. Even though two years had passed, Eulogio occasionally encountered his wife's *alma* (soul, Sp.) or ghost. Sometimes the alma appeared in the doorway to the kitchen, at other times in their fields planted with potatoes or corn. Frightened by the presence of the alma, Eulogio decided he could no longer live in the rural community. He left his children, a precocious five-year-old named Laura and a chubby toddler known as Gorda, in the care of his sister. Eulogio found work in the city as a vendor of plastic housewares: mixing bowls, plates, pails, and cups of all sizes and colors.

When Eulogio arrived back in Kallpa for a visit several months later, we spoke about his experiences in the city, struggling to make ends meet. Laura and Gorda, he had decided, would be going back with him to the city so that they could attend school there, rather than in the *campo* (countryside or rural region). An excerpt from my fieldnotes of 28 February 1996 reads:

Eulogio talked to me for a long time about Laura being in school in
Sucre. How he wants her to learn Spanish so that she can *caminar tran-*
quilo (Sp.), or "walk with tranquility." He said that when he'd first gone
to Sucre and was trying to get directions to the office where he could
buy pots and pans wholesale, he had trouble. Some people wouldn't talk
to him. People would refuse to give him directions, both on the phone
and in the street. He said, "I don't speak Spanish perfectly. And my pronunciation is different. And my Laura, she says to me, 'Papi, why are you
speaking Quechua?' She says to me, 'I am going to go to school and I will
be a doctor, a *médico*.'"

I said, "But it would be sad if you lose your customs (*costumbres*), if
you lose your Quechua, and if your daughters lose that too because it is
such a part of your heart."

And he said, "Yes, it is a part of me, but, doña Kristina, this is the way
it is. How can my daughters move about if they cannot speak Spanish?
I don't want them to be like me. I want them to be able to go to the city
calmly (*ven a la ciudad tranquilo*)."

Eulogio frames his experiences in the city through his admission that people
did not treat him with respect. In spite of having completed his mandatory service in the military and having worked in the mines, Eulogio suspected that he
was recognized as being "from the campo." Because of his accent and his im-
perfect Spanish, his clothing, and his mannerisms, he was treated poorly. At the
same time, he was determined to find work for himself. His wish for his daughters to learn to move about the city with tranquillity and dignity was paramount
in his decision to have them move with him to Sucre. Even so, Eulogio did not
completely sever his ties with his natal community or with the rural region in
which he had grown up.

Campo and Ciudad

Many Sullk'atas maintain a clear conceptual distinction between the *campo* (Sp.)
and the *ciudad* (Sp.), the countryside and the city. The opposition, at least in part,
reflects Sullk'ata experiences of discrimination in cities and provincial towns. The
opposition is also aligned with a far broader racial discourse that distinguishes between "Indians" and "whites" in the Andes (de la Cadena 2000; Wade 1997; Weismantel 2001). In national public discourses in Bolivia, the campo is associated
with romantic visions of the ancient civilizations of the Andean region and with
derogatory portrayals of the "backward" ethnic groups who impede the progress

of the nation. The city is associated with access to commodities, the Spanish language, western clothing styles, higher levels of education, and progress. At times Sullk'atas voice their aspirations to live a more modern life in the city.

Sullk'atas recognize that social networks, moral expectations, and political economies articulate in different ways in various places. Thus Sullk'atas also maintain the distinction between campo and ciudad by talking about themselves as "human beings" (*runa*). They deride as "naked" (*q'ara*) those people who are not properly socialized and do not live according to the moral economy of ayni. Sullk'atas who gain access to commodities and relationships outside the realm of the rural subsistence economy often fear the envy (*envidia*, Sp.) of others, hide their things and their comings and goings, and attempt to emphasize their connections of sociality within the local region.[1]

The conceptual distinction that Sullk'atas make between campo and ciudad is important in their everyday lives, but it also obscures the connections between places that are evident in their social, political, and economic relationships. Far from living in a timeless, isolated, and insular region, Sullk'atas live in a place with a long history of particular linkages with the social, political, and economic institutions of broader collectivities, such as the Bolivian republic and the Catholic Church. Like Eulogio, many Sullk'atas—men and women, married and single, young and old—move through and live in various places other than Sullk'ata over the course of their lifetimes, as they make a living or seek an education or simply visit friends and family. Maintaining economic, social, and political relationships in their rural communities and at the same time navigating the social and political institutions and relationships of the nation-state is often as complicated as it is necessary for Sullk'atas.

In trying to give voice to Sullk'ata discourses of place and identity, describe the distinctiveness of Sullk'ata social relationships, and at the same time recognize Sullk'atas as entangled in national and even transnational relationships, I have drawn upon the notion of "communities of practice" developed by linguists Penelope Eckert and Sally McConnell-Ginet (1995): "During the course of their lives, people move into, out of, and through" various communities, "continually transforming identities, understandings, and worldviews. Progressing through the life span brings ever-changing kinds of participation and nonparticipation, contexts for 'belonging' and 'not belonging' in communities" (Eckert and McConnell-Ginet 1995:469). Sullk'atas participate in various communities of practice—their natal families and the families of their urban employers, their labor exchange networks and the urban marketplace, rural and urban schools, and local neighborhoods and geographically dispersed ethnic groups—in any given historical moment and over the course of a lifetime. Moreover, certain

Pocoata is the provincial town where Sullk'atas attend regional festivals, access transportation, and buy commodities.

social, economic, and political relationships may cross-cut various communities of practice, mutually reinforcing or sometimes creating contradictions in their articulations. Because the practices of individuals are constitutive of these communities, the notion enables a vision of place that is not defined through a "counterposition to the outside" so much as through a "particularity of linkage to that 'outside'" (Massey 1994:156).[2]

In this chapter I describe the ethnographic context of Sullk'ata by explaining some of the significant social and political economic relationships and institutions at the local level and at a broader national level and by portraying moments when Sullk'atas navigate competing commitments, desires, and practices. In addition to the "prelude," in which I depict Eulogio's hopes and hesitancies about moving to Sucre, I include an "interlude," another ethnographic example that can only be understood by recognizing Sullk'atas' participation in overlapping communities of practice. Attending to the articulation of relationships illuminates the ways in which individuals identify as Sullk'atas and as Bolivians.

Exchange and Evaluation in Sullk'ata

The alma of Eulogio's wife would appear to him while he was entering the kitchen or planting the fields. This reflects the scenes his wife frequented while she lived and indexes the significance of the social relationships that accrued in those places. As they plant and harvest their food, raise their sheep and llamas, and care for their families, Sullk'atas establish relationships of reciprocity through several kinds of everyday and ritual exchanges of labor, energy, and food. The community of adults—that is, the group of married couples—is most responsible for maintaining relationships of reciprocity with the supernatural forces of Sullk'ata and with each other. Adults carry out their everyday activities with a constant awareness of the attention and evaluation of others. Their relationships of exchange tie Sullk'atas to the places and supernatural forces of Sullk'ata and to each other. Their sense of the attentive presence of others conditions the style in which an individual carries out an action as much as the action itself (cf. Desjarlais 1992, 1996). Everyday and ritual exchanges are thus intertwined with affective relationships and moral assessments, establishing a sense of conduct, enjoining collective effort, and maintaining the continuity of the community even as Sullk'atas navigate broader social, economic, and political contexts.

Exchanges within and between Households

Some of the most fundamental exchanges in Sullk'ata occur within the household, but many exchanges also extend beyond the household, linking individuals and households into ongoing social and material relationships. Within the household, exchanges take place between husbands and wives, mothers-in-law and daughters-in-law, and parents and children, as I describe more fully in succeeding chapters. Through cooking and feeding, for example, women play a crucial role in the circulation of labor, products, and energy inside and outside of the household. In cooking, many Sullk'ata women have a sense of rhythm and artistry: peeling potatoes with a knife, placing the thin curling strands of peel into a basket to feed the pigs, and dropping the potatoes into boiling water for a hearty soup; blowing chaff from the corn while shifting the kernels in a big metal basin; timing the cooking of dishes so that a snack of *mut'i* (boiled corn and peas) will finish before the main course; and ladling soup into wooden bowls and encouraging children to finish their meals and ask for seconds. Preparing, serving, and eating food is also serious business for the woman of the household, for through these material and social exchanges Sullk'atas produce relatedness.

Ilena's kitchen was like most kitchens in Sullk'ata, a small, adobe-walled building with a thatched roof. Inside, the walls of the kitchen were smooth to the touch and shiny black with soot; the floor was hard-packed earth. Ilena's hearth was immediately to the right of the door upon entering. She would sit on a low stool in front of the hearth, pushing thin branches and dried sheep dung into the fire. Her husband often sat on a low stool closest to the door. I would step carefully around him to sit on a sheepskin on the floor. Faviola and Marisa, their daughters, sat at the back of the kitchen, peeling *ch'uñu* (freeze-dried potatoes), grinding dried red chili peppers with the stone *batán,* and washing dishes. While Ilena worked, one daughter would tell stories of what had happened that day or during the previous fiesta when the adults were drunk and thus unable to remember, entertaining her parents. Nelson, the youngest of the eight siblings and Ilena's final child, would sit on the floor next to me, leaning against the wall, gradually slipping into a reclining position, and sleeping long before Ilena finished cooking the meal. Ilena called out, "Nelson, *jatariy!* Nelson, get up! *Mikhuy!* Eat!" and tried to rouse her son as she first served her husband and then proceeded to offer the rest of the family and me our bowls of soup.

As I discuss further in the next chapter, eating food grown from the same plot of land and drinking the same water makes people constitutionally similar (see also Weismantel 1988, 1995). This is true for daughters-in-law and anthropologists, who temporarily live in a household, as much as for children who are raised in a household. Moreover, because food is not so much exchanged as given within a household, feeding also sustains relationships of hierarchy and authority. A one-way flow of food reinforces the dependency of those who eat but do not feed (also see Harvey 1994). Exchanges of labor overlap exchanges of food. Children work with parents, caring for younger siblings and animals and contributing to agricultural tasks. A daughter-in-law may cook for her husband's parents and unmarried siblings, contributing labor power to her mother-in-law's household. If her mother-in-law serves the meal, she retains her position of superiority in the household. Even though a wife cooks and serves food, married couples recognize that the food has been produced or obtained through their joint efforts.[3]

At a broader level, most households depend on relationships of labor exchange in order to plant their fields (*chakras*). Both men and women develop independent networks of labor-exchange relationships over the course of their lives. As married partners, a husband and wife will ask others in their work networks to exchange labor with them in ayni during times when labor requirements are at a peak. Family members and compadres will help (*yanapay*) each other with no formal expectation of a return, but those working in ayni recognize that the person who has received labor is morally obligated to return an equivalent kind and amount of labor to her partner in the future.[4] Men plow the field into furrows using teams of oxen on flatter land or hand plows on steep mountain slopes. Women fold their carrying cloths into slings, fill the slings with

On steep mountainous terrain, Sullk'atas must use hand tools rather than oxen to plant potatoes and other high altitude crops.

seeds, and follow behind the plow, dropping seeds into the furrow. Older children, gringas, and elderly men and women use long-handled tools to push the soil back over the seeds. In this way, even larger fields may be planted in a single day.

On the day a field is planted, the people who receive labor offer food to their partners, as acknowledgment of their exchange. A woman typically begins cooking the midday meal immediately after her family has eaten a quick breakfast. She carries to the field a meal that is far more elaborate than the usual cold snack of mut'i. Once several hours of work have been completed, she serves peeled, boiled potatoes and ch'uñu (freeze-dried potatoes) with a spicy sauce made from ground peppers and peanuts. When everyone is nearly stuffed, an onion salad and mut'i are offered. Coca leaves and cane alcohol or corn beer follow, so that people may make offerings to the local mountains and Pacha Mama for the productivity of the field.

Within a household, the partnership between husbands and wives is crucial to maintaining Sullk'ata subsistence. Husbands and wives often operate independently of each other, maintaining control over distinct realms of everyday and ritual practice. At the same time, married partners depend upon each other.[5] If a man's wife dies, he typically remarries immediately—so necessary is a woman to food processing and distributing subsistence products, maintaining the house, herding, and contributing to agricultural production. Eulogio was an exception. After the death of his wife, he depended on his unmarried older sister, who was happy to care for Laura and Gorda as long as they lived in the rural community.

Married partners also, however, constantly negotiate competing material and emotional demands both within and between households. Because they do not exchange labor as a unit, husbands and wives do not always establish exchange relationships with individuals in the same households. Individuals must negotiate the competing obligations of their various work networks. Moreover, women often have more obligations than their husbands do. Women work for their mothers-in-law in an unequal exchange of labor and take on responsibilities for subsistence agriculture when their husbands migrate to work. Men and women thus have diverse experiences negotiating social, political, and economic relationships within and beyond households and communities, even though married couples have the primary responsibility for maintaining these exchanges that contribute to the life of the ayllu.

Exchanges within the Ayllu

Exchanges of food and labor also circulate through wider collectivities. The practice of planting, for example, forges associations with people beyond the boundaries of the household, especially when they travel to distant plots of land, assist parents, siblings, or compadres who live in other communities, or seek labor in ayni. The feast days and fiestas of the annual ritual calendar always include chewing coca, making libations with corn beer or cane alcohol, and offering food to participants. Some fiestas take place within a community, but others take place in the town of Pocoata, drawing people from hundreds of communities together to drink, dance, sing, and fight. During baptisms, weddings, and funerals, individuals and groups similarly create and remake connections with each other that extend beyond community boundaries. In each of these contexts, individuals recognize their obligations to broader collectivities and identify with different levels of social and political organization. Because of this, the *ayllu* (an indigenous sociopolitical grouping of people and territory) is an important aspect of the place of Sullk'ata and of Sullk'ata conceptions of relatedness.

For Sullk'atas, the term "ayllu" has multiple referents, including household, extended kinship group, community, and array of communities.[6] Throughout the Andes, ayllus have been characterized by a recursive political organization in which one ayllu is embedded in another. If one imagines a series of concentric circles, the Sullk'ata ayllu would be neither the innermost circle nor the outer-most encompassing circle. According to historical and ethnographic scholarship on the Andes, the Sullk'ata ayllu is classified as a "minor ayllu," encompassed by the "major ayllu," Majasaya, which is in turn encompassed by the "maximal ayllu," Pukwata. The Sullk'ata ayllu itself encompasses several communities, in-cluding Kallpa, and each community is further composed of smaller units (es-tancias, Sp.), extended kin groups, and even households. Quechua speakers may refer to *any level* of the social and political organization—from household to maximal ayllu—as their "ayllu."[7]

People also refer to ayllus, especially those more encompassing levels, as spe-cific places. The image of concentric circles does not, however, reflect the loca-tion or territorial possessions of ayllus. Ayllus often have widely dispersed, dis-contiguous territories. The Pukwata ayllu, for example, has territory that extends through highland, intermediary, and valley regions (Harris 1985:332).[8] Major and minor ayllus within Pukwata ayllu do not have continuous territories, and communities belonging to different ayllus are interspersed among each other. Nevertheless, Sullk'atas claim that particular lands "have always belonged" to their ayllu.

Significantly, the ayllu indexes a sense of imagined community (Anderson 1983) as well as a specific political organization and geographic location. De-pending upon the context of the situation, individuals may selectively identify with any one of the many ayllus to which they belong. People draw on the cate-gory of the ayllu to carry out common tasks and claim belonging to broader collectivities. For Sullk'atas, being a member of an ayllu is about identifying oneself in particular ways: celebrating fiestas of the ritual calendar; establishing relationships through compadrazgo; practicing certain styles of dress, weaving, and music; remembering common ancestors and histories; claiming a common identity in distinction to outsiders; practicing subsistence agriculture; and feed-ing the supernatural places of the ayllu.

When she claims identity with an ayllu, an individual also acknowledges her responsibility to the collectivity. One of the significant ways in which Sullk'atas sustain the ayllu is by guarding their relationships with the supernatural forces of the region. The mountains, in particular, are closely associated with certain locations. Sullk'atas constantly acknowledge, remember, and "feed" the forces of their lands through their ch'allas. During fiestas and community rituals, making libations is collectively organized, with corn beer passed to one person after another so that each may invoke one ch'alla before moving on to the next. Sullk'atas begin any series of ch'allas with an offering to the *esquina* (literally, "the corner of the house or of the place" and figuratively the married couple).

A woman drinks corn beer (aqha) after first making a libation to
Pacha Mama. Carved into the center of the wooden bowl is a team
of oxen, a symbol of fertility.

This is followed by offerings to the sun (Tata Santisimo) and moon (Mama San-
tisima) and to Pacha Mama and specific mountains. Variations in the order and
enumeration of blessings depend upon the occasion. During some fiestas, the
corrals of the sheep and the furrows of corn or potatoes are offered ch'allas. During others, sacred places beginning with Illimani and Illampu, the most distant
and powerful mountains, and ending with the mountains surrounding Kallpa,
are invoked so that wealth is brought to the speaker's doorway.

People also make invocations in more mundane situations. Once Ilena,

Marisa, and I arrived at the field below the mountain named Aramani to plant potatoes and fava beans. After unloading a set of tools and our lunch from the burro, Ilena bent down, took out her bag of coca, chose a perfect leaf, and buried it under a rock at the edge of the field. "For Pacha Mama," she told me. Later when we sat down to eat, she flicked food in different directions, voicing ch'allas to Aramani and to the other mountains that surround the field. Offering food and drink, chewing coca leaves, and whispering invocations open channels of communication and extend a cycle of exchanges through which energy, fertility, and productivity are cycled through the universe.

Thus supernatural forces pervade Sullk'ata consciousness and are recognized as crucial to the sustenance of human beings and the continuation of the ayllu. Pacha Mama and the urqus are themselves social actors, watching over and interacting with other beings in a hierarchy of power (see also Allen 2002). When Sabina and I were walking to the town of Pocoata, we noticed that several fields had been hit by hail, leaving the corn plants bent and broken, while many other nearby fields were lush and green. "Maybe they are bad [*saqra*] people. That's why their fields are ragged from hail," said Sabina. Mountains may destroy fields or the earth may simply fail to produce abundantly when people are not vigilant about their offerings. Sullk'atas thus have a deep respect for the places that are

Flowers and water are abundant during the short rainy season. This stone wall follows the contours of a stream that will dry to a trickle by the month of September. (Photo by Lawrence Kovacs)

Dancing is a typical offering to the supernatural forces, but only during particular fiestas do sponsors hire musicians.

familiar and sacred. Even as children, they display an intimate knowledge of the landscape—hills, rock formations, waterways, paths, chakras, houses, and grazing lands—of the ayllu and orient themselves by these places, remembering the names of the sites and the personal and storied events that happened there. As they grow up, however, individuals recognize that Pacha Mama and the mountains are capricious, easily angered, and more powerful than human beings. Thus, as adults, most Sullk'atas carry out their obligations to broader collectivities through exchanges of labor and food with other people and with supernatural forces; these exchanges also constitute relationships and enable individuals to identify with different levels of the ayllu.

Exchange and Evaluation in/of the State

Although even the nation of Bolivia may be seen as an ayllu, Sullk'atas most often used the category to refer to themselves as Sullk'atas, Majasayas, or Pukwatas. They are thus integrated into material, social, and imaginary networks that extend beyond the ayllu. Even their conception of the ayllu has been shaped by the broader state: the hegemonic notion of "ayllu" in Bolivia is of a rural and indigenous regional collectivity. Although my discussion of relatedness is embedded quite explicitly in the context of Sullk'ata ayllu, understanding this place also requires familiarity with a more general social and historical setting of Bolivia. The people that I knew sometimes traveled to or had children who lived in a city. They listened to national and local news broadcasts on the radio. They sometimes identified themselves as campesinos or Bolivianos. Like them, my attention to relationships, movements, and events extends beyond the territorial margins of Sullk'ata so that the experience of identifying as Sullk'ata may be illuminated more fully.

A Political Economy of Late Twentieth Century Bolivia

At the time of my fieldwork in 1995 and 1996, several households in Kallpa had a family member living in a city or lowland agricultural region in order to earn money or to attend school. Most Sullk'ata households cannot survive solely on subsistence agriculture or on wage labor. This uneven integration into the global economy creates a context in which people are continually juggling strategies for getting by. The youngest generation of Sullk'atas is more likely to travel to urban areas of Bolivia than to the valley regions of Pukwata ayllu or highland mining centers, as their grandparents and parents did. Increasingly, young couples migrate permanently to urban centers and raise their children speaking Spanish. Others talk about the possibilities of migrating: the elderly don Gregorio spoke resignedly about moving to Cochabamba because his adult children would not return to the campo. Middle-aged Sabina talked longingly of moving to Santa Cruz but admitted that she could not because she and her husband had too many young children. With children attending school in Cochabamba, Ilena and Marcelino began building a house there even though they preferred living in Kallpa. The talk about migrating to the city materializes in conversations when Sullk'atas ponder the work opportunities in the city and in the campo and attempt to piece together sustenance for their households and families.

The attention to migration among Sullk'atas is embedded in broader patterns of labor and migration in Bolivia, presently a nation of approximately eight million people living in an area (1,098,580 sq km) that is almost three times the size of the state of Montana. The majority of Bolivia's population has lived in urban centers only since the 1990s. From the earliest times, people have been concentrated at altitudes of 5,000 to 13,000 feet above sea level, even though some two-thirds of Bolivia's territory consists of semitropical and tropical lowlands. The highland region known as the *puna* or the *altiplano* (Sp.) is, in fact, a large

Sullk'atas arriving in Bolivian cities, like La Paz, negotiate traffic
and other aspects of urban life. (Photo by Lawrence Kovacs)

plateau stretching between two Andean mountain ranges, the virtually uninhabited Cordillera Occidental to the west and the long-populated Cordillera Real
to the east. Andean people have herded llamas and alpacas and have practiced
agriculture on the altiplano and the virtually treeless, semiarid, rounded mountains of the Cordillera Real for thousands of years. Highland peasants, like the
Sullk'atas, have produced the majority of Bolivia's food on plots of land that have
become smaller and less fertile with each succeeding generation. Rural migrants
to urban regions have sought out education and employment in hopes of better-
ing their lives and the lives of their children, and the populations of La Paz and
El Alto, Cochabamba, Santa Cruz, Potosí, and Sucre have expanded.

Although Sullk'atas have long been integrated into a global economy, in the past two decades the articulation of subsistence agriculture and market production and the pattern of migration have shifted rapidly. The increasing migration to cities is at least in part based upon the more general political economic context of Bolivia, which includes the demise of tin mining, the expansion of coca production in the lowland regions, and the demand for domestic service in urban areas. Tin was Bolivia's principal legal export until October 1985, when the price of tin collapsed on the world market. For centuries mining dominated the economy of Bolivia. The silver extracted from Bolivian mines funded the development of Spain in the colonial period; by the nineteenth century, tin mining took the place of silver, bringing wealth to a handful of Bolivian families. Throughout much of the twentieth century, Sullk'ata men would travel to tin mines in highland regions to earn money. After the crash, more than 8,000 miners, including many Sullk'atas, were laid off. By 1989 two-thirds of the labor force of the state mining corporation, Corporación Minera de Bolivia (COMIBOL), had become "permanently unwaged," and reductions continued until 1993 (García Argañarás 1997:71). Some Sullk'ata families migrated permanently to the city, joining thousands of those working in the unwaged sector of the economy. Others migrated to lowland agricultural regions; and still others returned to their natal communities in Bolivia's rural highlands.

The world tin crash came at a bad time for Bolivians, who were already struggling with rampant inflation, an international debt crisis of massive proportions, and a floundering economy. In 1981 Bolivia had become the first nation to fail to pay for the servicing of its international debt. Much of that international debt had been accumulated during a decade of military rule beginning in 1971 with Colonel Hugo Banzer. After Banzer was ousted in 1978 in a popular uprising, Hernán Siles Zuazo won democratic elections for the presidency. Before Siles Zuaso could take office, another military coup occurred, with Luis García Meza ascending to the presidency. Renegotiation of the international debt under García Meza's rule from July 1980 to August 1981 set impossible conditions on interest rates and terms for repayment. In October 1982 Siles Zuazo was installed as president on the basis of elections he had won in 1978, and he served until July 1985. As June Nash (1992:276) notes, by the end of Siles Zuazo's presidency, no "sector of the population (except those involved in the drug trade . . .) could endure the rampant inflation which exceeded 100 percent per month." By 1985 servicing the interest and annual amortization of Bolivia's $5 billion debt required 60 percent of the country's exports.

Shortly after he won elections in July 1985, the government of President Víctor Paz Estenssoro embarked upon an austerity plan in response to Bolivia's debt crisis. Following the neoliberal philosophy of Harvard economist Jeffrey Sachs and the demands of the International Monetary Fund (IMF), Paz Estenssoro's government carried out the reforms that closed down marginal mines and sold more profitable mines to private companies, revaluated the Bolivian currency (bolivianos or Bs), and began the process of privatizing national industries. In the mid-1990s inflation was under control, balanced in part on the influx of capital from the cocaine industry.

While Bolivians struggled to feed their families in the face of inflation and unemployment, the demand for cocaine and crack escalated in the United States and Europe. Coca leaves, the plant precursor to cocaine hydrochloride, are integral to the everyday and ritual interactions of native Andeans and have been grown, exchanged, and chewed for hundreds of years. The rising demand for cocaine in global markets meshed with the expulsion of miners and other workers from state-owned industry; land policies that supported increased migration to the eastern lowland regions of Bolivia; rampant inflation and unemployment without a state or international safety net; and radical IMF reforms.[9] Although Bolivians first simply shipped coca leaves to Peru and Colombia, they soon began processing coca paste and cocaine hydrochloride. By the early 1990s the coca economy in Bolivia generated as much foreign exchange as all other Bolivian exports combined (Andreas and Sharpe 1992:76).

Somewhat paradoxically, coca production became the foundation for the success of the economic austerity plan promoted by the United States and the IMF. At one level, coca production was a grassroots response to economic instability and insufficient resources: people from rural regions diversified, producing coca to provide a cushion in times of drought. Others, such as out-of-work miners, turned to coca production as an alternative to industrial production in state-owned businesses. The coca economy also enabled smallholders and those who could not access jobs elsewhere to generate some badly needed cash. At another level, the shift to the processing of coca paste and cocaine hydrochloride—which was dominated by agribusiness elites from Santa Cruz, members of the military, and cattle ranchers—positioned an already well-established minority to reap the lion's share of the profits. Paz Estenssoro implemented several measures that facilitated the absorption of drug profits into the banking system, so that the capital generated by the production and sale of coca leaf and cocaine could be reintegrated into Bolivia's economy.

The expansion of the coca and cocaine economy was closely tied to the growth of the service sector and the increasing availability of jobs for young women (García Argañarás 1997:70; Gill 1994). In the last two decades of the twentieth century, many young women from Sullk'ata and other rural areas traveled to

Santa Cruz and Cochabamba to work in the households of Bolivians who were profiting directly and indirectly from the coca trade.

The stabilization of the economy and the increase in service-sector jobs obscure the unevenness of the benefits and costs of the neoliberal policies and the coca economy for Bolivians. Informal economic activities as a whole were deemed to generate about 51 percent of the gross domestic product of Bolivia in 1991 and to involve about 32 percent of the labor force. The highly profitable illicit coca paste and cocaine hydrochloride trade, however, was categorized as part of those informal economic activities.

Thus, as Fernando García Argañarás (1997:70–71) points out, the economic weight of the small number of those involved in the drug trade "hides the poverty of the overwhelming majority of people—possibly 600,000—involved in informal activities not directly related to drug production or distribution." Thousands of Bolivians spend their days in the cities washing, cooking, and cleaning the clothes, homes, and bodies of middle-class and upper-class Bolivians or working as street vendors, peddling cups of jello, homemade drinks, plastic bowls, pencils, and innumerable other commodities, making just pennies a day. In recent years increasing numbers of people have arrived in Bolivian cities to work in the informal and service sectors of the economy, trying to escape the seemingly endemic problems of land scarcity, drought, and lack of educational and economic opportunities. Many have also maintained connections to their rural ayllus, supplementing their waged work with agriculture and hedging their bets in case migration fails to enhance their standard of living.

Privatization and Discourses of Exploitation

Sullk'atas sometimes told me that their national government was controlled by—or simply *was*—the government of the United States. Although they are integrated into national and global economies, Sullk'atas recognize that their lives and livelihoods are marginal to state and international agendas. Indeed, the president of Bolivia from 1993 until 1998, Gonzalo Sánchez de Lozada or "Goni," was an entrepreneur and multimillionaire who was raised and educated primarily in the United States. The vice-president at that time, Víctor Hugo Cárdenas, was hailed in 1993 as the first "Indian" to hold such high political office since Bolivia's independence in the nineteenth century. In a 1993 interview with the *New York Times,* Cárdenas expressed his criticism of the "internal colonialism" that for centuries has excluded indigenous peoples from the Bolivian nation and explicitly stated his intention to make indigenous participation in political offices of the federal government "the expression of something normal." Yet the policies and practices undertaken by Goni's government soon left many Sullk'atas angry that the president and vice-president had turned against the nation and its people.

In addition to the eradication of coca, Goni's government pursued a process of privatization, dismantled the political and economic structure of nationalized industries, and contradicted fervently held beliefs that the natural resources of Bolivia should remain in the hands of the state on behalf of its citizens.[10] By 1995 privatization of previously national industries was taking place in earnest. In 1996 some Sullk'atas participated in a national strike and road blockades mobilized to protest the government's plan to sell the national petroleum and natural gas company. Sullk'atas' unhappiness with the process of privatization is linked to material aspects of their daily lives—to local relationships of production and patterns of migration throughout the Bolivian countryside. The disaffection they express also reflects localized conceptions of the land as animate and a more broad-based understanding of natural resources as belonging collectively to the people of the nation. Sullk'atas also maintain a profound skepticism about the government's concern for the welfare of the populace.[11]

Sullk'atas' understandings of the history of exploitation in Bolivia have shaped their views of neoliberal policies. One morning after a conversation with Pascal, a father of seven children who spent his time in both Kallpa and Cochabamba, I wrote: "Pascal said that the government of Bolivia 'keeps people from advancing' . . . The government is privatizing the mines, the petroleum company, the airlines. People don't want it [he says] because the money will just leave Bolivia. None of it will benefit Bolivians, just like the mines that produced all those years and none of it for Bolivians" (fieldnotes, 21 January 1996). Pascal criticized the ways in which the national government ignored the needs of the poorest Bolivians. He and other Sullk'atas also understood privatization as action taken by the government, under the influence of the United States, to return Bolivia to the times of *patrones y peones,* the era of patronage and the hacienda system.

Sullk'ata reactions to the privatization of Bolivian industry are based on memories of extraction and exploitation within long-distant and more recent history. The time of patrons and peons to which Sullk'atas refer began with the Spanish colonization of the Andean polities, which had been under Inca control for less than a hundred years. The Spanish colonial system of *encomiendas,* in which huge tracts of land and the inhabitants of that land were given to Spanish conquerors and administrators, created long-lasting structural inequalities.

This system of serfdom intensified after Bolivia's independence from Spain in 1822 and was only abolished in 1953 in the Agrarian Reform that followed closely on the heels of the National Revolution of 1952. At that time Bolivia had

Two women chat outside a store in the town of Pocoata.

one of the most unequal distributions of land in the Americas: 82 percent of the country was owned by 4 percent of the population. Although Sullk'atas insist that they were never part of an hacienda, the huge herds of a nearby ranch (*finca*, Sp.) owned by a patron often encroached upon their agricultural and grazing lands. Some of the older men in the community worked on that finca as children, later marrying women from Sullk'ata communities. Sullk'atas also paid tribute and then taxes to the colonial and republican governments of Bolivia in order to maintain their status and their territories as *originarios* (indigenous communities). They were unable to vote or to attend public schools. The National Revolution and the Agrarian Reform ended the tribute system, established a national public education system, enfranchised the indigenous population, nationalized industries owned by a handful of elite families, and gradually redistributed land from the haciendas and fincas. In spite of even more recent political reforms, Sullk'atas are still excluded from many aspects of the political and social life of the nation.[12]

Interlude: Peon and Patron

The general assumption among Sullk'atas was that I, as a gringa and stranger, would take advantage of them in a variety of ways. Sullk'atas were certainly aware of the power and privileges linked to my class, national, and racial position. Their examinations of my tape recorder, camera, and other equipment; repeated questions and exclamations over the cost of flying between the United States and Bolivia; critical comments about the ways in which the U.S. government controlled Bolivia through conditions on foreign aid; and queries about how much I would earn in the United States once they had taught me about their lives and language implicitly and explicitly reflected the material and social dimensions of race and class in which we were enmeshed.

So when Basilia first expressed the opinion that I was Ilena's peon, I was taken aback. We were chatting about the approaching fiesta of Carnival when she asked me whether Ilena had given me any potatoes after I had worked with her the day before. I said that she had not. I ate dinner with her family every night, and I did not expect to be paid for helping. Shaking her head, Basilia characterized my relationship with Ilena as explicitly exploitative, naming Ilena as a *patrón* and me as a *peón*, an inverted reference to the old hacienda system.[13] Calling Ilena a patron placed her, not me, in the category of those who take advantage.

A few days later, Ilena told her sister who was visiting from another community that Basilia had been spreading rumors. Ilena did not direct her initial comment to me, but I was present at the time, watching the two women pass balls of yarn back and forth as they prepared a loom for weaving. Ilena said, "Basilia said that Kristina is paying me a lot of money and that I am making her work for me as well." We were sitting in the inner courtyard of Ilena and Marcelino's house, a relatively private location. Our conversation was interrupted only once when Ilena's eight-year-old son entered from primary school and greeted each of us in turn before disappearing to join his friends. My journal entry reads:

> I guess that . . . Basilia also asked Ilena how much I was paying. Sonia asked *me* the other day. I told her "I'm paying nothing—I just help out now and then." I hope she spreads it around. Then Ilena said to me,

"Now this is why I want to move to Cochabamba. People are saying I get a lot of money from you—and I make you work. They are envious. They are envious because I sell *chicha* [corn beer]. They are envious because my children, three of them, have graduated from high school." (fieldnotes, 22 January 1996)

Five months earlier I had dragged my two-burner camp stove, my propane tank, and my backpack across the plaza to Ilena's house, excited and relieved finally to have been accepted into a Sullk'ata household. It was only in January that I became aware of talk circulating in the community about my presence in Ilena's household. Not only Basilia, who was Ilena's sister-in-law (her husband's brother's wife), but other women voiced their suspicions about the financial arrangements between us. Some women said that I paid Ilena an exorbitant amount of money to live in her house. Others complained that I worked for Ilena without proper compensation (in money, produce, or an equivalent amount of labor).

People also categorized our relationship in another way by calling me Ilena's *qhachuni* or daughter-in-law. I heard this the first time from Ilena's godmother, who saw me squatting in the kitchen, pushing the dried kernels of corn off the cob in order to make mut'i. The label "qhachuni" recognized our joint living situation and the closeness of our relationship but also contained an evaluation of Ilena's actions, suggesting that she was not following the proper behavior of a native Andean person. Hierarchy permeates the relationship between mothers-in-law and daughters-in-law, to a large extent generated by the mother-in-law's appropriation of her daughter-in-law's labor power (Van Vleet 2002). This material and symbolic asymmetry is considered appropriate for Sullk'ata mothers-in-law and daughters-in-law (as much as daughters-in-law may contest the power asymmetry). Ilena's appropriation of my labor power was less acceptable. I was not, after all, married to her son.

Indignant that people thought she was taking advantage of me, Ilena countered their accusations of inappropriate behavior. She suggested that women were envious not only of my presence in her household but also of her ability to earn money by selling corn beer and of the success of her children. Her oldest daughter had just graduated from high school in Cochabamba, and her two oldest sons were attending the university there. Ilena recognized the talk of people in the community as problematic. "Now that's why I want to move to Cochabamba," she concluded, indicating her unhappiness about the state of her relationships within the community.

Three Discourses of Power and Place

In the context of increasing migration and wage work in a global capitalist economy, Sullk'atas intertwine local sensibilities of reciprocity and sociability with national discourses of modernization and progress. This creates at times contradictory evaluations of events and interactions. By turning attention to the discourses of progress and envy that circulate alongside a discourse of ayni in Sullk'ata, I demonstrate the ways in which Sullk'atas negotiate differing ideologies of what constitutes "civilized" behavior. I also balance a description of Sullk'atas' everyday understandings of themselves as Sullk'atas, campesinos, or Bolivians with an analytical understanding of identity as a dynamic process.

Discourses of "Advancement"

In their evaluations of themselves and others, Sullk'atas often locate themselves in a subordinate position, drawing on more general discourses of race, place, and progress that circulate in Bolivia. They say that as "Sullk'atas" or "campesinos" they do not partake of the "more advanced" (*awansadu,* from *avansado,* Sp.) life in Bolivian cities, where electricity and running water make streets, clothing, and people cleaner, where people can buy electronics and clothes, and where they speak Spanish rather than Quechua. As Bolivians, they say that they lag behind the United States, unable to develop industry and technology or to control their own political and economic future. In these and other statements, Sullk'atas draw on hegemonic discourses that valorize progress and modernization, sometimes explicitly voicing desires to become more "civilized" (*siwilisadu,* from *civilisado,* Sp.) or even more tranquil.

These discourses of advancement are often highly gendered. In national public discourses, the campo is imagined as existing in the past, as Indian, and as feminized; and the city is imagined as existing for the present and future, as white, and as masculinized. Married men in Sullk'ata, who migrate seasonally to cities more often than married women do, valorize their work as "more advanced" than that of their wives. This opposition emerges in the provincial judge's speech to the community, when he calls Kallpaños together to discuss the incident of violence between Marcelino and Ilena described in Chapter 1:

Why do I tell you the wives have double the work of men? Certainly, we [men] work and bring money back here . . . [W]e say, "I am more advanced than my wife." No, no, my friends. Women have double work . . . They wash our clothes. They cook our food. They raise the children in the

Two women carry their sleeping babies in colorful cloths (llikllas) down a Sucre street.

house. They bathe the children. When the children are little they carry them on their backs . . . Because of all this, we should say that women work without rest more than all of us . . . And who will tell me that it is not this way?

The judge attempts to champion women and encourage the men of the community, as "heads of the household," to recognize that their wives do "double work" (*doble trabajo,* Sp.).[14] The judge's comments also connect women more closely to the identity of "Indian," however, by emphasizing the ways in which they are embedded in the domestic and the subsistence economies (de la Cadena 1995). People of Kallpa and throughout the Andean region understand wage work to be linked to processes of "civilizing" and to more industrialized nations such as Argentina and the United States. In the judge's description Sullk'ata women do the work of "burros"—washing, cooking, and carrying loads.[15] In this context, the men's work is represented as more valued and valuable than that of women.

At least in part, the distinction between campo and city is intertwined with Sullk'ata notions of kinds and consequences of labor. Labor in Sullk'ata is embedded in relationships of reciprocity. Moreover, subsistence products are shared among members of a household and typically distributed by the senior woman. In contrast, money earned through wage labor is not exchanged or shared between married partners or among members of a household. People who earn money are free to spend that money on consumer goods, whether for "conspicuous consumption" or for household sustenance. Buying commodities is linked to attaining a higher level of education, speaking Spanish rather than Aymara or Quechua, and living in an urban area rather than in the countryside. In other words, money and other commodities are associated with modernity and with racial "whiteness" in Bolivia and other parts of the Andes (Weismantel 1997, 2001). Thus individuals may enhance their racial and class status through wage work and consumption.

The discourse of advancement also plays out in my conversation with Eulogio, when he speaks of wanting a better life for his daughters. Eulogio notes how people in the city looked at his clothes and heard him speak—and treated him without respect. He also recalls how his daughter admonishes him for using Quechua. Laura's emphasis on speaking Spanish rather than Quechua takes up the hegemonic discourse that categorizes people into a racial group based not only on their physical attributes and material possessions but also on their language.

Yet Eulogio also tells me of Laura's ambition to become a doctor. Just five years old, Laura actively identifies herself with various "imagined communities" (Anderson 1983) that show her connectedness to the modern nation and to her Sullk'ata family. Children growing up in Sullk'ata at the turn of the twenty-first century come into contact with urban hegemonic notions of national identity and are integrated into national arenas through education in rural public schools, migration to urban areas for work, consumption of commodities and mass media, and mandatory military service. They are engaged in realms from which their grandparents, and sometimes their parents, were excluded.[16] Saying that she will be a doctor, Laura imagines a different relationship to "the outside" than Eulogio imagined for himself or even for his daughters.

Discourses of Envy and Ayni

In Sullk'ata discourses of envy emerge in an arena in which national ideologies of modernization and desires to access commodities overlap local moral horizons of ayni and sociality. Envy is often directed toward those people who are able to earn money and buy consumer commodities or who have access to desired relationships that lie beyond the bounds of subsistence agricultural practices and relationships (see also Tapias 2006b). No one would admit to feeling envy for another, but the force of that emotion is realized in material, physical, and metaphysical ways on the envied person's body and relationships. For example, in 1996 Bolivian politician and millionaire Max Fernández died tragically in an airplane accident. People envied him for his wealth, I was told by more than one person, and this had caused his small plane to crash into the side of a mountain near the mining town of Huanuni. Community members sat all that afternoon and evening listening to local news broadcasts about the accident. The plane was said to have been filled with money, tens of thousands of U.S. dollars, that burned along with the plane and its passengers, which lent credibility to the power of envy to cause physical and metaphysical harm to the envied person.

Sullk'atas do not always valorize those who have gained access to commodities and relationships linked to the national economy. As noted above, Sullk'atas sometimes distinguish between those who are "naked" and those who are "human." Those who are naked (q'ara) do not live within the Quechua moral order of ayni: they are greedy, have become wealthy from the exploitation of others, "eat money" rather than food, and are improperly socialized.[17] In contrast, runa are people: human beings, usually Quechua speakers, who follow the parameters of local social order. Sullk'atas may criticize an individual as "uncivilized" or as q'ara when that person wants too much and fails to follow the appropriate practices of ayni.

For Sullk'atas the proper way to act and interact with each other and with the supernatural forces of the universe is grounded in reciprocity. Ayni is not so much a list of rules closely followed as a way of being in relation to human and supernatural others that is internalized through habitual actions. As Michael Taussig (1987:393) points out in his discussion of envy in shamanic discourse and practices in Putumayo, Peru, the sensitivity to envy can be thought of as "as a sort of sixth sense or antenna of 'implicit social knowledge.'" "[A]cquired through practices rather than through conscious learning, like one's native tongue, implicit social knowledge can be thought of as one of the dominant faculties of what it takes to be a social being" (Taussig 1987:393). Envy emerges when ayni, the underlying assumption of the way the world works, is disrupted.

In spite of the ideal of ayni in social relations, it should not be understood to connote a relation of equality. Only when the Quechua verb stem *ayni-* receives a reciprocal suffix (*-naku*), to create the term *ayninakuy* (to exchange with each other), does the term have the connotation of egalitarian exchange. Without this suffix, *ayni-* refers to one asymmetrical side of an exchange (Mannheim 1991b:19). In ayni, the return of similar labor or objects is *hoped* for, even expected, but ayni is not a contractual obligation.[18] The recognition that an initial offering may not be returned underlies conceptions of power among Quechua-speaking native Andeans (e.g., Earls 1969).[19] More powerful beings may not reciprocate in kind. Although a mountain is "fed," the mountain may not in turn feed Sullk'atas. The local elite in provincial towns, urban Bolivians, and gringos may also be dangerous and fickle, refusing to abide by local moral horizons. Those gringos who do not abide by the moral obligations of the Quechua universe, whether urban Bolivians or anthropologists, are criticized but cannot be penalized. In contrast, Sullk'atas may be socially ostracized when they fail to follow the moral horizon of ayni.

Among Sullk'atas, ayni may be implicated in local negotiations of hierarchy as much as it is highly valued and necessary to subsistence and sociality. From a local conception of "civility" (one that takes ayni into account), those who maintain their relationships with the supernatural forces, mobilize kin and compadres, and manage their labor-exchange relationships attain a position of superiority. This is particularly important for married women. Married women control the distribution and consumption of subsistence products in the household, including the sale of agricultural products. Women maintain their own herds of sheep and may own agricultural land as well. When their husbands migrate for work, women are in charge of subsistence production, which is crucial to the survival of family members. Women are also vital to community political and ritual events. Although the authority of individual women varies, those who have raised children to adulthood, developed extensive labor networks, and acted as "heads of household" are often quite formidable. Thus the meanings of the phrase "a woman is more Indian" (de la Cadena 1995) may have very different meanings depending on the specific contexts in which it is uttered (e.g., Canessa 2005b; Van Vleet 2003a).

Nevertheless, it is also within this understanding of "being civilized" that Sullk'ata women monitor the moral valuation of themselves and each other. Through their conversations about Ilena receiving money as well as labor from me without proper compensation, women privileged the moral values of ayni and revalued the hegemonic notions of "progress" and "advancement" against local standards of sociability. As Penelope Eckert has argued for a very different context, women may achieve symbolic capital (Bourdieu 1984) by proving their "moral worth" in relation to a social marketplace (Eckert 1993:34). In contrast to men's capital, the value of which is established by the marketplace, women's symbolic capital "must be evaluated in relation to community norms for their behaviour. The establishment and maintenance of these norms require regular monitoring, and because it is women [historically] who must compete in relation to these norms, it is they who have the greatest interest in this monitoring."

Although there are some senses in which women may have been concerned that Ilena was taking advantage of me, the resident anthropologist, the more likely interpretation revolves around a sense of Ilena gaining unfair advantage vis-à-vis other community members. Through the talk about the potential moral and social transgressions of Ilena, women reinforce the hegemonic value of ayni within the community but also enforce ayni among women who are engaged in, and more closely associated with, subsistence production.

In her talk about envy, Ilena also appraises the quality and condition of women's interactions with each other. Because women are typically without close kin when they move to their husband's community, they rely on ideals and practices of communality among women. Due to the local gendered division of labor and regional and national patterns of migration, relationships among women are integral to the subsistence production of any particular household. With her husband and oldest children in Cochabamba and her youngest children in school, Ilena depends upon labor exchange relationships with other women to carry out agriculture requirements of a subsistence economy. Her emotional, social, political, and economic well-being is balanced on the state of her relationships with other women.

Ilena claims to be envied and negotiates a stance from which to counter others' perceptions of inequality or improper action. Her later evaluation of her husband's violence as the result of the envy of community members is substantiated not only by the judge's presence but also by his insistence on documenting the incident and instituting a resolution prohibiting malicious talk in the community. Claiming to be *envied* thus provides a stance from which Ilena might assert her status as a proper person and wife—one who has not committed adultery and who has not taken advantage of others—and at the same time position herself as someone who has access to commodities or relationships associated with the urban sphere and market economy.

Conclusion

In this chapter I have portrayed the context of Sullk'ata through specific social and political economic structures as well as personal interactions. Exchanges of labor and energy and local conceptions of ayni structure social and economic relationships even as broader political economic relationships constrain Sullk'atas. It is through their very integration into various communities of practice that Sullk'atas create and re-create themselves as distinct from, but connected to, the urban and national. Eulogio went to the city in part because of his sorrow over his wife's death. She died in childbirth, a relatively common occurrence in rural Bolivia, where doctors are scarce and both infant mortality and maternal mortality are ranked among the highest in Latin America. Eulogio went to the city because of the particular historical moment in which his wife died. Years earlier he might have gone to work in the mines in Colquechaka or even the lowlands of Chapare. In the mid-1990s both were improbable options for re-creating a life. Instead he chose to become one of the many itinerant vendors selling commodities in the campesino market in Sucre.

The appellations "native" or "campesino," "Sullk'ata" or "Kallpa," and "backward" or "advanced" at once recognize and re-create a particular social reality structured through relationships of power. Campesinos like Eulogio who migrate to the city are faced with the unfamiliarity of a new place, language, and foods, the isolation from familiar people and social relationships of ayni, and the active maintenance of racial distinctions that limit choices. Yet people of different genders, generations, or life experiences negotiate the place of Sullk'ata in different ways. With her husband often in Cochabamba, Ilena mobilized local relationships of ayni and attempted other more novel kinds of exchanges as well. Her access to the labor, and relative wealth, of a gringa did not, however, result in claims to being more advanced or civilized. Understanding Sullk'ata as a place, and understanding the ways in which Sullk'atas identify themselves, requires analysis of the particular practices that constitute belongingness in multiple collectivities and of the ways in which these practices are structured by power asymmetries.

Although Sullk'ata is a territory marked on maps, in memories, and through material traces, the "place" of Sullk'ata is not static but changing over the course of time and constantly emerging through specific relationships, events, and people. In a context of increasing migration, rapid communication and transportation, shifting patterns of waged work, and differential ideologies of gender and race, how people position themselves as runa, as Sullk'ata, or as Bolivian may depend on the specific context of the situation as much as the place where they were born. Local discourses of being "uncivilized" may be laminated upon criticism of government policies that are returning campesinos to the "times of the patrons" and keeping campesinos, and the nation as a whole, from progressing. Sullk'atas may valorize becoming more civilized or more modern, living in the city and becoming educated, eating white bread and noodles rather than ch'uñu. They are also simultaneously, and excruciatingly, aware of the asymmetries of power that make attaining their desires difficult. Sullk'atas are thus intertwined in moral and political economies that unevenly overlap each other, at times mutually reinforcing and at times contradicting particular hierarchies and claims to belonging and identity.

THREE

Circulation of Care

A Primer on Sullk'ata Relatedness

TO BE ALONE (*sapalla*) in an Andean community is to be poor (*waqcha*). The word *waqcha* also means "orphan," a person without ties of kinship or compadrazgo. Most of the people living in Kallpa, the Sullk'ata community that I came to know best, either had been born in one of the small adobe houses that surrounded the plaza and lined the ravine or had married someone who had been born there. Although many Sullk'atas travel throughout the region and have lived in cities in Bolivia, Argentina, or even Spain, their everyday lives in the rural community are conducted in a style that creates and affirms relatedness. Relatedness in Sullk'ata extends beyond the genealogical relationships that we often assume to represent "kinship." People are related to the children they have raised, spouses and in-laws, compadres, and the supernatural beings with whom they maintain relationships of exchange. Sullk'atas are thus integrated into an intricate network of relationships, with human beings and the supernatural world, with runa and non-runa, with kin and nonkin.

Sullk'atas devote a great deal of effort to producing relatedness. Much of this "work," however, is accomplished through practices that are "sensible" yet "obscure to the eyes of their producers" (Bourdieu 1990a:68–69).[1] Implicit in my discussion of Sullk'ata kinship is a recognition that people are not always aware of or consciously negotiating and producing relatedness. I draw on Bourdieu's understanding that individuals acquire social schemas and dispositions through a "practical mimesis" (Bourdieu 1990a:72) in which certain ways of moving, presenting themselves to others, and orienting themselves to the surrounding space "pass directly from practice to practice without moving through discourse and consciousness" (Bourdieu 1990a:74). Dispositions, internalized in the body and reproduced without conscious effort, reproduce structures (Bourdieu 1977, 1990a) and generate affective relations among social actors. Understanding the ways in which people do, in some moments, quite actively negotiate relationships requires a preliminary understanding of the cultural schemas or dispositions that are the common sense of relatedness.

Although Sullk'ata relatedness may seem just like "ours," in many ways the underlying assumptions and dispositions or grounding of relatedness are quite different. In this chapter I argue that relatedness for Sullk'atas is grounded in a generalized conception of ayni: the cosmological and material circulation of energy and care through the universe. Although in certain contexts people mark—or set apart—their "true kin" (*parientes legítimos*, Sp.), Sullk'atas do not conceive of families as bounded by birth relationships. In fact, a North American understanding of "birth" as biological connection does little to explain Sullk'ata practices and understandings of true kinship or relatedness more generally. Moreover, a kinship grounded in ayni has quite different implications for the lived interactions among individuals than a kinship grounded in sexual reproduction. As I have already described, "reciprocity" has egalitarian connotations that "ayni" does not. Understanding the "common sense" of Sullk'ata relatedness provides a foundation for exploring the ways in which Sullk'atas navigate the hierarchies and intimacies of their relationships in subsequent chapters.

Javier's Mothers

The complicated ways in which people might claim relatedness became clear to me one day during Carnival in 1996 when I realized that Javier, a young man of sixteen, had two mothers. The sun had climbed high in the sky, sending rays of light through thick gray clouds that threatened rain. Most of the adults of the community had gathered in the small courtyard of Modesta and Luis that afternoon. Marking the beginning of the dry harvest season and the end of the rainy season, the fiesta in rural Andean communities usually lasts a week or more. Families bless their homes and fields; visit relatives, friends, and spiritual kin; and dance and sing to celebrate the fertility of lands and animals. Ideally, the adults of each household visit and host every other household in the community, receiving and offering food and drink and cementing bonds of sociality and conviviality.

On that particular afternoon, men and women sat around the perimeter of the patio, pouring drops of corn beer to the floor and whispering invocations before drinking the remainder of the cup. As people drank, Modesta presented a bowl of food to each adult. The new potatoes, pieces of boiled salted mutton, and small ears of young corn were a welcome treat after months of eating the freeze-dried potatoes known as ch'uñu. The food was also understood to be a gift from Modesta and Luis, and from the earth itself and was received by each community member with two outstretched hands in a gesture of respect.

Suddenly a woman began crying as she ate. A shy woman with a small nose and teeth that seemed too large for her narrow face, Silveria set aside her bowl of food and sobbed loudly, rocking back and forth. Sullk'atas sometimes move quickly between laughter and tears during fiestas; Silveria's crying was not unusual in a context where people had been drinking corn beer. The reason for her sorrow attracted my attention, however, and later that day I wrote in my fieldnotes about the event:

> Silveria was crying and talking to the woman who sat next to her. She was crying and talking about Javier, whom she said she had "lost" (*Javierta chinkapuni*). After listening for a few minutes I realized that I knew Javier as Silveria's nephew, her sister Julia's oldest son. I was confused. Why would Silveria be crying about Javier? Finally, another woman explained to me that Silveria had raised [*uyway*] Javier. When he was still a baby, Julia had fallen down a steep and rocky section of the mountain called Kinsa Kallpa. Julia had been herding sheep. She hurt her leg, an injury that has frozen her knee so that even today she walks with a limp. Silveria raised Javier because her sister was in too much pain to care for her child. Later her sister wanted the child back.
>
> Silveria sobbed, "I'll die and be forgotten. He's lost to me. He doesn't remember that I am his mother. I raised him."[2]
>
> The other woman listened, reciting, "Don't cry, don't cry!" as Silveria sobbed.
>
> Julia, who had been sitting across the courtyard, finally came over to her sister. "But he's still your son," she told Silveria. "He said, 'I will bring a radio.' But he said, he told me, 'I'm going to bring a radio for her.'"
>
> Silveria held onto her youngest child, a boy a little less than a year

old. As she bent down over him, her thin shoulders pulled together into her chest, and she cried, "Javier was just like this . . . just like this." (fieldnotes, 23 February 1996)

Tears continued to run down Silveria's face for several minutes. Eventually, however, her sister's intervention and acknowledgment that Javier still recognized Silveria as his mother seemed to have the desired effect: Silveria calmed down. She wiped her tears on the corner of her apron and began eating her bowl of food. Later Silveria walked across the plaza along with many of the other gathered community members to the house of her sister, where the process of drinking and blessing and eating began again.

As Silveria's public performance of affective and social connection—and disconnection—suggests, an emphasis on who gave birth to whom is in itself insufficient for understanding Sullk'ata relatedness. Silveria claims to be Javier's mother because she *raised* him: fed him and cared for him, carried him on her back, laughed with him, and comforted his cries. Indeed the ways in which kinship is established through everyday activities such as eating the same food, working on the same plot of land, or sharing the same space have been well established for other Andean communities (Harvey 1998; Weismantel 1995). Yet when women told me about Julia's injury and her sister's role in raising Javier, they referred to Javier as "Julia's son." Moreover, Julia's ability to reclaim Javier as her own remains undisputed by community members.

In the following pages I discuss how Sullk'atas make sense of the relatedness of Julia and Javier and of Silveria and Javier through the same conceptual framework. Sullk'atas understand kinship in reference to a cosmology built upon the uneven circulation of energy, food, and caring through the universe. By comparing the strength and flexibility of bonds between parents and children—even those who are not connected by birth, genes, or blood—with the fragility of bonds between siblings, especially brothers, I demonstrate the significance of ayni as an ontological principle in Sullk'ata relatedness.

Parents and Children, Part I: Naturalizing Ayni

In the Andean countryside, children are desired.[3] They are recognized as a significant aspect of familial and community life and appreciated for the enjoyment that they bring to a home and for their pragmatic value in a subsistence economy. Moreover, children are socially, emotionally, and materially important to Sullk'ata relatedness. In a region where patrilocal residence is the expectation, a woman establishes relationships of "true kinship" in her husband's community

Children learn to help with agricultural and household work at an early age.
After school, this girl often herded sheep for her mother.

when she has children of her own. Raising a child marks the transition between adolescence and adulthood: in an individual sense, for the woman who gives birth and, in a collective sense, for the couple that feeds and cares for the child. Moreover, through their children's hair cuttings, baptisms, graduations, and weddings, parents establish a series of relationships of compadrazgo with other adults, extending their networks of exchange and sociality. Children thus shape the relationships between people.

Discourses of Birth: Planting and Nurturing

Sullk'atas most often naturalize the relatedness between parents and children by linking the processes of pregnancy and birth with those of agriculture and herding and, more importantly, the cosmological cycles of regeneration. Sullk'ata women say, for example, that a child is born nine or ten months after a man plants seed (*muju,* Ay.) in a woman. A child ripens during pregnancy through the *actions* of the woman who nourishes her child, just as Pacha Mama nourishes the seeds of corn or potatoes, allowing those seeds to ripen.[4] Both the gendered actions of planting and nurturing are necessary to the reproduction of human beings, just as the gendered activities of planting and nurturing are necessary for the production of food that sustains Sullk'atas.

In a similar way, the people of Qaqachaka, a nearby ayllu where anthropologists Denise Arnold and Juan de Dios Yapita conduct research, emphasize the action of nurturing the seeds before birth. Women there say that a woman's menstrual blood "grabs" (Sp. *agarrar,* Ay. *katuña*) the seed of the man (Arnold and Yapita 1996:314).[5] A woman nourishes the seed, which eventually produces a human form; in particular, the blood of the woman is necessary for the production and ripening (*puquy*) of the child, who is like a plant. During pregnancy, the baby grows in the belly or intestines of the woman and nourishes itself from the blood inside the belly. The "food that is served to the mother passes directly to the baby 'through the blood,' and . . . the baby turns into a person 'with the blood'" (Arnold and Yapita 1996:317). The development of a fetus is thus contingent upon the blood of the mother and the food that she eats.

Distinct from either Spanish notions of "purity of blood" or North American conceptions of blood and genetic inheritance, Andean notions are drawn from an understanding of blood as a life force.[6] According to Pastor, regarded by many as one of the most accomplished birth assistants (*partero,* Sp.) in the region, a woman may only become pregnant when she has sexual relations during her menstrual period. Although recently converted to evangelical Protestantism, Pastor had been a healer and diviner (*yatiri*) for many years and spoke of his many experiences liberating (*libraykuy* from *liberar,* Sp.) babies from their mothers. During the birth of a child, he emphasized, a woman loses blood and subsequently loses life force and strength. To counteract this, the woman should eat a lot, especially meat and eggs, so that her blood has been fortified and she will not have a miscarriage (*aborto,* Sp). Ilena concurred when I discussed birth with her, saying: "I have already given birth to eight children. Each time I have lost blood. That is why you look so young. You have not lost blood even once." Sullk'atas link the loss of blood and the "thinning of blood" to disease and death. In a place where medical assistance is limited, the material significance of the loss of blood cannot be ignored. The meaning of blood as life force also extends beyond the individual body to a broader cosmological and symbolic system, further linking birth to Andean cosmology.

Cosmologies of Fertility

In particular, the circulation of the blood that sustains the life of an individual body and is crucial to the nourishment of the fetus is metaphorically related to the circulation of water and energy between human beings, the earth, and the cosmos that sustains and regenerates life.[7] Sullk'atas and other native Andeans describe the circulation of water through stories of the celestial Black

In the months of December through February, springtime rains swell the rivers.

Mother Llama (or Yacana). Since ancient times Andean peoples have observed the constellations, particularly the black spots in the Milky Way. Arnold and Yapita (1996:331) note that women in the ayllu of Qaqachaka say that when the constellation of "the Black Llama goes down below the horizon . . . she becomes stuffed by drinking the waters of the earth. Later . . . she gives birth, letting loose . . . first her amniotic waters as the water of the earth . . . and her blood like the rains and the vibrant colors of the rainy season." The Black Mother Llama animates llamas on the earth as well as in the heavens through the release of water and blood. Sullk'atas also associate the Black Mother Llama with birth and fertility. This association of human and animal birth with cosmological conceptions and productive practices points to culturally specific notions of "true kinship" that integrate human beings and supernatural forces and reinforces a widespread conceptual link between women and irrigation in the Andes.[8]

Moreover, when Sullk'atas say that a woman's blood nurtures a child before birth, they also allude to an animate Pacha Mama that sustains life. Pacha Mama is not inhabited by supernatural forces or spirits but is herself animate and agentive, watching over and interacting with people, plants, and animals. As a native Andean woman told anthropologist Catherine Allen (2002:29) during her fieldwork in Sunqu, Peru, in the late 1970s: "We owe our lives to her . . . She nurses the potatoes lying on her breast, and the potatoes nourish us . . . Pacha Mama doesn't teach us anything. She nourishes us. She nurses us." In spite of the different geographical locations and historical periods, Sullk'atas related to Pacha Mama in much the same way. Pacha Mama nurses Sullk'atas, feeding them with the potatoes and other food that grows in her body.

Because providing for Sullk'atas' sustenance initiates a relationship that must be maintained through reciprocal human actions, the women and men of Sullk'ata feed Pacha Mama and the urqus through their libations. Other anthropologists, working in Peru and Bolivia, have further suggested how the circulation of water and energy in the Andean cosmological cycle may be linked to individual actions of feeding Pacha Mama through libations. Drinking corn beer during the planting season or a fiesta animates or gives energy to the workers or feasters. As Peter Gose (1994:134) has noted, "By 'animating' the men in their work, corn beer promotes the productive expenditure of energy . . . As the men sweat in their labour, so they prove their spiritual worthiness." The corn beer circulates through human bodies and is returned to the earth in the form of sweat, urine, and the energy of labor. Moreover, when a person dies and the body is buried in the earth, Sullk'atas say that water is released from the body. Water, which was crucial to the life force of a living person, is then absorbed by plants. Just as water and energy are cycled through the bodies of human participants, integrating living and dead, water and energy are also cycled through the universe, providing a foundation for fertility, for the growth and regeneration of plants, and for the fecundity of animals and human beings.

Sullk'atas do not simply overlay understandings of relatedness upon a biological base of sexual reproduction. Instead, pregnancy and birth are intimately associated with the nurturing of Pacha Mama. The circulation of blood during pregnancy initiates a relationship of kinship through the "feeding" of the child. Before birth, a child is fed directly by her mother through her mother's blood and indirectly by her father, who provides food for her mother. Her mother's blood, or life force, circulates within her own body, just as the life force of the universe circulates between the earth, the heavens, and below the earth. The circulation of food and energy during pregnancy is linked to the circulation of water and energy in the cosmos, thereby integrating birth into the broader conceptual framework of ayni.

Parents and Children, Part II: Practical Kinship

In Kallpa as in other Andean communities, a household is typically composed of many members, some related "genealogically" and others not. An older and more established household, for example, may consist of three generations who cook, eat, and sleep together. Parents and unmarried children may live with at

Sullk'atas who have migrated permanently to Cochabamba and other
cities return to their natal communities for annual fiestas.

least one married son and his wife and children. When the household compound
becomes too crowded, a married son moves his family into their own house, re-
ducing the extended family to the configuration of a nuclear family. Occasionally, a young woman may leave her husband, usually prior to a church wedding,
and return to her parents' house to raise a child. Sometimes the youngest son
and his wife and children remain in his parents' household, cooking together
or separately, helping the parents as they age. A family occasionally takes in the
children of relatives or compadres who have died. An elderly couple whose children have grown and moved away may acquire a godchild or grandchild to live
with them so that they will not be lonely.

Those who share food and space with each other constantly reproduce and reinforce relatedness. Even those who are "true kin," related through the circulation of food and blood before birth, must constantly reproduce relatedness through everyday exchanges. Moreover, an adult who is unrelated to a child can produce relatedness by raising or caring for the child over the course of many months or years. As Mary Weismantel (1995:694–695) has noted for the people of Zumbagua, Ecuador, "ingesting food and drink, sharing emotional states with individuals or spirits, being in close physical proximity to people or objects" creates kinship. In Sullk'ata those who live in the same household eat together, sharing mut'i and potatoes from communal bowls and enjoying the warmth generated by the close physical proximity of many people in a tiny kitchen. Family members sleep in the same room, with two or three people sharing each single bed. They work together in the same fields, travel together whenever possible, and make libations to the same forces of the earth. These practices create and sustain relatedness.

Feeding others is one of the most important ways in which Sullk'atas constitute relatedness. Through the process of feeding and eating, a shared substance is created. Members of a household eat food cooked in the same pot and grown in the same field and over time become materially similar, made of the same flesh.[9] More generally, by drinking the water from the springs and eating the food grown in the dirt of the named mountains of the ayllu, a person who was not born in Sullk'ata may nevertheless begin to "speak the same Quechua," maintain relationships with the same supernatural forces, and become "from Sullk'ata." In practical and conceptual ways a person—whether an anthropologist, a new daughter-in-law, or a child—becomes integrated into a family by living in a household, sharing food, and taking on the practical and ritual responsibilities of everyday life.

To Make a Child One's Own

Sharing food is a crucial part of raising a child and of creating and maintaining the social, material, and affective bonds of relatedness. This is particularly clear in cases when an adult raises a child who is not her "true kin." In Sullk'ata and other parts of the Andes and the world, children circulate among households.[10] In 1996, when I conducted research, approximately 10 percent of families in the Sullk'ata community of Kallpa had either given (quy) a child to another family or were raising (wawachakuy) a child they had been given. "Giving a child" may take various forms; but in most cases the true kin no longer perform the practices, such as feeding a child, that establish and maintain relatedness. Although this situation is sometimes glossed as "adoption," Sullk'atas use the term *wawachakuy,* "to make a child into a son or daughter," to describe the processes through which everyday parents care for a child and make the child into kin. The complementary practices of "giving a child" and of "making a child into a son or daughter" highlight the ways in which relatedness is created through habitual everyday practices.

Most Sullk'atas give a child to or receive a child from relatives or compadres. Very few enter into a legal or contractual agreement or go through a state or private adoption agency. To a large extent the movement of children between households overlaps a variation in the wealth of households: a child almost always leaves a poorer household with many children and goes to a wealthier household with no or few children. An older couple with adult children (or no children of their own) often can support a child better than a younger couple whose resources are stretched thin by a shallower social network and many small children (also see Weismantel 1988:170–171, 1995). Sometimes Sullk'atas refer to "lending" a child, such as when a young girl is sent to her grandparents' house to live once they no longer have their own children living at home. Mariana often sent her oldest daughter to help her mother-in-law prepare meals and herd sheep and to spend the night. The child continually moved back and forth between the two households. In other instances, a child may go to her godparents' house in a city so that she may accompany them and at the same time "advance" herself, by learning Spanish, going to school, and becoming accustomed to the city (Leinaweaver 2005a, 2005b).

The contingencies of the situation in which a child is lent to another family often exceed the simple pragmatism of the subsistence economy or the pleasure of children. Lending children enables people to navigate potentially devastating social or economic circumstances. Sometimes, as in the case of Javier, lending a child is a temporary solution to illness or injury. The relationship established through wawachakuy may last far longer than the child's residence in a particular household. In other cases, lending a child is more permanent. After Leonarda gave birth to her sixth child, she became extremely ill and remained in the hospital for several weeks. She was too sick to care for her older five children, much less an infant. Leonarda and her husband, Nelson, gave their infant daughter to Leonarda's sister, Antonia. At least in retrospect, Leonarda also said that she gave the baby to her sister in hopes of ending a conflict between Antonia and her husband, Faustino. Antonia and Faustino have remained together and have raised the child, named Teresa, primarily in the city of Cochabamba.

Cared for, fed, and clothed by Antonia and Faustino since she was an infant, Teresa had grown to be a bright, sweet girl of twelve in 1996. She recognized Antonia and Faustino as her parents by addressing them as "my mother" (mamáy) and "my father" (tatáy). Although she knows that Leonarda gave birth to her, Teresa calls Leonarda "aunt" (tiya) and Nelson "uncle" (tiyu). She uses "aunt" and "uncle" as terms of respect and as indications of the relationship between the two sets of adults.[11] Antonia and Faustino have authority over her as well. Teresa lives with Antonia and Faustino and helps Antonia sell sodas and other refreshments after school. When she misbehaves, Antonia and Faustino are the adults who reprimand her.

In certain instances, Teresa's status as the daughter of Leonarda and Nelson is also acknowledged. Leonarda has an obvious affection for Teresa and a closer connection to her than does Nelson. When Teresa was visiting from Cochabamba, for example, Leonarda insisted that I take a picture of herself, Teresa, and another of her children so that she could have a remembrance of "me and my youngest daughters." When asked how many children they have, both Leonarda and Nelson include Teresa in their numerical count. In other situations, however, Teresa is acknowledged as the child of Antonia and Faustino. When Nelson visited Cochabamba, he gave money to their three other children (two sons and a daughter), but he did not give money to Teresa. Leonarda and Nelson do not provide food, clothing, or daily care for Teresa and do not dispute Antonia and Faustino's status as parents who have raised Teresa or their authority over her. Thus wawachakuy results in a material and social relatedness. A child who is not raised by a "birth parent" nevertheless becomes a daughter or son by receiving food from another adult. Giving a child to another person dilutes but does not completely erase the relationship of true kinship, especially for the mother, whose blood circulated through and formed the child.

Thus the everyday actions of feeding and caring for a child are also crucial for true kin to undertake in order to re-create and reconsolidate the intimacies (and the hierarchies, as I discuss below) of relatedness. Whether their actions are undertaken with forethought or embedded in the commonsensical habits of daily life, individuals produce relatedness through practices that move food, energy, care, and labor among other people. Just as food and blood circulate between mother and child before birth, food and energy cycle between parents and children afterward. Sullk'atas do not explicitly describe the relationship between parents and children as ayni. No account is kept, for example, of the labor or food given and received. The relationship between parents and children nevertheless partakes of the moral horizon of ayni through the exchanges of substances.[12] Common substances accumulate in people's bodies but also circulate among them. Wawachakuy is aligned with the circulation of energy and blood that is naturalized in true kinship. Conversely, Sullk'atas recognize some people as true kin, but true kin also are part of a larger category of those who feed each other.

Creating Authority

The everyday actions of Sullk'atas also contribute to the creation and maintenance of hierarchy among kin. As anthropologist Penelope Harvey (1998:74–75) has noted for native Andeans in Peru, the unidirectional flow of food from parents to children inscribes a relationship of unequal exchange and of power asymmetry. Feeding children in a household is embedded in a wider context of giving and receiving food in conjunction with exchanges of labor, the annual cycle of fiestas, the system of rotating community political offices (*kargu; Sp. cargo*), and the maintenance of reciprocity between human and supernatural beings. In contrast to the ways in which Sullk'ata adults feed Pacha Mama through ch'allas and other offerings, children do not "feed" their parents, at least initially. Until they are engaged in productive relationships, children are dependent on and subordinate to their parents. They are fed but do not feed others.

As Harvey (1994:69) has noted, successful kinship relationships in the Andes are relationships where a hierarchy remains intact. The local value system that children are born into and are taught as they grow from childhood to adulthood also includes a hierarchical relationship between generations (grandfather, father, [male] self, and son; or grandmother, mother, [female] self, and daughter), with the youngest generation being the most subordinate.[13] The hierarchical relationship between different generations is also associated, at least ideally, with the hierarchical relationship between siblings, who refer to each other as "my older" (*kuraqniy*) or "my younger" (*sullk'ay*). As part of these relationships of hierarchy, the subordinate (younger) acts respectfully toward the superior (older) person.

This genealogical and generational hierarchy is conceptually and practically linked to the hierarchical relationships among the four ranked political authorities in Andean communities, who are usually adult men and their wives.[14] The political and moral influence of the male community authorities is derived from the local ancestral deities—the mountains, hills, stones, and places of the ayllu. These places possess and control powers having predominantly masculine qualities, including the power to speak authoritatively and to control natural forces such as rainfall, wind, hail, and frost. The political power and authority of women, derived from Pacha Mama and other female deities, is more diffuse, though no less potent.[15] Multiple hierarchies are superimposed in this conceptual framework.

Although this framework guides individual actions, in practice continuous reiterations of respect and authority, as much as nurturing and caring, are required in everyday interactions to maintain relatedness. Parents use a variety of means to reinforce their position of authority and to designate the hierarchies within the family, from serving food to meeting a child's defiance with varying degrees of verbal or physical reprimand (Van Vleet 2003a). As part of this hierarchical relationship, children are expected to work for their parents, obey them, and behave in a respectful manner. Children help care for the animals and other things that are important to the reproduction of the household; from an early age they are engaged in herding and agricultural production as well as daily household tasks. Children are expected to carry out tasks readily, watch over younger siblings, and address adults in a proper manner. Children always greet an adult first with the kinship term appropriate to the adult's gender and generation. By calling out "Good day, Uncle!" or simply saying "Grandmother!" with an upward inflection, a child conveys respect. No matter what their genealogical relationship, adults respond by saying "My child!" Adults do not typically reprimand other people's children, but children know that their behavior is visible to people other than their parents.[16] In Sullk'ata, then, children become social beings by learning to give respect through the proper actions and to the appropriate individuals.

The bonds between parents and children—that is, those who are engaged in everyday practices of relatedness whether or not they also share a birth relationship—are strong and flexible. Through the daily circulation of energy, food, care, and labor over time, Sullk'atas establish affective and social attachments. Just as Sullk'atas feed Pacha Mama, parents feed, nurture, and raise their children. In other words, caring for and feeding children is simply what people do. It is part of the simple experience of common sense. But because children do not feed parents, these daily habitual practices also constitute and elaborate differential degrees of authority and relationships of power.

The circulation of care integrates both birth and everyday practices into a broader conceptual framework. Nurturing a child before birth is not sufficient to constitute relatedness, to maintain authority, or to create a sense of closeness and conviviality. True kinship, however, is recognized as a crucial set of relationships in Sullk'ata. Although Weismantel (1995:690) asserts that "true kinship" or kinship based in birth is simply "one of a large set of beliefs and practices that governmental and religious workers attempt to impose upon local people" in the Andean region of Zumbagua, Ecuador, this does not reflect the complexities of Sullk'ata relatedness. Raising a child does not completely erase the ties established through the circulation of blood between the bodies of the mother and the baby. In contrast, even the relationship between birth parents and children may be experienced as tenuous when children no longer live, eat, work, or visit with their parents.

Brothers and the Fragility of True Kinship

Reading the relationship between parents and children through ayni suggests that the hierarchies and intimacies of relatedness extend into a broader matrix of relationships among people, within and beyond any particular household. Within a household, hierarchy is established and negotiated not only between parents and children but also between older and younger siblings, husbands and wives, mothers-in-law and daughters-in-law, brothers and sisters, and sometimes godparents and godchildren. The authority of parents and the strength and flexibility of their bonds with children stand in contrast to the fragility of bonds among siblings. Here I briefly discuss the fragilities of bonds and ambiguities of power among siblings as a way to complicate the picture of relatedness and reinforce the significance of ayni for Sullk'atas.

Like parents and children, siblings are referred to as "true kin" and from a western perspective are linked through "biological ties" that are essentialized through sexual reproduction. For Sullk'atas, siblings are ideally close. Siblings grow up in the same household, eating the same foods grown from the same plots of land. Brothers share beds, clothing, and jokes as children. Sisters often care for younger siblings, helping to cook food for them, carrying them on their backs, and keeping them out of harm. As adults, brothers tend to remain in the same community, living in close proximity. Although sisters attempt to maintain close contact with siblings of both genders, women tend to move out of their natal communities when they marry. Unless they marry men from the same community, two sisters will find it difficult to visit each other regularly. A brother and sister may maintain closer contact by establishing labor exchange relationships with their respective spouses.

Sharing corporeal substance by having eaten, worked, and slept together from birth, siblings are socially and materially intimate. They are also enmeshed in a well-recognized kinship hierarchy that places the older sibling in a position of authority over the younger one. Siblings address each other or refer to each other in conversation as *kuraqniy,* "my older [sibling]," or *sullk'ay,* "my younger [sibling]." If a parent should die, an older sibling of the same gender may undertake that parent's responsibilities. As adults, older male siblings typically enter into positions of political authority earlier than younger siblings.

As children grow into adulthood, the clarity of this hierarchy is blurred. Al-

In their youth, older brothers watch over younger brothers, but as
adults, brothers are often embroiled in disputes over resources.

though the older brother is structurally dominant, the youngest brother traditionally takes over the natal home when his father dies. Because of their proximity in terms of residence, overlapping obligations to family and community,
and participation in community fiestas and work projects, brothers are aware
of differences in what they receive from their parents and what they give to
their parents. In a context of patrilocal residence and patrilineal inheritance of
land, brothers inevitably compare responsibilities and recompense. Household
resources are limited in Sullk'ata, and parents often distribute material and affective resources unevenly. The oldest son might be more likely to receive education beyond high school, whereas the youngest may receive the greater share of

land and often the most affection from the parents (also see Nash 1993:67–69). Moreover, although parents may call on all of their children to assist them with agricultural labor, the obligations to work and care for parents require unequal amounts of time and energy from various family members. The most appropriate person to help elderly parents is the youngest son, who eventually inherits the household compound of his parents. The obligations of a son may create tension within households and between households, as sentimental and economic attachments to parents compete with the often jealous interest of siblings and the developing economic, social, and affective relationships with a spouse and children.

Brothers are thus often embroiled in disputes. In particular, the negotiation and competition involving land inheritance may take place over many years, as siblings perceive inequalities in a context of scarcity. While I was living in the community, tensions over land inheritance and labor erupted numerous times into verbal conflict, and less frequently into physical violence, between brothers. Agricultural land is ideally divided equally among sons sometime after one of them marries and before the father dies. A father may refuse to divide his land when his oldest son marries, however, maintaining control of production by continuing to sow the fields. A son often assists with the agricultural labor on the land that he will eventually inherit; but until his father gives him his plot, he receives only a share of the produce. As the father of two grown boys pointed out to me, in giving lands as inheritance parents are often constrained by the small size of their holdings. Some parents maintain that each son should have a portion of each plot, because plots at different altitudes enable one to grow different crops. Dividing already small parcels in a region where ecological and climactic parameters vary considerably creates a situation in which no one can subsist off any single plot or even off a combination of very small landholdings. Sometimes parents haphazardly give the son who marries first a plot in one region and the son who marries next a plot in another, without leaving a parcel of land for the third son's inheritance. Parents may favor one son over the other. Or a father may die suddenly before he divides land between his children.

Antonio and Teodoro's father died suddenly, after Antonio had married. Although Antonio had received some land, his father had not divided all the land before his death. After Teodoro, the youngest son, reached adulthood, the conflict between the brothers over land intensified. One night after dark, when the plaza was usually silent, I heard shouting. Looking out the window, I could make out the figures of two men repeatedly hitting each other and falling to the ground then shouting again. The next day, I learned that the fight was between the brothers. Antonio wanted additional land as his inheritance. One elderly woman shook her head disapprovingly, saying: "They were fighting like dogs, those two brothers who should only help each other."

Brothers may use any excuse to gain the upper hand in negotiations over the access to inherited land. In Sullk'ata, brothers may also direct witchcraft at male kin in disputes over land resources. One Pukwata man told me the story of the terrible affliction that befell a young boy when he took two stalks of corn from his uncle's field. The boy's uncle (his father's brother) hexed the child so that large boils appeared on his legs. Rapidly becoming infected, the boils began to ooze, and the boy's legs smelled like rotting flesh. As the story goes, the child just wanted to chew the ends of the fresh corn stalks for the sweet liquid inside. He did not even take the ears of corn. As one Sullk'ata man explained, "Brothers are jealous of each other. They punish the children of their siblings even for such a small infraction!" In spite of the ideal that siblings—especially brothers—are close companions with strong bonds, in practice Sullk'atas recognize that the ideal of intimacy obscures the very real dangers that brothers pose for each other.

These conflicts between brothers often seep into the relationships of other family members. The dispute over land between Antonio and Teodoro, for example, reemerged the morning after their fight. This time, however, their sister, Anacleta, and their mother became embroiled in an argument with Antonio's wife, Nicolasa. Nicolasa shouted and cried, almost coming to blows with Anacleta, as she argued that Antonio should inherit some of the land that remained in their mother's possession. Anacleta and her mother refused to give in, saying that they were saving the land for the youngest brother, Teodoro, who was not yet married.

Even more common than conflict between a woman and her brother's wife is conflict between the wives of two brothers. The wives of brothers do not grow up sharing material and social relatedness and rarely live within the same household after marriage (see Chapter 7). Even those siblings and affines who do generally get along may become entangled in conflicts as they protect the perceived interests of their children. For example, Teresa, the girl who had been cared for, fed, clothed, and disciplined by Antonia and Faustino since she was an infant, became the focus of a dispute between Antonia and her sister-in-law. Sullk'atas generally considered Antonia and Faustino to be Teresa's mother and father; but when Teresa reached adolescence, Faustino's brother's wife began claiming that Teresa "was not really Antonia and Faustino's child." She argued that Teresa should not inherit land from Faustino. Instead, all of the land should go to Faustino's brother and eventually to their children.

Conflicts such as this are typical not only because of the constraints on avail-

Sullk'atas formalized their social connections with me through
spiritual kinship. Here I talk with my two comadres. (Photo by
Lawrence Kovacs)

ability of land and the subsistence economy but also because of the ways in
which bonds of relatedness are created and maintained among parents and children and among siblings. Siblings share common substances and experiences
as they are raised in the same household. Older siblings may demand respect
and obedience from younger siblings and may in fact reprimand a younger sibling verbally or physically. However, one brother does not typically feed another.
Because there is no one-way flow of food between siblings, no clear hierarchy
is produced. When the youngest brother eventually takes control of familial resources, previously understood hierarchies among siblings are often disrupted.

Thus both the process of exchange and the directionality of exchange have an impact on the development of relationships and condition the trajectories along which relationships of affection and authority among kin are established and negotiated.

The Peripheries of Relatedness

Relatedness emerges in the cycles of giving and receiving among people that may begin before birth but do not end there. The ways in which parents and children constitute relatedness—and brothers do not—have implications for understanding the relatedness of broader networks of individuals in Sullk'ata. Affinity is one arena in which the sharing of food, labor, and space is particularly important. Women and their husbands and women and their mothers-in-law and sisters-in-law undertake a variety of means to produce relatedness and to navigate the ambiguities of relatedness (see Chapters 6 and 7). Like a daughter-in-law, an anthropologist may become integrated into the social and affective relationships of a community through living in a household, eating the food, drinking the water, and sharing the spaces and activities of others over a long period. Those Sullk'atas with whom I developed the closest relationships were also those with whom I established a variety of relationships of exchange.

Most Sullk'atas devote daily effort to reproducing relatedness and to negotiating both the ideals of close connection and the hierarchies that emerge among people who are linked in partial cycles of exchange. Although the circulation of substance and energy is required for the maintenance of close ties of respect, intimacy, and hierarchy, this does not mean that individuals interpret relationships in singular ways. Moreover, in spite of the flexibility and processual nature of relatedness, the relationship does not extend outward indefinitely. My relationships with Sullk'atas were formalized as compadrazgo—another significant aspect of sociality that also depends on certain kinds of exchanges but that overlaps relatedness of kinship.[17] Thus I turn to some of the limits of relatedness as produced in daily interaction.

Unfulfilled Cravings

Even relationships between parents and children may show the fragilities and strengths of networks of relatedness. Depending upon the specific situation and the history of relationships among particular individuals, Sullk'atas may highlight or elide various aspects or discourses of kinship. People also interpret their relationships within the constraints of particular historical contexts or variable life experiences. The moral and affective horizons through which people come to know and experience themselves as *related* are dynamic in spite of historical and regional continuities in discourses and practices. The articulation of relatedness with national ideologies and individual life experiences creates contradictions in people's lives and in their relationships with each other.

Analyzing the disjunctures that arise in relationships among Sullk'atas requires understanding not only an ontology of ayni but also the wider relationships of production and consumption which play into discourses of relatedness. I remember, for example, my conversation with Pastor in which we talked about conceptions of birth and his experiences as a midwife. At one point, he described the differences between babies born at term and miscarriages. Pastor's analysis of why miscarriages occur brings together material, moral, and physiological relationships with understandings of how relatedness is produced. Miscarriages occur because women have cravings that are unfulfilled:

> They wish—most [of the women who miscarry] have cravings [for food] . . . Why wouldn't [her husband] put down money for her cravings, for whatever she wanted? It makes *me* so mad! Instead she gives birth as she's walking along! . . . [I wonder,] "And what should you have bought for your wife?" This is the way it is; some men earn money just to *earn* it.

Feeding a woman eggs and meat during her pregnancy is crucial to the development of the fetus. By feeding his wife, a man also feeds the child and develops a relationship with it. Yet a husband may decide not use his money to buy the food that his wife craves.

Earning money just to have it, to hold onto it, epitomizes the power and mystery of gringos, who desire money as human beings would desire food. In this sense, and in Pastor's evaluation, such a husband's actions are immoral. Most Sullk'atas eat potatoes, however, not meat and eggs. It is more typical for a woman to have had at least one child die early in life than to have all of her children survive to adolescence. Thus the material and physiological contingencies, as well as the social, political, and economic parameters of the reproduction of daily life in a capitalist system, are implicated in the negotiation of relatedness and hierarchy among kin in Sullk'ata.

Modern Children and Unfinished Cycles

Pastor's evaluation of those "who earn money just to *earn* it" may be played out in another way for those whose children live to adulthood. What happens when sons are resituated by their experiences so that the hierarchical relationship between parents and children established through birth, work, and feeding children is inverted? Increasingly Sullk'atas are put into the position of relating to children who live out their adolescent and adult lives away from the place of their birth in urban and predominantly Spanish-speaking places. These children live outside of the daily relationships of reciprocity.

Sullk'atas recognize that during adolescence children not only become less dependent on and connected to parents but also identify themselves with urban ideologies of sociality and modernity, creating contradictions in the structural relationship of hierarchy between parents and children (Van Vleet 1999:160–171). Children or grandchildren may increasingly position themselves, or may be positioned, as Sucreños or Cochabambinos instead of Sullk'atas, through their life experiences and attributes (such as their ability to speak Spanish, education in public schools, an urban lifestyle, and access to commodities through wage work). When Sullk'atas become less involved in the daily practices of relatedness, they at once live through those dispositions established in childhood and reinvent what it is to be kin and to be native Andean.

Moreover, as adolescents increasingly leave rural communities to work in cities, temporarily or permanently, their means of maintaining relatedness shift. Adult actions are crucial in establishing and maintaining kinship relationships, but children are not simply passive recipients of relatedness (Van Vleet 2003a). Children's actions and words also sustain relationships. Rather than contributing labor on the family agricultural plots, herding sheep, or cooking meals, children carry home gifts of sweaters and jeans, radios and blankets, and food such as bread, fruit, and rice. Carnival is one of the most prominent times when Sullk'ata youth return to communities, bearing gifts for family members as well as displaying their own commodities. In fact, Sullk'ata women expect these gifts primarily from their children rather than from their husbands, as expressions of relatedness and affection.

There is, however, an *unevenness* to the value placed on reciprocal action in ayni and the sacrifices required to raise a child. The very practice of feeding is a primary way in which kin relationships are continuously established and naturalized: this is true for children raised by their "birth" parents and for children raised by "adoptive" parents. Unlike the relationship of reciprocity between human beings and the supernatural forces of the universe, the relationship of reciprocity between parents and children is attenuated. Although children contribute to the production of the household, they are not expected or obligated to remain in the household. They work with their parents but do not feed their parents. Children, especially daughters, eventually leave their parents, fraying the fabric of everyday kinship. Elderly Sullk'atas may hope that their children will help them in their old age, but this and other returns are described as an expression of tenderness rather than as the second half of a cycle of reciprocity. Thus the sacrifice of raising a child may not be repaid or even acknowledged.

Conclusion

Sullk'atas often expressed concern for me because I was alone, living far from my family. On numerous occasions one woman or another said to me, "Don't you wish for your own child to accompany you?" or "Wouldn't you like to take this baby home with you?" (reinforcing her words with gestures as she presented her baby to me). Both North American and Bolivian friends in Sucre and La Paz had warned me that in rural regions of Bolivia stories circulate about strangers, especially gringos, who steal babies, having no children of their own. More concerned with giving further voice to the rumors than with people's consternation over my state of being alone or my lack of interest in the babies, I generally explained that I was still finishing my studies and too far from my family to have a child. In another instance, however, a young mother repeatedly offered to let me take her infant back to the United States with me until her three-year-old daughter burst into tears. Only then did I realize that most Sullk'ata women were simply teasing me, pretending to offer me something of value that they had but I did not. At the same time, mothers were also taunting their children, reminding older siblings of the affection and protectiveness they should feel for the youngest of the family. Thus in offering to give an infant away, Sullk'ata women reinscribed the significance of relatedness among kin and of sociality more generally.

In this chapter I have argued that kinship is grounded in ayni, not sexual reproduction, in Sullk'ata. Both the degree of intimacy and the transparency of authority in a household are linked to the circulation of food and energy. This has implications for how Sullk'atas live out their daily lives and navigate hierarchies and intimacies. If ayni is the ground to relatedness, then true kin, as much as everyday kin, must do social, emotional, and material work to maintain their relationships. Nurturing, feeding, and caring for that child, teaching how to work and to contribute to the sustenance of the household, and disciplining and receiving respect are practices that create and maintain relatedness. Moreover, people may emphasize different relationships in different contexts. Individuals may recognize more than one set of adults as parents, performing and negotiating relatedness with each. With reciprocity as the ontological ground of relatedness, the discourses of true kinship and everyday kinship are not contradictory ones that oppose an essential (biological or genetic) kinship with a chosen kinship.

This chapter revolves around the relatedness between parents and children. Ayni as the ground of relatedness emerges most explicitly in relation to parent and child. To a certain extent, my emphasis on the relationship between parents and children reflects my own cultural and intellectual background, in which sexual reproduction is both assumed and challenged as the foundation of family. My emphasis also reflects my experiences in Sullk'ata, however, shaped as they were by conversations and everyday activities with women and children. The relationship between parents and children is salient, both because it is one of the strongest and most flexible, based on long-term unidirectional care, and because it is one of the most frayed by the transforming political economy.

Reading the relationship between parents and children through ayni suggests that the hierarchies and intimacies of relatedness extend into a broader matrix of relationships among people, within and beyond any particular household. In the story with which I began the chapter, Silveria's public expression of sorrow about Javier's failure to bring her a radio evolves into her sister's insistence that he is still Silveria's son. Her sister locates the legitimacy of being a mother in the work of caring for a child, which requires maintaining a circulation of food, energy, and emotion. Although Silveria's expression of pain at having been forgotten by Javier turns on his failure to express his affection for her by bringing a promised gift from Cochabamba, this story also raises a question. When Silveria expressed such sorrow, was it *only* her relationship with Javier that she was navigating? She cried during a fiesta, when she and others were drunk. She cried in the presence of her sister and her sister's husband and in the presence of her own husband. How might Silveria, and other Sullk'atas, be engaged in maintaining other relationships as well?

As this case and the others described in this chapter suggest, the reproduction of relationships between kin and the construction of the household on an everyday basis are profoundly political matters, crosscut by power relations and emotional ties, by social expectations and economic interests. As I describe in the following chapter, Sullk'atas draw attention to their own positioning in a network of kin and to specific events or relationships through emotional talk and displays of emotions. Sullk'atas also at times interpret events as morally and socially relevant, intertwining relatedness with commentary on the broader political-economic context. Relatedness is lived in emergent interactions that take place among individuals; thus investigating how talk is embedded in particular situations highlights the ways in which relatedness extends beyond but is shaped by the ideals of ayni.

FOUR

Narrating Sorrow, Performing Relatedness

A Story Told in Conversation

I REMEMBER ONE of the first times I visited Lorenzo and María. When I arrived at their house in the afternoon, Lorenzo was in the courtyard. He invited me in but told me that María was still away from the house, herding her sheep. I reminded him that I had come to visit him as well as María. Lorenzo possessed a far-reaching understanding of the political organization of the ayllu and had agreed to tell me about its history. As the *alcalde,* the highest-ranking authority in Kallpa, he had the knowledge and authority to advise me about the ayllu. I also learned that he had personal experience of the ways in which everyday circumstances impinge upon ideal structures. We sat down against the far wall of the courtyard, so that we could face the sun; but instead of talking about the political organization of Sullk'ata or the events and experiences that had shaped the ayllu since 1952, Lorenzo began talking about his children.

Lorenzo and María's children, like those of many other elderly Sullk'atas, did not live in the ayllu. They had each initially gone to the city to earn money for a few months or to take part in mandatory military service. Their temporary migrations had become permanent. Two of Lorenzo's sons lived in Sucre, and one son and two daughters lived in Cochabamba. All of them were married and had children of their own.

"Not one has stayed here with us," he said, beginning to weep. "My sons are no longer Kallpaños. They are Sucreños." He cried, saying, "Aaaay, *llakikuni*. I feel such sadness."

And I—not yet knowing that I should respond by saying, "*Ama waqaychu! Don't cry!*"—did little to comfort him.

"After this year, we will have to move to Sucre," he said. "They want us to come to live in the house they are building. What will we do? We have no one to help us plant our fields here."

Many of the men and women in Lorenzo's generation found themselves growing old with their children far away. Lorenzo's sorrow was particularly sharp because neither his sons nor his daughters lived in the rural community. Most of the men of Lorenzo's generation had remained in their natal communities and had contributed to their fathers' subsistence-based production until they were given land of their own to farm. Even Lorenzo's youngest son, who would inherit the household compound, did not live in Kallpa. He preferred to visit only occasionally with his wife and three young children. Lorenzo, I discovered, had undertaken the year-long responsibility (*cargo*, Sp.) of serving as the alcalde of the community in place of his son. This was an unusual situation. Typically a community member—usually a married man—serves in each ranked political position and sponsors each fiesta only once over the course of his lifetime. In addition to the financial and personal burdens of the cargo itself, Lorenzo also despaired over the futility of attempting to maintain his son's connections to the ayllu. When a loved one moves permanently from the ayllu, the sensual and material tenor of daily exchanges of labor and food is lost. Sullk'atas recognize the uncertainties and potential ambiguities of relatedness—the sadness that comes of not knowing whether what has been given will ever be reciprocated. Tied up with value-laden understandings of reciprocity, and the contradictions of living at the conjuncture of divergent moral economies, *llakikuy* (to feel sadness, to sorrow) expresses a gap between the expectations of relatedness and the actualities.

In this chapter I explore the ways in which Sullk'atas navigate relatedness in embodied, affective, and storied interactions among individuals. In particular, I focus on a narrative told to me in conversation about the death of a woman's brother. I discuss both the conventional aspects of the expression of llakikuy in Sullk'ata and the ways in which relatedness is performed and produced through the expression of llakikuy in a particular situation. As anthropologists have pointed out, emotion is culturally and socially situated; the expression, meanings, material bases, and corporeal consequences of emotions vary widely across cultures.[1] Moreover, emotions are not "raw" modes of access to "the truth," no matter how spontaneously expressed and deeply felt (Abu-Lughod 1990b:27; Abu-Lughod and Lutz 1990; Appadurai 1990; Lutz 1988). Rather than trying to guess Sullk'atas' intentions or "true feelings," I raise the question of how sorrowful talk and talk about sadness act upon the world.[2] Sorrowing is also a performance that enacts connection, points to ruptures in the social fabric, and influences an audience and is thus implicated in the interpersonal politics of a small community.

Narratives of Exploitation and Sorrow

Over the course of the time I lived in Kallpa, I visited Lorenzo and María often. Soft-spoken yet friendly, Lorenzo was delighted with the bags of coca leaves that I brought to him first as a gesture of respect and goodwill and later also as a token of friendship. María, a tiny yet spry woman in her seventies, had eyes that twinkled amid the wrinkles that radiated across her face. The two would invite me into their kitchen to sit on the edge of the bed, listen to stories, or simply talk about the day's events. Eventually I met their sons, their daughters-in-law, and their grandchildren when they arrived in Kallpa to visit. Before long I began visiting Lorenzo and María's children whenever I traveled to Sucre. I carried ch'uñu from Lorenzo and María to their children and returned with gifts of clothing or coca from the children to their parents.

One evening, after I had been living in Kallpa for over a year, I dropped by Lorenzo and María's house to find out whether they wanted me to take anything to their children when I left the next day on the bus to Sucre. Our conversation about my plans to travel turned into an array of warnings and stories about lik'ichiri. Neither mythical beings nor spirits of the dead (aya; or alma [soul], Sp.), lik'ichiri are human beings who are quite alive and pose a very real danger to people as they travel.[3] Lorenzo and María warned me not to sleep on the bus. I was vulnerable, they said, to a lik'ichiri sucking out my fat and blood. Stories about lik'ichiri have circulated in the Andean region at least since the seventeenth century. Anthropological accounts have interpreted these stories as being implicit theories of social subordination in which the life force of the poor— their fat—is taken by the rich.

The narrative I include here shares details with many other lik'ichiri stories. Central to this narrative, however, is María's account of how her brother died from the attack of a lik'ichiri many years before. Emotion may be produced and sustained through a myriad of discourses (talk *and* actions) that do not directly refer to any particular emotional state.[4] As she spoke of her brother's death and the dangers that a person may encounter when traveling far from home, María also evoked a sense of the despair engendered by her brother's absence and of the sustaining attention that emanates from the people and places of Sullk'ata. I draw on this conversation in order to introduce three of the conventional contexts of sorrowing in Sullk'ata: a loved one's death, migration, and a daughter's marriage. I also use this story, told in the course of a conversation, to raise the question of what the expression of llakikuy accomplishes. Told jointly by an elderly married couple, with my minimal but crucial participation, the narrative is part of an emotional exchange that acts upon the situation at hand and, at the same time, refers back to another moment in time.[5]

Don't Ever Sleep on the Bus

María was sitting in front of the hearth on a small wooden stool, with her clay pots and some plastic and wooden bowls arranged on a ledge and on the floor behind her as she cooked the evening meal. Just behind her, in the small kitchen, Lorenzo sat on the bed. Leaning against the wall, he shelled corn, rubbing the dried kernels off the cob and into a large basin. I greeted them from outside their gate. Hearing their call to enter, I made my way carefully through the dark courtyard to the kitchen. We talked for a few moments of my plans to travel to Sucre. Then Lorenzo said to me, "You know, the husband of the woman who lives below our comadre was killed by a lik'ichiri." He added, nodding toward María: "Her brother was killed by a lik'ichiri too."

"But how did it kill him?" I asked.

"He was extinguished. Perhaps he came down with the sickness really fast. *All* his fat was sucked out with a machine!"

Just as Lorenzo began to repeat that the fat was sucked out, I made a scared sound and said, "Oh, they extr—they took out all of his fat? With a machine?"

And he emphasized again, "Yes, with a machine."

"What is that machine like, anyway?"

"I don't know," Lorenzo replied in Spanish. Then switching back to Quechua, he wondered: "What could it be like? I haven't ever seen it either. But with a machine, they say."

I paused, thinking about what he had told me. This was not the first time I had heard about lik'ichiri. On one of my first trips to Sullk'ata while I was still looking for a field site, our guide had warned my husband and me that people might suspect us of being lik'ichiri. Fragments of a description followed: lik'ichiri extract fat and blood from human beings with a small black machine; they travel without a specific destination; they are gringos and strangers; they wear sunglasses. On that same trip we encountered our guide's compadre, who was recovering from a sickness caused by a lik'ichiri. He showed us a small round red mark on his side, where, he said, the lik'ichiri had sucked out his fat and blood with a machine.

I asked Lorenzo whether the lik'ichiri are like almas, the souls of the dead.

Both María and Lorenzo answered at once: *Runallataq a!* (They're just people!).

Then each one tried to speak again, but María held the floor. "When we sit next to each other," she said, "we don't come down with lik'ichiri sickness."

"Now on a bus, we would sit like this," added Lorenzo, demonstrating that they would sit side by side. "Now [when] you sit with someone who you do not know, don't you fall asleep?" he asked me.

María spoke up for me: "'I will go!' she says." She was not convinced that Lorenzo's story was having any affect on my decision to take the bus to Sucre. "You tell him: 'Traveling makes me fall asleep.'"

"Ayyyy," I groaned. I always fell asleep on the long bus trips to and from Sucre. The bus traveled during the day, and I rarely slept for long, as the bus jounced along the rutted dirt road. During the past several months, however, I had been traveling to and from La Paz to visit my husband. The return trips were always at night. The bus from La Paz to Llallagua, a mining center from which I typically caught a truck to Pocoata, left at seven in the evening. Arriving in Llallagua at three in the morning, I usually tried to catch another few hours of fitful sleep on the bus before the terminal opened for business. Although I was always nervous about spending the night on the bus, I was more concerned about someone stealing my backpack than about a lik'ichiri stealing my fat and blood.[6]

"Fall asleep, then he puts that machine . . . right up to you until your fat is sucked out . . . And you, you will sleep!" cautioned Lorenzo.

"That's what I don't like," I explained. "From La Paz to Llallagua the bus travels only at night."

Lorenzo reiterates, "Don't sleep . . . don't sleep . . ."

A Black Sheep Could Have Cured Him

As our conversation continued, Lorenzo told me that a long time ago Sullk'atas did not know how to cure the wasting that follows a lik'ichiri's attack. Because no one knew how to cure an attack, the poor individuals who had their blood and fat—their life force—removed just slowly withered away. Their family members and neighbors watched helplessly as they died. "Now they know to slaughter a black sheep for someone who has lik'ichiri sickness. They drink the blood of the black sheep and eat the meat, and with that they get better."

María picked up the narrative, saying, "A long time my brother walked in pain, slowly." When her brother was not yet twenty, he went to Argentina to work. Most travel then was by foot, at least from the rural community to the mining town of Llallagua.

"He had a fever for a long time," Lorenzo added.

Her voice rising, María remembered: "I said, 'Just cure him, just cure him, just *cure* him!'"

"With herbs you tried to cure him," Lorenzo said, shaking his head.

I broke in, asking if he just died, little by little, with his fat sucked out.

"Yes," María answered. "We would have fed our brother a black sheep. And then he might have gotten better, gotten better . . . until we had cured him completely. Yes . . . with the ones who know, we would have cured him. But no! Until [inaudible], he died."

María continued by remembering the sounds her brother made as he died: "He said, 'Guuuuu' [*groaning*]. So many people arrived. 'Guuuuun,' he just said. People just kept arriving to be with him. Like that he died, that brother of mine. Ayyy! He was so young!"

Interrupting María's story, I asked where lik'ichiri were encountered and again queried whether they actually were living human beings. Once more they told me: lik'ichiri are just people. Realizing that what was hard for me to imagine was common sense to them, I reiterated the point with which María had begun her story: a long time ago people did not know how to cure the sickness.

"We did not know," María agreed. "We would have made him well if we had known." She added: "And he had a wife. And then his wife left after he died. She went back to her parents' house."

"Did he have children when he died?" I asked.

"No, there weren't any children."

María then told me about the relationships of her seven siblings, naming each one in order of birth, from oldest to youngest. She placed the brother who died between her two brothers who still lived in the community. As she named each sibling's younger brother or sister, I repeated every name.

"Now you know Ércoles, right?"

"Yes," I replied.

"Ah, that one, that one was Ércoles' younger brother."

"Ércoles' younger?"

"Yes, he was Ércoles' younger brother. And *his* younger sibling was Primo."

"Ah, Primo."

"And Primo's younger sibling is Hermelinda."

"And were there more?"

"Next, Hermelinda's younger sibling was Reina."

"Reina?"

"And the next was Máximo. There were a lot of us."

"Did they also die? Reina and Máximo?"

"Those two also died."

Lorenzo then broke in, "Now you won't ever sleep going somewhere [on the bus]!" He laughed.

Also laughing, I promised him, "I won't sleep anymore."

Shaking his head, Lorenzo noted that many people sleep on the bus as they are traveling, perhaps unaware of the danger in which they put themselves. He then pointed out that lik'ichiri not only profit from stealing fat and blood but also steal money and other commodities as well. "They sell that fat for money."

"They sell it?"

"Yes, they sell it to priests, they say. With that fat they baptize those little children, with fat from those people."

I was surprised. "Ahhiiii!"

"For lots of different things they sell the fat . . . Priests, they buy it and with that human fat they baptize the children."

"Really?"

Until this conversation with Lorenzo and María, I was under the impression that I was more suspected of *being* a lik'ichiri than of being vulnerable to sustaining an attack from one. Scholars have interpreted the stories of lik'ichiri, who are often characterized as gringos, as commentary on the exploitation of native Andeans by more powerful others or as indigenous analyses of extraction.[7] Lik'ichiri extract and sell the life force of poor campesinos on the open market. As Weismantel (1997, 2001) points out, the stories are intimately linked to racial discourses that associate commodities with whiteness. The unequal exchanges between lik'ichiri and campesinos parallel those between gringos (anthropologists, tourists, missionaries, the urban elite, provincial authorities, shop owners) and campesinos more generally. Yet most anthropological interpretations of lik'ichiri rest almost exclusively on an analysis of the relationship between gringos and campesinos (Mannheim and Van Vleet 1998:332); interpretations of these stories do not address the relationships among campesinos themselves.

The relationship between campesinos and gringos, or self and other, is not always of paramount concern for Sullk'atas. Moreover, Sullk'atas may engage in activities and interpret events in ways that are not readily apparent to "outsiders," even though "foreign" institutions influence the social and historical milieu in which they live. Taking María's part of the story seriously and examining the ways in which it is embedded in the conversation illuminates not only the interweaving of political economy and sentiment in the interactions of individuals but also the attempts to maintain relatedness among individuals. If what we need to know, as Lila Abu-Lughod (1990b:28) has written, is "how discourses on emotion, or emotional discourses for that matter . . . are implicated in the play of power and the operation of historically changing systems of social hierarchy," then tracing the linkages of political economy, social hierarchies, and affective interactions in specific circumstances is crucial to understanding llakikuy in a broader social and historical context. By attending to the ways in which the story is embedded in a particular situation, I show that this narrative is as much about loss and sorrow among those who care about each other as it is about the exploitation of native Andeans by gringos.

Conventional Expressions of Sorrow

When María took up the story of the lik'ichiri, she highlighted her brother's illness and death and how his death affected other people. Although Lorenzo first introduced the fact that her brother died from the attack of a lik'ichiri, María was the one who remembered the moments of his dying and the futility of their attempts to save him. She recounted how her brother had walked for many miles, sick and in pain as he returned on foot from Argentina. She evoked the room where the sick young man finally lay down and embedded her brother's speech, even his groans, into her narrative. María lamented that they were unable to cure her brother. Her voice rose as she remembered pleading, "Just cure him!" She mourned the lack of knowledge at that time about how to heal the sickness caused by lik'ichiri. Emphasizing the network of ties between her brother and many others, she recalled the large number of people who arrived for his wake, "because of him."

Even many years after the event, María's eyes filled with tears. As much as her expression of llakikuy reflects a personally felt engagement, sorrowing also draws on "discursive public forms" that are anchored in particular cultural settings and ideals, styles of performance, social formations of power and authority, and histories of personal interaction (Appadurai 1990:93). Sullk'atas explicitly name the feeling of llakikuy in relation to both themselves and others in everyday contexts and ritual occasions. They express sorrow through particular styles of speaking: the high-pitched, slower-paced speech of a person expressing sorrow sharply contrasts with the rapid, low-pitched, and almost monotone everyday speech. Sullk'atas most often express sorrow or say that they feel an existential pain when an adult or child dies, when children are living far away, and when a woman marries. In each of these circumstances, the everyday cycling of energy, labor, and gifts among people is attenuated in ways that are not easily altered. These conventional contexts shape the expression of particular emotions and constrain the ways in which interlocutors interpret the meanings of interactions, events, and stories.

When a Loved One Dies

Perhaps the most conventional, though not necessarily most frequent, expression of llakikuy is during a funeral or other ritual events that evoke the memory of a person who has died.[8] When people die, their immediate relationships of reciprocity with family and community members are ended, although, as Gose (1994) and others have pointed out, ancestors continue to participate in the cycling of water and energy crucial to the lives and livelihoods of native Andeans. Ideally, a person dies after having grown to old age. Children, particularly sons, have the responsibility of caring for their parents in their old age and of burying their parents properly. As Arnold and Yapita (1996:320–21; my translation) report for the people of the ayllu Qaqachaka, Bolivia, "Although the son brings a daughter-in-law to the house, he will cry for his parents and he will bury them. In contrast, they say, the daughter will be far away and will just say: 'Oh, they died, and they went to bury them after a while.'" Sullk'atas in some ways also see daughters, like daughters-in-law, as though they are "of other people." When a daughter marries, her parents know that she will leave her natal community, will become integrated into another kinship network, and may not maintain relatedness with them, as I discuss further below.

A death is a marked occurrence of loss. Funeral rituals place great emphasis on separating the living from the dead and symbolically transforming individual souls into a collective body of ancestors (Gose 1994; Harris 1982). Until the corpse is buried and sent on its way to the afterlife, family members, who are considered to have an almost physical connection to the person who has died, are in a state of ritual danger (Gose 1994:117). When people are about to die, Sullk'atas say that their almas or souls may wander to the places they often visited in their life. Almas may cause sickness or misfortune as they attempt to pull the living, especially those close to them, to the afterlife. People, particularly family members, drink cane alcohol and smoke cigarettes to protect themselves from the alma. Close family members—brothers and sisters, children and parents, and spouse—express grief through crying during the funeral. Affines, compadres, and neighbors comfort the "true kin" but do not express grief as much as fearfulness of the soul.

The sorrow expressed for those individuals who have died is also reiterated during two annual fiestas: All Souls Day (Todos Santos) and Carnival. During the Catholic feast of Todos Santos, entire communities spend a day in the cemetery. Living family members of those who have recently died "remember" the soul by decorating an altar; offering corn beer, cane alcohol, and cigarettes to ayllu members around the grave; reciting prayers; crying; and offering children bread made into the shapes of babies, snakes, and flowers in return for prayers recited. Relatives create altars on Todos Santos for the first three years after the death. A few months later, on the eve of Carnival, ayllu members remember the men who have died in the past year. The young people from each community in Sullk'ata travel in a group to each household where a man died that year. At each *alma wasi* (literally, soul house) living relatives serve corn beer and ritual food throughout the night to adults and to young people who arrive from the surrounding communities, dancing and playing flutes. The rites on the first night of Carnival are said to "welcome the souls" to the fiesta; on the final night of Carnival the souls are dispatched. In spite of the rituals of transformation that shift the focus away from individual deaths, some Sullk'atas may continue to emphasize their feelings of sorrow for spouses, parents, siblings, or children for years after they die.

When a Loved One Leaves

Sullk'atas also express sadness when a child or a spouse migrates to the city or to lowland regions for work, mandatory military service, education in urban high schools or colleges, or even just to visit. Sullk'atas have long histories of traveling between highland and valley regions of the ayllu and of migrating to mines and cities for wage work. In the past entire families would walk with their herds of sheep and/or llamas to their valley lands. Now most migration is by truck or bus, undertaken by individuals seeking work in Bolivia's cities or eastern lowlands. Some adolescents remain in the city and through their life experiences, desires, and attributes identify with urban life and practices more than with ayllu life and practices. Many Sullk'atas are thus in the position of relating to children who live out their adolescent and adult lives away from the place of their birth and outside of the daily relationships of reciprocity.

In addition, many Sullk'atas, like Lorenzo, find themselves in the position of doing the majority of the agricultural work at a time in their lives when they

Sitting on top of almost any kind of cargo, truck passengers have a view of the surrounding countryside as they travel to and from the campo.

had hoped to rely on the help of their sons and daughters-in-law. María and Lorenzo's three sons all eventually built houses in Cochabamba and Sucre. After working as domestic servants, their daughters married and remained in Cochabamba. Lorenzo and María's children visited them in Kallpa, but only for brief periods. Lorenzo mobilized labor for planting his fields through ayni or *mink'a* (unequivalent exchange) relationships or by requesting the help of his compadres. His sons had initially participated in the cargo system and had each sponsored a fiesta. For the past several years they had refused to serve as community authorities or sponsor additional fiestas, practices that would have helped them maintain connections with the ayllu in spite of their absence. Lorenzo and María's grandchildren were growing up in the city, attending schools there, eating the food of the city, living in apartments, and traveling on buses each day. None of their grandchildren could speak Quechua, although they understood a little. María also cried at the prospect of someday having to leave the community of Kallpa and live in a city "filled with gringos" when she and Lorenzo could no longer subsist in the community.

When a Daughter Marries

The loneliness of elderly couples who no longer have children in the rural community is associated with relatively recent shifts in migration patterns.

The sorrow that emerges in this situation, however, is similar to that expressed by parents when their daughters marry. Because a woman typically marries a man from another community and patrilocal residence is the expectation, most women leave their families when they marry. Most young couples spend from a few months to a few years living in the household of the husband's parents. Sometimes a newly married couple will move to a city together to work and earn money for their wedding fiesta. In each case, a woman leaves the network of kin with whom she grew up and the pantheon of sacred places with which she is familiar.

Parents realize that when a daughter marries they will no longer have the benefits of her labor and affection. They also recognize that a daughter will have a difficult time in her new community (see Chapter 7). Many parents scold their daughter for running off with a young man and express llakikuy when a daughter marries. During the first days of a wedding fiesta, as the groom's community celebrates with music, dancing, and drinking in one household compound, the bride's community sits outside the walls of the compound drinking and making libations in somber silence (see Chapter 6). Even though most women are less than a day's travel from their natal home, they rarely return to visit their parents. One young woman who returned to her parents' house during Carnival was in fact criticized for "making her mother-in-law cry." Women who are recently married and not yet integrated into their husband's natal household are especially vulnerable to criticism, especially if they do not yet have children of their own.

Women, young and old, also say that they feel sorry for themselves, taking up this discourse of loneliness. Newly married women who live far from their kin may cry about being alone even if their days are filled with cooking and washing clothes for several of their husbands' family members. I have also heard women who have lived in a community for several years crying about being alone and saying, "I have no mother or father," whether or not their parents are dead. In Chapter 7 I return to the ways in which power asymmetries, emotional discourse, and relatedness are intertwined in relationships among women who are affines. Here, however, I discuss the more general issue of sorrow in Sullk'ata and how María's narrative fits into these conventional contexts.

Convention and Engagement in María's Narrative

Sullk'atas expect that people will feel sorrow because of a particular state of affairs (such as being far from one's kin), a series of events (such as a death and funeral), or a social position (such as being a daughter-in-law). In each of these conventional contexts, sorrowing is associated with a rupture in bonds and an attenuation of the cycling of care. Ayni, as I have already described, organizes much of daily life, including the raising of children. Yet children may not reciprocate their parents' care or sacrifice. Siblings may not engage in the ideals of mutuality. The incompleteness of an exchange engenders both hierarchy and ambiguity in those interactions in which a long-term reciprocal action—children helping their parents in old age, bringing gifts of food and clothing, or burying and remembering their parents after their deaths—may be desired but never be realized (cf. Trawick 1990).

This sense of loss and sorrow is also more generally expressed among native Andeans in ritual and songs as well as in everyday interactions. Mannheim (1991b:19; see also Gose 1986) has argued that this expression of sorrow is perhaps

> an implicit recognition that every reciprocal action is always one-half of a cycle, that reciprocity requires an initial surrender of the self to the gift of labor or object, and that the cycle of reciprocity is ever liable to rupture. "Why have you come from the mountains alone, why have you come single?" they will sing to an animal at an increase ritual. Andean economy and culture turn a famous anthropological principle on its head: all exchange is, at base, sacrifice.

Llakikuy is intertwined with the connection and caring for others that is implicit in ayni and with the fragilities of relatedness, the potential pain in caring for others, and the more general recognition that a loss of mutuality in exchange is an inherent part of everyday life.

The conventional aspects of ruptures in social relationships are evident in María's story and her expression of sorrow. Her sorrow emerges as she remembers her brother's absence and return and his illness and death. Before his death, her brother had traveled far away from those who cared about him: his siblings and parents and his wife. María's emphasis on the ways in which her brother was enmeshed in social and affective relationships creates a sense that those relationships made "here" a place of safety. "Here" is where people know and love you; "there" is where you stand outside of a network of relatedness. After the death of María's brother, his wife returned to her own natal community to live with her parents and be close to the people who cared for her, rather than remain alone among her husband's kin. The particular painfulness of the death of María's younger brother in his youth at the hands of a stranger also draws upon a long history of exploitation and individuals' experiences of discrimination.

Sullk'atas generally agree that lik'ichiri attack when their victims are unaware and that they profit from the sale of fat. Whether the fat is the necessary ingredient of the baptismal oil that priests use to anoint children, as Lorenzo explains to me, or of cosmetics and creams or of the grease that lubricates airplanes, these commodities are associated with a powerful world that is organized according to a different moral and economic system.[9]

Rather than being tangential to the lik'ichiri narrative, as I initially supposed, María's emphasis on her brother's social relationships highlights her understanding of where and how she lives and the value-laden understandings of relatedness among Sullk'atas. By pinpointing her brother's place among the siblings, María indicates that he was her younger brother. She actively cared for him as a child. By acknowledging the large number of people who came to be with him as he died and to participate in his funeral, she gives evidence of the strength of his ties to others. By enacting through her words and style of speech the efforts that she and others put into curing him, María underscores their relatedness to him.

Dialogic Production of Affect

The narrative thus points to the engagement of social actors in social and affective relationships, an engagement that is not negated by the conventionalities of the expression of llakikuy. María's words are "seeped with the apprehension that 'I am involved'" (M. Rosaldo 1984:143). In the remainder of the chapter, I draw on Michelle Rosaldo's proposal that emotion bespeaks the "difference between a mere hearing of a child's cry and a hearing *felt*—as when one realizes that danger is involved or that the child is one's own" (1984:143; emphasis in original).[10] Her purpose was to highlight the simultaneously felt and cognized aspects of emotion.[11] I use the concept of "engagement" to point to the ways in which affect, though "phenomenologically experienced," arises between social actors as they are involved in social and linguistic interactions with each other.

From this perspective, individuals may produce those emotions or more subtle sensibilities, dispositions, or sentiments through talk and actions that do not directly reference particular emotions. In her analysis of women's songs, for example, Regina Harrison (1989) has demonstrated that for Ecuadorian Quechua speakers moving someone to sorrow through a song and making someone feel love are inextricably linked. As much as sorrowing marks disconnection among Sullk'atas, evoking sorrow is also a means of establishing care between people.

Anthropologists do not, of course, have access to the unspoken feelings or thoughts of their interlocutors, but they do engage in affective, social, and linguistic interactions. In this case, I participated in a conversational narrative. Like other Quechua narratives, this one was triggered by a previous topic of conversation and required the active participation of the listeners.[12] Fragments of stories and references to details and characters of other stories were interwoven in the conversation. Lorenzo initiated discussion of lik'ichiri in response to my announcement that I would be traveling. Although he mentioned the deaths of María's brother and a neighbor's husband, he primarily described the typical characteristics of lik'ichiri, drawing on other stories that circulated about them, as a way to warn me not to sleep on the bus.

María's story of her brother's death was embedded within the broader margins of Lorenzo's narrative of lik'ichiri. She highlighted the sense of loss and helplessness among people as they watch a loved one die. She listed the names of her siblings after she told of the family's inability to cure her brother. I supported their talk by providing back-channel responses like "yes," "and then," and "umhunh" and by asking questions. Finally, Lorenzo took over the conversation again to tell me that lik'ichiri sell the fat that they steal to priests; but before doing so, he emphasized the impact of María's story by saying, "Now you won't ever sleep on the bus!" In this interaction, we jointly produced a conversational narrative, but we also jointly produced a sense of affective engagement.

Embedded Sorrow

By analyzing the embedded speech in the narrative, I illuminate the ways in which the narrative is socially produced and productive of interpretations and perhaps even "feelings." Embedded speech, most typically the use of citation and indirect discourse, is typical of all Quechua narrative (Mannheim and Van Vleet 1998:327; see also Howard-Malverde 1989, 1990).[13] María creates dialogue more than Lorenzo does, by embedding speech into her description of her brother's death from the sickness caused by being "grabbed" by a lik'ichiri. She embeds her brother's groans and her own cries of "Just cure him!" into her story, bringing the moment of her brother's dying into the here and now. She transports the mood of her brother's death into our conversation about lik'ichiri, which up to that point has been dominated by details of the existential nature (real or imaginary, human or supernatural) and the practices of lik'ichiri. María's use of embedded speech emphasizes her personal experience of a lik'ichiri attack and of her brother's death.

An important consequence of any narrative with reported speech is that an implicit theory about the relationship between speech and action is carried within the story (Urban 1991). María's use of quotation—of herself and of others those many years before—may enable her to claim a certain authority on the matter. Her use of embedded speech also highlights the affective involvement that she had with her brother and that he had with others. As Judith Irvine (1990:130) has noted of a very different context, verbal performances or interactions

> do not simply represent our own social identity, our own feelings, and the social occasion here and now. They are full of allusions to the behavior of others and to other times and places. To put this another way: One of the many methods people have for differentiating situations and marking their moods is to draw on (or carefully avoid) the "voices" of others, or what they assume those "voices" to be.

Drawing on the voices of herself and her brother, María conveys the desperation of caring for someone who was wasting away from a sickness brought on by the greed of another. She also creates a bridge between the context of the story and the context of our conversation, as she re-creates the sorrowing at the time of her brother's death, crying: "Just cure him! Just cure him! Just *cure* him!" She also contributes to our conversation about lik'ichiri and the danger of travel.

Evoking Care

At the end of our conversation, Lorenzo reiterates that I should not sleep on the bus. "This is the secret," he says. "Someone told me. I have told my children. Now I am telling you." Over the course of the conversation, both María and Lorenzo work hard to warn me about lik'ichiri and to convince me of my vulnerability. They tell me about lik'ichiri not only because of my lack of knowledge—evident in my questions to them—but also because of my plans to travel and their fear for my safety. Lorenzo and María thus offer knowledge that I might use to protect myself from harm; and at the same time, through nonreferential aspects of talk, they produce a sense of identification and collaboration.

Lorenzo also establishes his knowledge of a certain danger and of the ways to avoid it. The details of his narrative include the small black machines that lik'ichiri use to extract the life force of unsuspecting travelers; the baptismal oil that is actually human fat sold to priests at exorbitant prices and then used to baptize Sullk'ata children; and the availability of a potential cure for a terminal illness available only to those with knowledge and wealth. Through these elements, he directs attention to the economic, social, and political relationships in which Sullk'atas are engaged, which extend far beyond the kitchen where we spoke. Later in the conversation, Lorenzo reemphasizes the potential dangers of sleeping on the bus. "We come back here from Cochabamba, and we don't sleep at all." The trip from Cochabamba to Kallpa is at least forty-eight hours long. "At times," Lorenzo continues, "the two of us go together, and we sit in just one seat. That's all. I don't know how to sleep [on the bus]."

"I always sleep," María interjects.

"She sleeps, but, anyway, she is with me," replies Lorenzo. He reiterates his cautionary advice, distinguishing between the habits of their gringa anthropologist, who travels alone on buses, and the habits of campesinos, who always travel at least two together.

María explicitly aligns herself with me socially and linguistically. Both of us fall asleep on buses. Both of us have experiences of being far away from loved ones. Her sorrowing for her brother is at once a warning that relationships of caring can be lost, stolen, or extinguished and a performance which evokes my care for her. At certain points in the conversation María also embeds my speech into her own. She uses shifts in footing (Goffman 1981) to align herself with Lorenzo and me. In one instance, María speaks for me, saying: "She says, 'I will go.'" Addressing her husband, she embeds a statement indicating a future action attributed to me ("I will go") within a statement of reported speech ("She says"). Next she addresses me, embedding a statement of hypothetical, unbounded action ("Going makes me fall asleep") within the immediacy of a command ("Say"). Future and past, hypothetical and immediate contexts of interaction, are layered on top of each other as María mediates their emphasis on my vulnerability and attempts to explain what is to them a commonsensical danger.

Lorenzo sums up the narrative when he interrupts María, saying: "Now you won't ever sleep on a bus." And I finally agree. In different ways, then, these two elderly people show that they care about me and attempt to engage me in an affective and social exchange. María's story about her brother's death evokes a sense of sadness and caring. Lorenzo states that they also told their children not to sleep on the bus. Ideally, I should reciprocate the care that they have shown me.

Conclusion

In this chapter I have retold a story about beings who steal the life force of campesinos and have explored the conventional contexts and productive performances of sorrow in Sullk'ata. It might seem that a story of lik'ichiri has little to do with llakikuy, until we remember that lik'ichiri cause profound suffering in people's lives. Beyond the existential connection, as any storyteller knows, the meanings of any story are not limited to its purported topic. Meanings are embedded in layers of dialogue within the text that are interpreted by participants as they tell, listen to, or even read a story. Meanings also are lodged in the situation in which the narrative arises among participants. Tracing these meanings broadens our understanding of a story, in the process of its telling or even years later.

Similarly, when people sorrow, they may reflect upon already existing relationships and tell stories about events that cause distress. Although sorrow is not always named explicitly, the conventional styles and contexts of llakikuy may be resources that differently positioned individuals draw upon in different ways as they interact with others. Even when people do not put their sorrow into words, their actions are interpreted by others, who respond in some way. From this perspective, people jointly produce affective discourses and social relationships. By integrating discussion of the conventional contexts of llakikuy with analysis of dialogical emergence of llakikuy in a particular case, I argue for an understanding of affect as relational rather than individual and an understanding of Sullk'ata kinship that includes emotional performance.

In spite of anthropological critiques of assumptions about the internal and psychobiological locus of emotion, scholars have continued to center analyses on individual actors expressing emotion. As Donald Brenneis (1990:115) points out, this reflects an implicit assumption that the relationship between the internal state of the original "feelers" and the form and content of their message—or, alternatively, the speakers' intentions and the discursive strategies they use in pursuing their ends—are the most important issues. Yet, as this chapter has shown, audiences (including audiences of one or two people) are active, forming their own opinions, speaking as interlocutors, expressing their feelings, evincing disbelief, sympathy, or appreciation, and evaluating the affective "load" of the speaker even as an interaction is taking place (see also Irvine 1982:40). The issue for analysis is thus not only how those emotive messages are received or how messages might affect the audience but also how emotion is shaped by those active interpreters.

From this perspective the story in Chapter 3 in which Silveria cried about losing Javier might also be understood as a story expressing sorrow and evoking care. "I'll die and be forgotten. He's lost to me. He doesn't remember that I am his mother. I raised him," said Silveria. As her sorrow turned to sobbing, another woman responded, "Don't cry, don't cry!" Silveria's sorrow over having lost Javier turned on his failure to express his affection for her, as I have already described. Children who work away from the rural community often bring commodities such as clothing, food, and electronic items to their loved ones. These commodities become symbols not only of the givers' status as modern people but also of their caring. Lorenzo's sorrow about his sons who are "no longer Sullk'atas" is intertwined with their absence and their integration into a different moral economy. Their visits are few and far between; and though they send or bring clothing and other gifts, their absence weighs heavily. They cannot care for their parents as their parents have cared for them. Silveria's and Lorenzo's sorrowing provides explicit commentaries on the contingencies of their relationships, drawing on a conventional context of llakikuy for parents.

At the same time, Silveria and Lorenzo each navigate the contingencies of more immediate relationships—Silveria with her sister, who is present to hear her crying, and Lorenzo with me. Silveria and Julia have a complicated relationship; they are sisters-in-law and comadres as well as sisters. Silveria married the younger brother of a Kallpa family, and Julia married the older brother. Their husbands often fight with each other, and the disputes between the men frequently overflow into their own relationship. Although Julia does not at first respond to Silveria's sorrow, she eventually comes over to Silveria and says: "But he's still your son. He said, 'I will bring a radio.' But he said, he told me, 'I'm going to bring a radio for her.'" Silveria thus enacts relatedness with Javier by sorrowing and evokes caring, expressed in Julia's attempt to quiet her.

At least in Sullk'ata, sorrow and caring are jointly mobilized and produced in relationships among people. Conversely, through their interactions with each other, Sullk'atas performatively establish relatedness. Expressions of existential pain or llakikuy are particularly tied up with Sullk'ata performances of relatedness, moving relationships into new configurations, reinforcing moments of collaboration, or interpreting gaps in mutuality. The sorrowing of Lorenzo and María and other Sullk'atas is intertwined with local histories of personal relationships and the broad political-economic context of Bolivia at the turn of the twenty-first century. Spouses, parents, and children may die. Daughters marry and leave the care of their parents. Children leave home and increasingly remove themselves from the exchanges of the ayllu. Emotional performances thus enact particular moral and affective stances, enabling Sullk'atas to navigate relatedness in their everyday interactions.

FIVE

Storied Silences

Adolescent Desires, Gendered Agency,
and the Practice of Stealing Women

Intertext I: Julia Gets a Husband

JULIA WAS WASHING her clothes by the stream when I went down to get water. I squatted down next to her where she was sitting on top of the concrete-covered reservoir. She poured a little extra powdered soap into her basin even though the suds were floating over the rim. Women who could afford ACE powdered soap rather than a bar of laundry soap used it to wash everything from dishes and clothing to hair. I asked her when she'd be going back to Santa Cruz, where she worked as a domestic servant in the home of a wealthier Bolivian woman. "Soon," she said, "maybe tomorrow."

"And will you be coming back for San Juan?" I asked, referring to a fiesta that would take place in June. She said that she did not think so: now that she had a husband, things were less sure.[1] She did not know when she would be coming back to Kallpa.

"As a *soltera* [single woman, Sp.] you can go at any time, as you please. But now I have a *marido* [spouse, Sp.]," she said, nodding over to the young man who had been hanging out with her in the shade of the eucalyptus trees until I showed up. "I will have to save money for a wedding."

"You're married! Since when?" I asked.

"Now. Just this Carnival," she said. "I didn't plan on it. I was very drunk."

"Where is he from?"

"He's just from here."

"From Kallpa?" I clarified.

"Yes."

"What's his name?"

"Wilberto."

"What's his last name?"

"Mamani."

"He's not from Kallpa, is he?" I said, having lived in the community long enough to recognize that "Mamani," though prevalent in the region, was not a family name of the community.

"No . . . from Arana," she said, referring to a nearby community. "He's—you know doña Alsira, right?—he's doña Alsira's sister's son."

"Did you know him from before you went to Santa Cruz?" I asked.

"Yes, I knew him."

"But you weren't planning on this?" I queried.

"No," she said. "I don't really want a husband, but now I have one."

"How did it happen?"

"It just happened—like that," she said, shrugging her shoulders.

"What did your mother say? Did she scold you?" I asked Julia.

"They didn't say anything."

"Nothing?"

"No, my mother didn't say anything. My father didn't say anything either."

Wilberto wandered back over. We talked a little more, and then I left. Julia continued washing. She scrubbed the clothes that she had worn the past week for Carnival: polleras, eyelet blouses, and white slips trimmed with lace. Her polleras were made of the most fashionable materials: a nylon fabric that draped like silk in deep purple, another in turquoise, and a third in a green patterned fabric that reminded me of the grain of wood or of oil on water. The yards of fabric were gathered at the waist, with three horizontal pleats at hip level, and fell in loose folds to the knee. "I don't like it here," she said. "There's too much dirt, too much dust."

Warmi Suway: Asymmetries and Ambivalence

Marriage is a process as well as an event for Sullk'atas; if the beginning of a marriage could be marked, however, that event for Sullk'atas would be when a woman is stolen from a fiesta (*warmi suway*) or carried from her house (*warmi pusay*). Julia was one of two young women "stolen" during Carnival the year that I lived in Kallpa. Stealing a woman, or initiating a marriage without the consent of parents, is the most typical way for marriages to begin in the region. One married woman explained to me that young women (*sipas; cholitas* or *jovencitas,* Sp.) who are stolen from fiestas have gotten drunk and may not even know the person they follow home. "They wake up in the morning having never seen each other's faces," she said. Yet Sullk'atas recognize a range of circumstances when they use the phrase, from a young woman who is taken against her will and raped or forced to spend the night at the home of a young man to a couple that plans for months before eloping during a fiesta.

Described as custom (*custumbrilla; costumbre,* Sp.), the practice of warmi suway is normalized by Sullk'atas in ritual arenas and more daily occurrences. In the weeks preceding the fiesta, I heard several people in the community laughingly wonder, "How many cholitas will be stolen during Carnival?" Cholitas, in this case young unmarried native Andean women, often return to their natal Sullk'ata communities during Carnival to dance and sing for the fiesta. Carnival songs, which are played by local radio stations, reproduced on cassette tapes, and sung under the breath as the fiesta approaches, express the love and desires, and the love lost, of the young men (*jóvenes,* Sp.) and cholitas of the region. On the final night of Carnival, the young men of the community—some dressed as cholitas—enact a comic rendition of suway, to the delight of onlookers. In more everyday contexts, Sullk'atas retell stories about girls who are stolen by the huge Andean condor, bears, or supernatural beings and gossip about the most recent instances of suway in the ayllu.

The practice of warmi suway, however, is also embedded in layers of silence and ambivalence. Although older women joked with me about the cholitas who would be carried away during Carnival and encouraged me to buy or borrow a pollera so that I too could dance, they also evaded my more direct questions about particular instances of suway. Women would do little more than acknowledge whether or not they had been stolen themselves. Many denied that they had any role in the course of events of their own marriages. Married men would happily recall that they had stolen their wives, but they condensed the details of those events into generalities. Some men told me that warmi suway was only practiced in the campo, not in cities such as Llallagua or Cochabamba, where people were "more civilized."[2] Others distinguished between the local practices of warmi suway and warmi pusay, in which a young man first requests permission for marriage and the young woman is carried from her parents' house. Sullk'atas' silences about suway do not suggest that the practice is socially inconsequential. The ways in which people talk about warmi suway are shaped by local and national discourses of gender, sexuality, and power.

In this chapter I focus on the ways in which Sullk'atas talk about—and also decline to talk about—suway in order to trace how variously positioned individuals negotiate conjunctures of power, authority, and knowledge in the process of marriage and in their everyday interactions. In attempting to understand warmi suway, in spite of the unevenness of people's willingness to talk about the practice, I draw on a notion of intertextuality developed by philosopher and literary critic Julia Kristeva (1980). Based on the work of Bakhtin (1968, 1981), Kristeva (1980:66) argues that "any text is constructed as a mosaic of quotations; any text is the absorption and transformation of another." The meanings of one text, in other words, are partially shaped by other texts that a reader may draw upon. Kristeva, like Bakhtin, used a narrow definition of "text," working primarily with words on the printed page. As anthropologists have shown, a textile, ritual performance, conversational narrative, or spontaneously spoken poem may also be a "text" (e.g., Howard-Malverde, 1997). Interlocutors, including ethnographers, make use of incompletely overlapping arrays of texts, or intertexts, to interpret a story in the process of their interaction and afterward as they remember and retell a story.

The intertexts that I analyze—my conversation with Julia, a passage from my fieldnotes about the final night of Carnival, a folk story told in conversation, and an excerpt from an interview about marriage—are admittedly different from those of my Sullk'ata companions. Among other things, I have a shallower understanding of the personal histories and relationships of individuals to bring into play. These intertexts are not, however, idiosyncratic or private. Each of them opens the door to different perspectives on warmi suway. The first introduces stealing women as a customary practice that may nevertheless take one by surprise. The second highlights the ritual performance of young men as cholitas in order to illuminate Carnival as a context for the practice of stealing women and young men as the agents of suway. I analyze the third intertext, a folk story about two young lovers who run away together, in terms of referential and non-referential meanings in order to give voice to the agency of young women. The fourth intertext is a brief excerpt from an interview that acts as a springboard for further discussion of the ways in which the performances of young women as cholitas highlight their sometimes ambivalent desires for money and material goods, for socioeconomic mobility, and for a husband, a household, and children.

I draw upon these texts to make two overlapping points, the first primarily ethnographic and the second methodological. First, I argue that the actions and interpretations of adolescent girls and boys are crucial to interpreting the practice of suway, and of marriage more generally, in Sullk'ata. Much anthropological scholarship on marriage has focused on the authorization or validation of an exchange of women between groups of men or the incorporation of a woman into a man's lineage (e.g., Collier 1988; Leach 1968, 1977; Lévi-Strauss 1969). Indeed, whether they begin by stealing or by carrying away, Sullk'ata marriages are reaffirmed by parents, communities, and church and state authorities, as I discuss in the following chapter. As in more recent analyses of marriage, I direct attention here to the contingencies of interaction through which marriages emerge between differently positioned individuals.[3] In particular, I show that young women are agents in the process of marriage but are at the same time constrained differently than young Sullk'ata men.

Second, I show that examining intertextual references enables a more thorough understanding of a practice that people are hesitant to discuss. The silencing of suway occurs at the level of conversation, through interruption or nonresponse. Like Julia, young women may refuse to elaborate upon their experiences of suway or their interest in marriage. Although arranged marriage is not an ideal background to suway, most Sullk'atas explicitly highlight the young man's choice and actions in initiating marriage. Silencing also occurs at the level of public discourse, through interpretive control (Lakoff 1995). For example, Sullk'ata adults may interpret suway as an aspect of the immaturity and "uncivilized" nature of adolescents and emphasize the importance of validating marriages through a ritual called *warmi mañay* (to lend a woman). Later state and church authorities confirm partnerships through legal documentation and Catholic rituals, reinscribing notions of "civility" that are aligned with participation in the nation. By analyzing stories that are told and retold in different contexts and by different people, and by bringing attention to what remains unspoken, I highlight some interpretations of suway that push the boundaries of hegemonic interpretations.

Carnival: The Context of Suway

Welcoming the Souls of the Dead

For Sullk'atas Carnival is the yearly fiesta during which houses are blessed, the fertility of animals and fields is solicited and celebrated, and the male ancestors, especially the men who have died in the past year, are remembered and honored.[4] Carnival is also recognized by Sullk'atas as the preeminent time during which warmi suway takes place. Unlike other fiestas, in which adults are the only people ratified to make libations, during Carnival teenagers also drink and dance. Over the course of the fiesta, each household within the community ideally hosts every other household and each community in the ayllu sends its young people to dance and sing in other communities. The presence and practices of unmarried men and women are thus crucial to the overall success of the fiesta, for dancing, drinking, and singing are the offering that communities and households make to the supernatural forces of Sullk'ata.

Moreover, during Carnival it is the unmarried young men of the ayllu who welcome the presence of the souls (almas) of men who have recently died and dispatch them at the end of the week. The souls are honored with an altar (*misa,* Sp.) in their family homes. As dusk falls, the young unmarried men from each community gather together and travel from one "soul house" (*alma wasi*) to another to greet the souls throughout the night. Dressed in jeans or homespun white pants, shirts with colorful belts or scarves tied around their waists, and cowhide helmets (*muntiras*) decorated with small balloons, feathers, and tassels, the young men play the large flutes characteristic of Carnival music. Dancing and flute playing "invite the almas to come to Carnival" and embody the presence of the almas, who are closely related to the fertility of the earth and the availability of water (Earls and Silverblatt 1976; Gose 1994; Harris 1982). Although married men and women as well as some unmarried women may dance on the eve of Carnival, that night is considered the time when young men dance. The groups of dancers return to their own communities only in the late morning or early afternoon of the following day.[5]

Throughout the remainder of the week, as adults reciprocally exchange food and drink between each other within a community, young unmarried men and women travel between communities of the ayllu. Leaving late in the afternoon, the young men and women walk together to another community. Once there, they go from house to house, where they are invited in; they sing in high-pitched voices, dancing in a circle; they are given ritual food and drink; and then they go on to the next house, becoming increasingly drunk as the evening wears on.

Stealing women occurs when the unmarried men and women traverse the uninhabited spaces between communities, in a context that is at once sacred and permeated by the camaraderie and sexual innuendo of the youthful participants. Sullk'atas assume that sexual encounters between men and women occur prior to marriage and take place in the puna, often when young women are herding their sheep, or during fiestas.[6] Sullk'atas also assume that suway occurs when the two people are drunk. Drunkenness is linked to dream states and the long distant past (see Chapter 7); when they are drunk, individuals are not responsible for their actions. The significance of the fiesta as an arena for suway extends beyond the claim to drunkenness, for Carnival also links the fertility and sexual

promiscuity of supernatural forces of the universe to the actions of young unmarried men.

Intertext II: Young Men, Ancestors, and Mountain Spirits

Sullk'atas closely link the sexual energy and excess, and unpredictable actions, of
young men during warmi suway to their embodiment of the spirits of their male
ancestors. In Sullk'ata cosmology, male ancestors are linked to the supernatural
urqus or mountains. *Apu,* the Quechua term commonly used in Peru for mountain spirit, is also the word for father's father's father's father (Earls 1969:68; Gose
1994:223). The sexual voracity of mountains has also been documented by several Andean scholars.[7] For example, according to Gose (1994:220), mountains
take the form of "tall good looking mistis [or mestizos], to seduce and impregnate" women. This notion is reinforced through the observation of John Earls
(1971:87–88) that Quechua speakers in Peru explain illegitimate children as the
result of encounters between mountains and women. Stories also circulate in
Sullk'ata about mountain forces that impregnate women.

During the fiesta of Carnival, the conceptual association of young men and
male ancestors is ritually linked with the practice of warmi suway when young
men perform an exaggerated rendition of warmi suway in the public space of
the community on the final night of the fiesta. The *kacharipaya* or farewell to
Carnival takes place at the end of the week on a Sunday. That night, I was told,
the young men would put on polleras; cholitas would put on pants; everybody
would dress up. During the farewell of 1996, four young men did dress up and
perform an exaggerated gendering of cholitas, to the amusement of many appreciative onlookers.

> Aurelia said that they had started the "farewell." "That's Raúl in the poll-
> era," she said. Raúl was clowning. Wearing a pink pollera, a black and
> green shawl, and a bowler hat, he was speaking in a high, hoarse voice
> and kicking the backsides of the two jóvenes near him. He was sur-
> rounded by a group of kids and women, a few men. The crowd roared
> as one of the young men pulled Raúl, the "cholita," onto the ground and
> jumped on top of him. "Get off!" (*Jatariy!*) Raúl yelled, struggling to get
> up from his prone position.
>
> The group crossed the creek to [the other side of] Kallpa, dancing,
> playing music, and singing into two different houses.
>
> By now three other male "cholitas" had joined the fun as well as many
> more young men and women. Raúl would lift up his skirt and plaster his

body to the front or the back of a young man. Little boys would lift up the skirts of the "cholitas." There was much grabbing, the jóvenes grabbing the "cholitas" in ways that they might not so obviously grab young women.

The "cholitas" walked arm in arm, singing and dancing around the circle, speaking and singing in high voices. They walked with lighter steps than usual, almost on their toes, and they bent their torsos down with the dance . . . tap tap TAP tap tap TAP. Two "cholitas" walking arm and arm to the mayor's house were being harassed, grabbed by a joven. "Jatariy! Jatariy!" they said in high voices, holding each other, arms linked and trying to escape the horsefly-like attentions of their suitor.

None of the young women put on pants. "Aren't you going to change your clothes?" asked one young man. "What are you going to change to?" I countered. "Superman," he replied.

As a group, the jóvenes and cholitas and their followers left the mayor's house and walked out of town, at first walking on the path toward Pocoata but then swerving left down through someone's field. We walked up a slight hill and then after some standing and sitting around, a few pieces of dynamite were lit . . . After only a few minutes, the group walked down the hill and began singing and dancing, around and around in a circle. Every one of the young people was dancing, their voices lifting clearly in the night. One charango carried the tune of a song for several verses. The older generation who had come to watch and listen to the young people also danced, shuffling around counterclockwise. *Somos Kallpaños, Norte Potosiños,* they sang . . . Dynamite booms crashed in the air along with flashes of light from nearby communities. "Everywhere they are taking leave of Carnival. *Tukuyniqpi carnavales kacharipunku.*"

In the farewell, young men like Raúl take on the bodily stance and practices of native Andean women—clothing, gestures, and voices.[8] The pollera, a full pleated skirt, is iconic of ethnically native Andean women. The blanket-like shawl (*manta,* Sp.) and bowler hat complete the outfit. Although little girls are often dressed in western (used) clothing (which is less expensive), young women eventually choose which type of clothing to wear: western or native dress. Most living in the communities of Sullk'ata choose to wear a pollera. The young men do not solely borrow and wear the clothing of women but also alter their voices, using a higher-pitched register. The voices of women are of course naturally

Young men dramatize warmi suway on the final night of Carnival. The center figure is a youth dressed as a young woman, or cholita.

higher than those of men, but during fiestas the preference in the region is for women to attain an even higher range, a falsetto, when they sing.[9] The young men also mimic the dancing movements of women: the rhythm of stomping feet, the bodily position of bending from the waist, with the head bowed down.

The performance of young men as cholitas is a gendered performance which is doubled as the audience recognizes both the masculinity and femininity of the cholita. The performances of the jóvenes might best be described as performances of androgyny, for they are both male and female, not one or the other. This reflects the androgynous aspect of the supernatural and of the active landscape. Although the Sullk'ata landscape is gendered, the dualism of male and female is symbolically recursive: levels of dual relationships may encompass one another. Thus, when earth and water are opposed, the earth is male and the water female. The earth is also at once female in the guise of Pacha Mama and male, as specific mountains (see also Isbell 1997; Salomon 1997).

The performance is doubled in another way as well: the "cholitas" are aggressively sexual with the young men yet constantly deflect their advances. The excess sexuality of these performances links young men with the power of patrilineal ancestors and of mountain spirits that are closely related to the fertility of the earth and the availability of water. Because they steal women, young men are like the ancestors, sexually unpredictable and not properly socialized but necessary to the wealth and fertility of households and communities. The "cholitas" also, however, portray young women, who in actuality often protect themselves and each other from being stolen. The audience is aware that the jóvenes "quote" (as in Weismantel 2001:126, using Bertolt Brecht's 1963 concept) both male ancestors and young women.

The sexual transgressions enacted in the gender performances of young men who play cholitas may in addition serve as examples of the ritual "reversals" or "inversions" of Carnival.[10] Sexual energy and excess is enacted by the young men who play cholitas and by other jóvenes (playing themselves). Although the performance takes place in a public space, with adults looking on, jóvenes are able to portray with "cholitas" some of the excesses that actually occur between young men and cholitas during Carnival dancing. As I have noted, whereas sexual relationships between unmarried young men and women may take place (and are to a certain extent expected), these relationships are understood to occur in places outside of the community and away from the married adults. Meetings between unmarried young Sullk'ata couples typically take place on Sunday visits to the market in Pocoata. Young men and women also experience greater freedom to meet with each other in cities, where they seasonally migrate and live with older siblings or aunts and uncles. During Carnival, stealing women occurs when the unmarried men and women traverse the uninhabited spaces between communities. On the final night of Carnival, these interactions between young men and women may be performed in the public, socialized space of the community, under the observation of the married adults.

The ritualized performances of suway highlight the expectations of Sullk'atas that warmi suway will occur during the fiesta and that young men are the primary actors. However, the performances obscure the trauma of the actual event. Warmi suway, at least in some instances, is characterized by forced sexual intercourse. A young woman may indeed wake up out on the puna or in her new husband's house without knowing him or without "having planned" to get married. Understanding warmi suway as gendered as well as sexual—as an experience in which varying levels of coercion and desire might be implicated—thus requires further exploration. For a young woman, spending the night away from home is just as significant as whether she had sex with a young man. Before turning to a story of two lovers, I describe the typical reactions to warmi suway by adult Sullk'atas.

Suway: Convention or Transgression?

However conventional the practice is in the campo, parents are often angry and concerned when they realize that their daughter has not returned home after a fiesta. Parents are angry with the young man who stole their daughter and with their daughter for following him, as Cecelia makes clear (see also Carter 1977). Cecelia, a woman in her fifties with married children of her own, told me that she was carried away from a fiesta when she was a teenager. "What did your mother say?" I asked.

"She scolded me. She said, 'Why did you go with that man? He will beat you [*maqasunqa*]. You will have to work for him.' She scolded me."

Cecelia then turned the question to me: "But what did your mother say to you?" she asked me.

"She scolded me," I said, remembering my parents' reaction when I left home to live with a boyfriend after college.

"See," she said, "that is what mothers do: they scold. That is what they should do."

"So then," I asked, "what did you do?"

"From then I lived with my husband. I lived here. My mother didn't have me to help her anymore."

Suway marks a relationship as not only sexual but publicly so, with the aim of cohabitation. After spending the night away from her natal home, a young woman will move to the house of her in-laws, usually in another community. Parents lose not only their daughter's labor power but also the company of a beloved child.

From the perspective of the young woman's parents, the young man acts in an uncivilized manner when he steals their daughter. Within the context of Quechua moral discourse, the immoral and improper relationships of human beings are sometimes described through an opposition between human and animal worlds.[11] In Sullk'ata, as in nearby Laymi ayllu, sons-in-law may be called condors or bulls (Harris 1994:54); people who fight are likened to dogs. Nondomesticated animals may also be used metaphorically to talk about different types of people or different stages in the life cycle of human beings.[12] Adolescents are "uncivilized" in Sullk'ata in the sense that they are incompletely socialized. They are on their way to becoming adults but must continue the process of maturation by getting married, having children, and eventually taking on responsibilities as members of the ayllu.

Whatever the contingencies of the events leading up to warmi suway, marriages initiated by suway must be affirmed by the families of both the young man and the young woman through local rituals of betrothal called *warmi mañay* (to lend the woman). As I discuss in the following chapter, usually within a day or two after the suway the young man and his parents go to the young woman's home, bringing alcohol and coca to her parents in order to request that the children marry. In most cases, the parents eventually reach an agreement, and the young woman who "wakes up to" a husband will live with him (*tantanakuy*) and his parents for several months and even years before civil and church ceremonies take place.

In some cases the young man and his parents will not show up at the young woman's house at all. A young woman who becomes pregnant but is abandoned by the young man usually remains in her parents' house. While living in Sullk'ata, I knew two women who were raising their children while living with their parents. One told me that she had been stolen from a fiesta but that the young man never came to her parents to ask permission to marry her. He married another woman instead. The other young woman, whose child was less than a year old, had lived for a few months with her husband. He had hit her, so she returned to her parents' house. It is not unusual for a couple to separate (*t'aqay*), particularly if they fight and if a Catholic wedding ceremony has not yet consolidated the partnership. The young woman's parents will usually take their daughter back. Although a single mother may have a more difficult time getting married, people in her natal community do not stigmatize or isolate her or her child.[13]

Grandmother's Authority and Young Woman's Agency

In spite of parents' consternation with specific instances of suway, arranged marriage does not figure as a convention or ideal background to warmi suway. Sullk'atas emphasize that in all cases the young man should be the one who chooses the young woman to marry—not his parents. The practice of warmi suway, and the emphasis on the young man's agency, is normalized outside of the context of Carnival through folk stories that circulate throughout the ayllu. In mythical representations of Andean marriages, and in the personal stories told by elderly Sullk'atas, tellers often—though not always—highlight actions of the not yet properly socialized being—the young *tullqa* (son-in-law). Sometimes the young man is likened to a condor, mountain spirit, or bear who steals and impregnates a woman. In one folk story or *kwintu* (*cuento,* Sp.) told to me while I lived in Sullk'ata, a young man wants to marry a young woman, but his father refuses to agree to the match. The referential content of the story details the dire consequences that transpire when the two young people run away together. The young woman's degree of participation in the event is obscured by the actions of her partner and his father.

The meanings of a story also extend beyond the content of what is said. I heard the story that I call the Lovers' Story for the first time from an elderly woman, whom I will call Seferina. In her version of the story, the actions of the female characters (a young woman and a grandmother) are central. Examining the nonreferential content of the narrative—specifically the embedded speech and the relationship between the narrative and the context of its telling—provides a counterbalance to the view that women are simply passive victims of such encounters. In this narrative the grandmother and the young woman have agency and authority.

Intertext III: The Lovers' Story

Seferina related the story to me in the midst of our conversation about my intention to travel to La Paz to visit my husband. I had come to visit Seferina and her husband, Bartolomé, with one of their granddaughters, a teenager named Reina. That particular afternoon had been filled with radio announcements of a strike and roadblocks throughout the province of Chayanta. The roadblocks were to begin the next day, in reaction to increases in gasoline prices and the privatization of the Bolivian petroleum company. I was anxious about the roadblocks but still determined to see my husband, who was to return to the United States from La Paz. As Bartolomé listened to the radio, Seferina and I talked about the possibilities for travel. Seferina told me that she and her husband had planned to go to Llallagua, a large mining town on the way to Oruro and La Paz. They had postponed their trip until after the strike. She encouraged me to postpone my trip as well. As I tried to explain that my husband already had his airline ticket and that he would not be coming back to Bolivia, Seferina responded by asking why he did not come and visit me in the community anymore. "You should stay here and buy some sheep," she concluded.

To my ears, the story came out of the blue. In the dialogue below, I am "Kristina," the name Sullk'atas used for me. Seferina began by announcing that someone's lover (*enamorado,* Sp.) had died.[14]

SEFERINA: So maybe that one's lover died.
KRISTINA: Died?
SEFERINA: Oh, that one died.
KRISTINA: Ooh.
SEFERINA: Then the girl,

the girl was crying REAlly hard as she traveled, they say.

Then the alma, they say, saw her.

After that "Le . . . Let's go, let's return now," he said.

He did not show himself to the girl.

"Come on, show yourself to me!" she said.

KRISTINA: And?

SEFERINA: He didn't show himself.

And after that they probably just went along, just went along.

"There was a lake [*lago*, Sp.]," she said, "a lake [*qhucha*]."

KRISTINA: And then?

SEFERINA: Yes.

Then [yawning] perhaps on the shore of that lake there were houses.

KRISTINA: Unhuh.

SEFERINA: Um.

KRISTINA: That house, there, (next to) the lake? [pointing]

SEFERINA: Yes.

"I will slaughter. We will cook," she said.

The girl went, they say, to slaughter,

Saying, "We will cook at that house."

And then, a dog

Awu^uu^uuuu^aw_auwauwau awau^uu^uuuuuu^auwau^w_auwauwaw!

A dog was howling!

KRISTINA: Ooooh!

SEFERINA: And then that dog was howling.

"Over there," that one with the house said,

"Stu ^Stuuu^pid giiirrl!"

Saying, "What taught her to herd a cadaver?"

"A cadaver, OH yes!" she said.

Yes, a ghost!

"Why do you know how to herd a ghost?" she said.

Ohh she was a pretty girl, they say!

KRISTINA: Uuuum.

SEFERINA: Unhuh. "Now stop being stupid!

Uuum, pass by that lake again.

That lake, that lake, inside that lake [inaudible] . . . leave a brush and a mirror there," she said.

KRISTINA: And?

SEFERINA: From that the girl was saved from the cadaver.

Yes, he didn't pass the shore of that lake.

No, he just wasn't able to, they say.

They say the cadaver had been slaughtered.

KRISTINA: Umm.

SEFERINA: Maybe it was a condenado.

But that condenado maybe he cries,

[Seferina begins singing]

> Qhapallayta qupuway hukumwarum
>
> Qhapallayta qupuway hukumwarum.

And perhaps he comes and goes, comes and goes to the lake.

KRISTINA: Auhuuum.

SEFERINA: And after that the girl came back to that one who had a house,

There she arrived.

"GRANDmother!" she said.

"From the precipice she arrives," she said, that one with a house.

And that is how girls follow cadavers they say! Yes!

KRISTINA: Oh no!

SEFERINA: But maybe they were lovers.

KRISTINA: And?

SEFERINA: Well, then maybe he went there to steal his father's money, maybe

that's why he went there.

Then it was just his very own father who killed him, that young man, they

say.

Saying that, they used to talk.

KRISTINA: Really?

SEFERINA: The story was like this.

Although I quickly understood that what was happening was the "telling of a story," I was still unsure (as you undoubtedly are now) what the story was about even when Seferina had finished. As in other stories told in conversation among Quechua speakers, Seferina included only a fragment of a much longer story and tied the fragment directly to our conversation, as I discuss further below. A few weeks after this conversation with Seferina, I asked Dario, a middle-aged man from the region who lived in Sucre, if he had heard of the story. Dario had arrived in Sullk'ata to help me conduct interviews on marriage practices. After listening to a segment of the tape, he told me that the grandmother had told the story "very poorly." He told me the story again. Dario's formally solicited version, told in a continuous sequence from beginning to end, enabled me to get a sense of the plotline and to understand what piece of the story Seferina had recounted. In fact, Seferina's and Dario's versions of the story are similar in referential content, and I summarize the story below. Analyzing Seferina's story in terms of the nonreferential content, especially the relationship between the story and the context in which it was told, suggests additional meanings. Seferina recognizes the agency and the mobility of young women while at the same time sending an implicit message to heed the knowledge and authority of a grandmother.

Summarizing Myth, Interpreting Reference

In this folk story, two young lovers run away together. The young man's father does not approve of the young woman he has chosen to marry and refuses to give his son land or money with which to begin married life. As a result, the lovers go to another community to live, but so desperate is their situation that the boy returns time after time to his parents' home in order to steal food to survive. Eventually, the father notices that food is missing from the storeroom. He stays awake one night, hiding in the shadows, in order to catch the thief. The darkness that protects the father from a potentially dangerous intruder prevents him from seeing the identity of the thief. When the thief enters, the father strikes him with a machete, slashing his throat. Calling for his wife to bring a light, he realizes too late that he has killed his son. Heartbroken, the parents bury their child.

Soon after, the young man rises from his grave as a *condenado* (a condemned soul) and returns to the young woman who is his wife. Like the father, who does not realize that the thief is his son, the young woman does not recognize that her husband is a condemned soul. Her husband walks with his shirt tightly pulled around his neck, moaning in his pain, but still she does not see the transformation. The young woman follows the cadaver, walking along until they come to a house, where she asks if they may spend the night. The older woman agrees, but the condenado does not want to sleep inside the house. In the middle of the night the older woman awakens, realizes that the young man is a condenado, and alerts the young woman to the state of her husband. The grandmother encourages the wife to run away from the condenado and gives her instructions so that she can protect herself.

Sullk'atas fear souls of the dead (*aya*s; *almas,* Sp.). A soul, however, is eventually integrated into the cosmological and agricultural cycle. A condenado is a person who committed a moral transgression while alive and is not integrated into the generalized realm of ancestors. Dario vividly enacted the father slashing the intruder with a machete and said that the son was *nak'asqa* (slaughtered).

Native Andean herders typically slaughter a sheep or llama by cutting its throat (*ñak'ay*) on the rare occasions when meat is to be eaten. *Ñak'aq* (the nominalized form of the verb) is, as I have already mentioned, another common Quechua expression in Peru for *lik'ichiri* (which is an Aymara retention) or *phistaku* (beings who steal the fat and blood from others). A ñak'aq is someone who slaughters another human being.[15] The boy in the story is nak'asqa (slaughtered), killed as if he was an animal for his immoral actions.

In stealing from his parents the young man disrupts the one-way gift of food between parent and child that establishes relationships of affection and hierarchy. Yet the consequences for stealing food or disobeying a father seem quite dire. The moral infractions would not seem to require—even in a myth—that a father kill his son and that the son become a condemned soul. Marcin Mróz (1992) suggests in his analysis of a version of the same myth told by Quechua speakers in Peru that the young man steals not any woman, but his own sister. As Claude Lévi-Strauss (1969:51, 481) has argued, incest is not so much a prohibition against sex among family members as an injunction to give a sister or daughter away to another man (see also Rubin 1975:173–177). From this perspective, the young man's parents lost a daughter, a potential daughter-in-law and son-in-law, and relationships with other families and communities when the young couple ran away.

Sullk'atas agreed that the young man must have committed a terrible offense to become a condenado, but they did not interpret the story as a prohibition of incest, at least not explicitly. For example, Dario commented to me that the story is a warning to a young man's parents not to choose the woman their son should marry. Once the young man has chosen, Dario said, his parents must "shut their mouths." That is what his sister had to do, he said, when her son stole a young woman who already had two children from a previous marriage. Although the young woman's parents may disagree with the match, a young man's parents accept the choice of their son and invite the young couple to live with them. Parents are morally obligated to feed and care for their children until they are adults. In many senses, Sullk'atas remain children until they have children of their own to feed and clothe and until they have established their own labor networks and relationships of reciprocity with other adults in the community. In the story the young man's father persists in his disapproval, refusing to allow the couple to live at home and refusing to give the son money or land so that the two young people may live on their own. Interpreting the story as an injunction to allow young men to choose their wives reinforces the agency of boys and the obligations of parents.

Meaning beyond Content

Lévi-Strauss (1955:430) once claimed that the "mythical value of the myth remains preserved, even through the worst translation . . . Its substance does not lie in its style, its original music, or its syntax, but in the story which it tells" (Tedlock 1983:40). The story which this myth tells is based in part in the referential content; Seferina assumed my knowledge of the story's plot when she began her telling. As linguistic anthropologists have emphasized, however, reported speech and other types of citation may have particular importance for the interpretation of narratives (Hymes 1981; Irvine 1996; Nuckolls 1996; Tedlock 1983; Urban 1984). Pauses, onomatopoeia, archaic words and phrases: these poetic subtleties, as citations within narrative, are significant to style but also "have a potential for radically altering surface meaning" of what is said (Tedlock 1990:154). Although direct quotation is nearly universal, an important consequence of a narrative having reported speech is that the story contains an embedded theory about the relationship between speech and action (Mannheim and Van Vleet 1998; Urban 1984).

Thus meanings emerge in the embedded speech of the characters that are not evident in the referential content of the story. The relationship between reported speech and action suggests the importance of the sense of hearing (and speech) among Quechua speakers for gleaning information crucial to everyday life (Classen 1993:70–73). Seferina begins the story with the young woman walking along and crying, wondering where her lover is. Soon she sees her lover—but sight alone does not indicate to her that her lover is dead. The reported speech in this excerpt does, however, alert the audience that the young woman is following a condenado. The reported speech includes the young woman telling what she will do (slaughter and cook), a dog howling, and a grandmother commenting upon the young woman's actions. That the young woman was "herding" a cadaver is first explicitly recognized by the old woman when she exclaims, "Stupid girl! What taught her to herd a cadaver?" Although herding sheep and llamas is a daily activity of girls and women throughout the rural Andes, beings that have died but that return to walk the earth are feared and avoided.

A Quechua speaker listening to this story would already have been clued into this turn of events by the howling of the dog. Many people in the community, including Seferina and her husband, noted to me that a howling dog, especially at night, is a sure sign that a condenado or an alma is walking about. On a previous visit when Reina's grandfather told of his encounter with an alma as a young man, Reina added to the conversation a story of her father's more recent encounter with an alma. A truck had been in the area just two days before, picking up men to bring them to large farms near Santa Cruz to pick cotton. Reina's father had gone that evening to find work. In a town not far away, there was an accident on the road, and he decided that it was a bad omen. Walking back to the community in the middle of the night, her father heard a dog howling. "It is an alma," he said. Making libations all the way back to his house, he arrived drunk but safe. Had she been listening, reported speech would have provided the young woman in the story with information that was crucial to her proper course of action—information that was not gained by sight.

Later in the story the grandmother not only recognizes the condenado but gives instructions to the young woman that save her life. Through the actions and words of the grandmother and those of the young woman, Seferina establishes the authority of the grandmother. The young woman listens to the grandmother and obeys her instructions to return to the lake, carrying a brush and a mirror. Now instead of her following or herding the cadaver, the cadaver follows her. The young woman walks in front of the cadaver when she goes back to the lake. Once she has carried out the instructions of the grandmother, throwing out the brush and then the mirror, the young woman returns to the grandmother's house. The cadaver is not able to follow her; he cannot cross the lake, which has risen beyond its shores.[16] The young woman, having listened and properly followed the grandmother's instructions, saves herself from the condenado. Seferina, who was herself a grandmother, told me at the end of her story (but not the end of our conversation): "And that is how girls follow cadavers they say! Yes!" But after my exclamation of dismay, she added, "But maybe they were lovers." The story told by Seferina emphasizes the lovers' lack of knowledge of the world but not their lack of agency.

Moreover, the situation in which a story is told, including the identities and life experiences of the various interlocutors, is not tangential but substantive to the potential meanings of the narrative. The two versions of the story emerged in very different situations, told by people with different life experiences. Seferina was a monolingual Quechua speaker who lived her entire life in rural communities of Bolivia. Dario was a middle-aged man who grew up in a rural community in the region but migrated to a Bolivian city in the early 1980s. Although Seferina was accustomed to telling stories and told them extremely well, like many Quechua narratives, Seferina's begins "in the middle" of the story. She keys the action of the characters to our conversation. She may not have remembered the presence of the tape recorder, which had been rolling throughout our conversation as we ate roasted potatoes in the semidarkness of her kitchen. In contrast, Dario speaks Quechua and Spanish. The recording of his formally elicited version of the story took place in my room, with the tape recorder on the desk between us. Dario had the explicit aim of clarifying the story for the listener, an anthropologist. His formally elicited narrative follows a form that many North American readers are familiar with: the story has a coherent plot-line with a beginning, middle, and end. Dario also incorporated many details of plot and character that are left out of Seferina's story, a recording of which he heard immediately before he began his narration.

Seferina's story as told in the context of a broader conversation contains an implicit message that is brought out in the relationship between the story and the situation in which it was told. My intention to go to La Paz even though my husband did not come to the community to visit anymore (and was leaving to return to the United States) and in spite of the roadblocks was a not unimport-ant factor in Seferina's telling me that story. My living in Bolivia, rather than living with my mother-in-law, might also have motivated the abuela's narrative. Moreover, Seferina's granddaughter Reina, who had just danced in her first Car-nival and was dreaming of going to Cochabamba to work, was also listening to the story. Just as Seferina recognized my ability to go to La Paz—and Reina's ability to go to Cochabamba—she indicated that following a lover might have dire consequences if the lover/condenado were to come after me instead. Seferi-na's story might also reveal her speculations about me and my husband: was our marriage, in fact, legitimate? If so, why were we living so far from our families?

In establishing the grandmother's authority within the narrative, Seferina also establishes her own personal authority in her relationships with Reina and me. The personal authority of the speaker of Quechua is not taken for granted, and storytellers themselves may be more or less effective in manipulating claims to social or political authority. Authority must be established socially, as par-ents establish authority through feeding or sometimes hitting their children, and grammatically through such devices as evidentials that distinguish claims to knowledge based on personal eyewitness experience versus hearsay.[17] The nar-rative is embedded in the broader context of the conversation between Seferina and me about my decision to travel to La Paz. The grandmother's attempt in the story to convince the young woman that her husband has become a dangerous being is laminated on Seferina's attempt to convince me that I should stay in Kallpa and herd sheep.

Reading these versions of the story in conjunction with each other suggests that multiple interpretations of stories are possible, even likely, and that the con-text in which the story is told and the relationships among interlocutors are sig-nificant in how people interpret the story. The two versions of the story highlight different arrays of social, political, and cultural relationships and enable different interpretations of warmi suway. The story of the lovers who run away together may, of course, be interpreted as a prohibition against incest. This story also describes the will, the agency, the ambiguity, and the immaturity of the young lovers, both the boy and the girl. The recognition of a young woman's actions and the grandmother's authority within the story suggests that we turn our attention to the (potential) desires and actions of young single women in Sullk'ata, at the same time taking seriously the structural constraints under which people live their lives.

Intertext IV: A More Civilized Marriage

The term "stealing" at once points to an unequal exchange and also requires further interrogation: Who or what is stolen? From whom? And by whom? Although Sullk'atas sometimes use the term *suway* to indicate a marriage that began under violent or coercive circumstances, at other times the term is used to refer to a situation in which a young woman has exercised some choice in the matter of her marriage but does not want her choice to be recognized. Some Sullk'atas used another term in their descriptions of the initiation of their marriages. Julio and Juana married in the Catholic Church in 1986 and told me that they had affection for each other long before they married. Recounting their marriage to me in 1996 in an interview, Julio first stated that the marriage had begun when he stole (*suway*) Juana from a fiesta. Then he said:

> We knew each other not . . . we did not meet in a fiesta or anything like that. From being friends we knew each other, and knowing each other, well, we went to Pocoata. And in Pocoata we surely got drunk; yes, we drank corn beer. And say that we came back. Early in the morning. I carried [her] to Kallpa, here to my house [laughter]. Yes, sure, after that we knew each other really well.

Julio is careful to recount that they knew each other before the fiesta, reiterating that they went to the town of Pocoata and drank corn beer together. He shifts away from using the pronoun "we" to the pronoun "I" when he states "I carried [her] to Kallpa, here to my house" (*Chay Kallpaman kaypitaq um wasiyman pusarqani a*). As linguistic anthropologists have noted, first person pronouns—in contrast to second and third person pronouns, proper nouns, and common nouns—are more likely to be found in the position of agent rather than object (Ahearn 2001b:122–123). Julio's shift from the plural to the singular first person pronoun makes Juana into the object of the verb.

Although grammatical agency does not necessarily overlap social agency, close attention to the words used by Sullk'atas in their personal narratives of suway also reveals that girls may have some role in their marriages. Rather than using the term *suway,* for example, Julio uses the term *pusay.* The Quechua verb *pusay* (to carry) is used when the object moves of its own volition and uses its own energy. When women asked me to help them go to the United States, they would say, *Estadus unidusman pusariwaqchu* ("Wouldn't you carry me to the United States?" or "Take me with you to the United States"). In contrast, the verb *apay* (also meaning to carry) is used when the object of the verb is inanimate. Sullk'atas might say, *Papata apasaq* ("I will carry these potatoes"). Julio in this way indicates the young woman's capacity to act, her movement of her own volition, while at the same time positioning her as an object of someone else's actions. As Laura Ahearn (2001a:112) has argued, agency can be understood as a "socioculturally mediated capacity to act," a definition that is at once flexible enough to incorporate various modalities of action yet bounded enough to challenge simplistic notions of agency as "free will" or "resistance." Although Sullk'atas did not use the terms *suway* and *pusay* to categorize marriages into different types, the contrast between the meanings of the words suggests that the agency of young women in the arena of marriage deserves further exploration, as do the constraints on girls' capacity to act and to acknowledge their own actions.[18]

In spite of the emphasis on young men's choice of a wife, and on parents' validation of the choice, a young woman may have exercised some agency in the matter of her marriage, yet may not want her actions to be recognized. Indeed, claiming to have taken part in planning an elopement or to have agreed to be stolen is particularly problematic for young women. Voicing a desire to marry in general or to marry a particular young man indexes not only sexual desires but also geographical and emotional distance from natal families. Once married, a young woman will (in all probability) never again live with her natal family. Marriage usually removes daughters from their own natal household to the households of strangers. Living in her in-laws' household is quite difficult for a young woman, as I describe in the following chapters. A daughter's suggestion that she would prefer to live with her mother-in-law and husband rather than with her mother and family, whose love and affection she has known all her life, would be considered quite strange by most Sullk'atas.

Moreover, local and national gendered and racial ideologies differentially constrain the actions of girls and boys—as well as the ways in which they talk about their actions and interactions. Living and traveling between rural and urban communities, going to public school, serving in the army, working as domestic servants, Sullk'ata adolescents engage in communities of practice with diverse and sometimes contradictory ideologies. In local discourses boys are closely linked with male ancestors and the promiscuity of mountain spirits. Boys in Sullk'ata are far more openly engaged in sexual joking and wordplay than girls are (cf. Isbell and Fernández 1977). Teenaged boys are also exposed to racialized and sexualized discourses and practices of hypermasculinity that only partially overlap local gender ideals for men during their required army service.[19]

In local discourses girls and especially married women are associated with Pacha Mama and the Virgin Mary, both of whom are considered productive, fecund, fertile, and powerful. Among Sullk'atas, giving birth to a child before marriage (in this case, before warmi mañay) typically results in the young woman's continued residence in her parents' household. Neither the young woman nor her child is ostracized by family or ayllu members. In contrast, national gender ideologies attribute conceptions of purity and chastity to the Virgin and maintain expectations of chastity and containment for the actions of young women. Upon more than one occasion I heard the mestizo teachers at the local junior high and high schools speak disparagingly of young Sullk'ata women who dropped out of school, implying that they were pregnant.

Similarly, some Sullk'atas describe warmi suway as "uncivilized," drawing on national and international discourses of family, progress, and modernization rather than local moral discourses of sociality. When I asked Claudina, a middle-aged woman with married children of her own, about whether she had been stolen, she denied that she had been carried away from a fiesta at all. She emphasized that *some* people in the campo do not want to get married in that way even though it is customary. Contrasting the rural community with Pocoata, the nearest pueblo, and the cities of Llallagua and Cochabamba, Claudina noted, "Men do not steal women there, just here in the campo." There a boy may be introduced to a girl by a parent, and a young man may go to the parents of his beloved to ask permission to marry her. "They are *civilizado* [civilized] there," she told me. Like a civilized person, her husband, Hernán, had come with his parents to her house and asked permission of her parents to marry her. "Hernán carried me from my house [*Wasiymanta pusapuwan*]," she said. Claudina and Hernán may have had many encounters, sexual or otherwise, but these were undiscovered by their parents. Hernán and his parents began the process of warmi mañay without having to apologize for Hernán stealing Claudina.

Claudina's distinction between "civilized" and "uncivilized" goes beyond the practice of warmi suway and links the process of marriage in the Andes to a wider discourse on progress and modernization and to oppositions between the campo and the city, the poor and the rich, the United States and Bolivia, Spanish speakers and Quechua speakers. The racialization of local courtship and marriage practices by Sullk'atas as well as outsiders—such as teachers, anthropologists, and missionaries—is often based on the characterization of suway as violent. Anthropological discussion of the violence in Andean courtship practices, though written from a culturally relativist position, may reinforce racial discourses without deepening insight into the cultural and political parameters of violence. As Weismantel (2001:155) has demonstrated, however, the history of the Andes is saturated with unequal exchanges—including nonconsensual sex—that are structured by racial and gendered asymmetries. Discourses of more "civilized" marriage draw on standards of morality and progress that obscure the history of coercive sexuality between (white) men and (Indian) women and the more general material and symbolic asymmetries—the structural violence—permeating Bolivia and other Andean polities.

Women's selective silences and sometimes contradictory discourses on warmi suway both reflect "eloquent assumptions about local knowledge" (White 2000:77) and indicate constraints on production of meaning—the personal meanings of experience and more broadly accepted meanings of individual and collective practices. Although Daza (1983:73) argues that the term *suway* should not be taken literally but instead as a way of categorizing "a joint decision to elope with the initial purpose of cohabitation and procreation," both what is said and what is unsaid about warmi suway by Sullk'atas indicate that the experience of warmi suway is gendered and racial as well as sexual, an experience in which varying levels of coercion are implicated. As in other contexts, however, "women, even as subordinate players, always play an active part that goes beyond the dichotomy of victimization/acceptance, a dichotomy that flattens out a complex and ambiguous agency in which women accept, accommodate, ignore, resist, or protest—sometimes all at the same time" (MacLeod 1992:534). Although the acknowledgment of girls' capacity to act in the context of marriage, or suway more specifically, is pushed to the margins of discourse, Sullk'atas also recognize that young women are not simply objects to be taken and cannot be understood solely as victims in spite of the coercive and sometimes violent conditions of their transition from unmarried to married woman.

Dancing toward Marriage

Months after my conversation with Julia by the stream, in which she emphasized the spontaneity of her new partnership and her drunkenness on the night when she had gained a husband, another woman recounted an additional series of events. Julia and Wilberto, she said, had come to her sister Alsira's door asking to be let in, late, late in the night on one of the last days of Carnival. Alsira initially had refused, but Julia had pleaded with her, saying, "I really want to marry this young man, but my brothers are angry. They are chasing us." Alsira, who also happened to be Wilberto's maternal aunt, let them in, allowing them to spend the night together. They shared one of the three single beds in the household with Alsira's ten-year-old daughter that night. Alsira's brother-in-law, who was also in town for Carnival, woke up still drunk the next morning and could not stop laughing at the sight of the three of them in one single bed.

The intentions and purposes of individuals are often left unspoken, and beyond the scope of ethnographic analysis, but the outlines or shadows of those subjectivities may be traced in the interactions of differently positioned individuals. Although Julia may have had many reasons for remaining quiet about her own role in gaining a husband, listening to the silences, observing interactions, and extrapolating from both spoken and unspoken clues are necessary for writing about the subjectivities and activities of those engaged in warmi suway. We might return to the context of Carnival in order to explore the subjectivities and activities of women in the process of marriage, for dancing in Carnival is part of a transition to marriageability for young women. Cholitas dance for Carnival, many returning to the rural community from urban areas where they have migrated to work as domestic servants. They arrive in the community carrying huge bundles of clothing, as many Sullk'atas excitedly reported to me before the fiesta began: "a different pollera for every day they dance!" Displays of fashion, consumer consumption, and ritual prowess (including singing and dancing) are significant facets of cholita behavior during Carnival and relevant to what people remember and tell each other about Carnival.

By focusing on the performances of young women as cholitas, we may begin to perceive the subjectivities and activities of women in the process of marriage in the Bolivian campo, which is increasingly affected by a growing consumer economy. Like the young men who perform as "cholitas" during the farewell to Carnival, young women also perform as cholitas themselves, though in a more habitual and constrained sense, reiterating gendered and simultaneously ethnic, racial, class, sexual, and age-based positionalities.

Although the term "performance" most readily brings the scholarship of literary critic Judith Butler (1990, 1993) to mind, here I also invoke the work of Carolyn Steedman. In her exploration of her mother's life and of her own childhood in post–World War II Great Britain, Steedman (1994:68) suggests that social theorists might turn attention to the productive labor of women in the process of marriage. Women may come to understand that they possess themselves and may exchange themselves or their labor for something else: for the ability to buy new clothes or for a particularly envisioned future (Steedman 1994:68). Steed-

Young women proudly display their best clothing when they dance during
Carnival.

man's insights into women's recognition that they may exchange their productive and reproductive capacities complicate Butler's (1990) emphasis on gender
as iteration by bringing to the forefront of her analysis the question of the social,
cultural, and economic constraints on women. The performances of women as
cholitas might, then, be understood as productive labor by which they attempt
to maintain and transform themselves as domestic servants, as consumers, as
native, as urban, as wives, or as daughters even as they are translated as objects,
gifts, hands, or workers (Steedman 1994:68).

Whereas boys' performances as "cholitas" are laminated upon a traditional
Andean cosmology, hierarchy, and subsistence economy, the usually more ha-

bitual performances of young women as cholitas intertwine femininity with production and consumption *outside* the arena of subsistence. Dancing during Carnival requires a significant outlay of capital by young women. A few of the young women who typically wore western-style clothing borrowed polleras from their friends, many of whom had returned to the community from Cochabamba or Santa Cruz, where they worked as domestic servants. Even Nelida, who was said to have male energy (*qhari kallpa*), who wore jeans not a skirt or a pollera, and who knew how to ride a bike and to plow with oxen, had borrowed a pollera, slicked back her bangs and worked her hair into two long braids against her back, and gone with her sister and brothers, cousins, and community-mates to sing and dance for Carnival. The dancing continues for seven days, and the single women returning from the city bring several polleras, each costing between sixty and eighty U.S. dollars. They also carry the specialized clothing to complete their outfits: blouses made of eyelet lace, straight slips trimmed with lace, bowler hats, shawls, and sandals or slip-on shoes, sometimes even nylon stockings.

By wearing their new clothes the cholitas are displaying their success, their ability to consume commodities, to attain a higher standard of living, to speak Spanish and become more educated (or at least cosmopolitan, living in a city with electricity, television, cement floors, and running water).[20] Although they may, in fact, go into debt borrowing money to buy polleras, they nevertheless distinguish themselves from the women who do not have the cash or the access to commodities for conspicuous consumption. At the same time they actively identify themselves as native Andeans. Moreover, young women coming from the city also bring with them gifts for family members—from food to clothing to electronic items such as radios. They pay for their bus or truck fare to and from the community and for the wages which are lost during the time they are away from their jobs. Most significant, however, is the expenditure they undertake for this display of fashion. Fashion here is a medium for communicating a particular gender, ethnic, and class position. Rather than assuming that the clothing reflects an essential identity of "Indianness," we might well consider the ways in which clothing refers back to polleras worn at other times, with other purposes, and in other places.

Moreover, the clothing that cholitas buy is understood to be part of the property that they take with them into marriage. Young women who work in cities do not typically send money to their parents and younger siblings but spend their earnings to increase their personal material wealth and to purchase gifts. Young women accumulate as much clothing as possible (polleras, slips, blouses and shawls and blankets, carrying cloths, and belts may be purchased or made).

In addition, women buy kitchen appliances and tools in order to have property to take with them when they marry. Although a young woman will also receive an inheritance from her mother in the form of animals (sheep, llamas, cattle) and other movable property, this property will not be given to her until after she has been married for a while.[21] This inheritance sometimes exceeds in value the property that the young man brings to the marriage. The cholita who has accumulated a number of polleras, displayed during Carnival dancing, is thus also perceived as a hard worker and as owning property necessary for her new life as part of a married couple.

The cholitas, then, are desirable and marriageable in multiple ways. The songs that they sing express the longings and unfulfilled desires of both young women and unmarried young men. And women are represented not simply as objects of exchange (Rubin 1975; Steedman 1994:68) but as consumers of commodities. Similarly, the expectations of women who dance are more complicated than simply desiring to be stolen, and their own desires for marriage may be ambivalent. Although some cholitas are stolen during Carnival, the majority of young women who dance for Carnival protect themselves from being stolen. Moreover, young men of the community also protect young women from being stolen. Particularly the young women who work in cities recognize that their lives as unmarried employed women are quite different from the lives of married women living in the rural community, as exemplified by Julia, who was stolen during Carnival. Young women's displays of fashion in their performances as cholitas enhance their desirability as marriage partners but require us to incorporate the lived and material experiences of transformations in Andean economy and society into ethnic and gendered positionalities of Native Andean women.

Conclusions

Adolescent girls and boys are active in the process of marriage, both as agents and as objects, transforming themselves as they are transformed, taking on different positionalities and subjectivities in the transaction. Even Lévi-Strauss admitted in *Elementary Structures of Kinship* (1969:xx) that each woman, in contrast to women in general, is "a person . . . a generator of signs . . . never purely what is spoken about." Of course, his insistence on the significance of the models of social structure as opposed to the on-the-ground contingencies of social interaction obscures the historically embedded activities and subjectivities of human beings. In his well-known analyses of marriage, women and men as individuals who marry have no place in the scheme of things. Women figure as objects of exchange between groups of men. Although at least some Sullk'ata adults would agree that maintaining the relationship between families is the most significant aspect of marriage, the individuals undergoing the process of marriage are also integral to the ethnographic and theoretical picture of marriage.

In this chapter I have raised the question of how to incorporate subjectivities (that are embodied and interacting) into an analysis of marriage. People's positionalities (of gender, ethnicity, age, and socioeconomic class) cannot be extracted from their desirability as marriage partners; nor can marriage be extracted from the shifting social, economic, and political milieu in which people live. Local gender ideologies and power asymmetries, conceptions of sexuality, and the specific constraints of adolescence articulate with national discourses of modernity as young men and women enter into or avoid suway.

Although the gender, ethnic, and class positionalities of single men and women are enacted in both exaggerated and unremarkable ways in performances of "cholitas," the performances complicate rather than reinforce a simple notion of gender or gender hierarchy. The ritual performance of young men as cholitas illuminates gender difference by which men are linked to male supernatural forces, subsistence agriculture, and marriage exchanges. But these male "cholitas" also direct attention to the performed aspect of gender in an everyday sense. The performances of young women as cholitas, though more habitual than ritual, highlight the desires of young single women for money and material goods, for socioeconomic mobility, and for a husband, a household, and children. Young women's displays of fashion, often made possible by their wage work outside of Sullk'ata, enhance their desirability as marriage partners. In order to understand young women's performances as cholitas, and to understand warmi suway more generally, both the broader context of the Bolivian political economy and the lived experiences of gender and ethnicity must be taken into account.

For Sullk'atas, gender is at once a state of being, an immanence, and a process. Gender is developed throughout life and solidifies in some senses with marriage, when two single people enter into a relationship conceived of (in ideal terms) as *yanantin* or mirrored pairs, a dual relation reflected in cosmological conceptions and everyday activities (Platt 1986). Adolescents are well on their way to being adults and fully gendered beings, but they do not yet carry out their daily and ritual activities in that particular configuration of relationships required by marriage (Van Vleet 2003a). I have argued that adolescence is understood as ambiguous for both men and women, but young men somehow epitomize this positionality more than young women do. It is a young man who becomes a condenado (a being caught between life and death) in the story; and it is young men who perform as cholitas during Carnival (or dance as bears). Cholitas do not perform as jóvenes. Why is the ambiguous facet of gender more obvious in the ritual practices of young men? The ambiguity that young men embody links them, as I have argued, to the mountain forces and patrilineal ancestors. In this sense, young men perform from a position of power. In another sense, the young men's activities are marked. Maleness stands out against a more pervasive feminine background (which is unmarked) for native Andeans, as Billie Jean Isbell (1997) has argued. From this perspective, within the typically female-headed household and through his marriage, a young man might play a special role in the transmission of authority from the mother-in-law to the daughter-in-law.

Finally, notions that warmi suway only happens in the campo and is "uncivilized" constrain young women in different ways than they may constrain young men. Women's refusals to voice their opinions about warmi suway or to describe their experiences of warmi suway in particular and personal terms, then, should be suggestive of social constraints and contradictions, in which and through which individuals still must act and live. Being attentive to actions as well as words, structured constraints as well as structuring discourses, may provide a way of listening to those silences of subaltern women (Spivak 1985; see also Coronil 1996) and acknowledging the materialities of sexuality and gender, ethnicity and affinity. Tracing the ways in which multiple texts speak to each other, sometimes reinforcing and at other times contesting particular meanings, enables a fuller though not a complete rendering of Sullk'ata experience.

SIX

Reframing the Married Couple

Affect and Exchange in Three Parts

To Become a Married Couple

MARRIAGE IS SO much a part of the experience of almost every adult in Sullk'ata that the practices and the everyday contingencies of married life are assumed as "simple experience" and "common sense" (Williams 1977:110).[1] In many Andean regions, including Sullk'ata, a person must be married and have children, and ideally contribute to the ayllu by farming the land and participating in the cargo system, in order to be a mature human being. Yet in regard to this transition from childhood to adulthood, the Sullk'atas that I know would agree with the words of a Peruvian mother of the bride: "Do you think it's easy to begin to walk the road of life, the life of a marriage? It's one thing, the life of youth, and it's another thing, the life of a married couple" (Valderrama and Escalante 1998:304; my translation). Only with the help of responsible adults and through the passage of time do the young man and woman learn how carry out their economic, social, political, and ritual responsibilities to each other, to their children, to the community and ayllu, and to the spiritual forces of the universe.

Marriages are consolidated, or sometimes dissolved, over the course of many years through the contingencies of daily life in the campo. Families, communities, and state and church authorities also reaffirm marriages through rituals and rites. At the turn of the twenty-first century most Sullk'ata couples engaged in multiple forms of ceremony, including a betrothal (*warmi mañay*), civil marriage (*matrimonio civil,* Sp.), and a Catholic wedding ceremony and community fiesta (*kasarakuy; casar,* Sp.). For the oldest generation of married couples in the ayllu, warmi mañay was ample validation of the marriage partnership. José and Mariana had been living together as husband and wife for some twenty years when they were married in a Catholic ceremony in 1973. One day the priest came to their community in search of those who had not been married in the Catholic Church. José told me that the priest married many couples that day in a large group ceremony. In contrast, Julia and Wilberto began planning immediately for the years of saving money and working for others that would be required to accomplish a Catholic wedding ceremony and fiesta. Most Sullk'atas state publicly that they "have a husband" or "have a wife" after their parents legitimate the relationship in the betrothal ceremony. In the following months or years they undertake a (usually perfunctory) civil ceremony, begin having children, and ultimately sponsor their own wedding fiesta.

The discourses of the marriage process produce and legitimate social, moral, economic, and emotional bonds between the married partners, creating a qhari-warmi (married couple, "man-and-woman") from a joven and a cholita. These discourses and the relationships they produce also extend beyond the couple. The marriage process integrates a daughter-in-law into her husband's family, creates social and economic bonds between parents, reinforces relationships between two communities, and establishes a married couple as an economic-political and social unit that contributes to the community and ayllu.

In this chapter I explore some of the discourses through which Sullk'atas forge affective and moral stances toward each other and social, economic, and political bonds between themselves and the ayllu. Each of these discourses entails economic and social exchanges of people, ideals, things, money, and labor. The first discourse highlights the authority of parents and immaturity of the young couple. Most closely associated with betrothal, this discourse originates in everyday relationships between parents and children and most closely approximates Lévi-Strauss's (1969) notion of the exchange of women between groups of men. The second discourse emphasizes the companionship, love, and compassion between spouses and overlaps more general discourses of progress and modernization. Highlighting exchanges of a different order, the discourse is promulgated by the Catholic missionary nuns in the region during a course on marriage that is required for all Sullk'atas who wish to be married in the Catholic

Church. Finally, a discourse of indebtedness is embedded in the multiple acts of giving and receiving labor and commodities during the wedding fiesta. Associated with the circulation of energy and labor, this discourse also indexes shifting economic relationships that have resulted in an increase in access to commodities and gift-giving during weddings. The two individuals, who may not know each other well at the initiation of their marriage, become enmeshed in, draw upon, or challenge facets of the talk and practices of these three discursive arenas. In the process, they shape and are constrained by their affective, social, and economic relationship as a married couple and as individuals in a wider community of human and supernatural beings.

In the experiences of Sullk'atas, these discourses are not bounded but intertwined. Individuals may draw upon any of these conceptualizations of partnership to make sense of an interaction or event or to navigate a relationship. The aim of the chapter is to describe these discourses as they emerged in interactions of Sullk'atas at the turn of the twenty-first century. Of course, each generation goes through adolescence and approaches marriage under different economic, social, and political circumstances than their parents and grandparents did. Prior to the 1970s, for example, a priest only arrived intermittently in the region to conduct necessary rites. By the early 1980s a priest from Great Britain resided in the town of Pocoata, and an order of nuns from Canada founded a mission in a nearby community. More generally, those growing up in the second half of the twentieth century have been increasingly exposed to national and transnational ideologies of gender, family, and modernity through education in public schools, media broadcasts, and migration to urban and lowland regions.

However, attempting to make an argument about historical changes in marriage practices based on information collected in a relatively short period from individuals of different generations and genders would result in what Arland Thornton (2001) calls the problem of "reading history sideways." My data are primarily based on a year and a half of intensive research, not on long-term ethnographic research that followed individuals and their practices, attitudes, and beliefs over several years. I draw from my observations of weddings and wedding classes and my audiotaped interviews and informal conversations with Sullk'ata men and women in 1995–1996 and 2001. Without discounting the historical moment in which I conducted fieldwork, I explore the competing and overlapping affective practices and discourses of identity and exchange through which Sullk'atas produce husbands and wives.

From Adolescent to Adult

Warmi Mañay: Reestablishing Parental Authority

However marriages are initiated, many of the succeeding events reconstruct the authority of the parents and the immaturity of the *novios* (bride and groom or boyfriend and girlfriend, Sp.). Marriages initiated by suway must be affirmed by the families of both the young man and the young woman through local rituals of betrothal called *warmi mañay* (to lend the woman). A young man's parents cannot completely control their son's actions. As adults, they are nonetheless responsible for his actions and must make amends to the parents of the stolen young woman. As I have already noted, a young man and his parents will usually go to the young woman's parents within a few days of the suway in order to tell them that he has carried her away. Coca and cane alcohol or, if possible, corn beer are brought along. The parents stay up late into the night, talking and negotiating, drinking and making libations, scolding the young man and the young woman if she is present. Through the warmi mañay, parents reassert their authority over the young people and negotiate their future relationship with each other.

Parents make the couple aware of their new obligations through the scolding (*rimanakuy*) that takes place during warmi mañay ritual.[2] The parents examine the characters of their children, enumerating their failings and chastising them for acting irresponsibly. During the scolding, the parents of the novios also impress upon the young couple that their lives have changed, their obligations have shifted, and different conduct will be expected from them. Although the young man and woman will already have helped herding sheep, plowing a field, cooking, or hilling up potatoes for many years, now the *way* in which they do these things must change. The couple will no longer be able to rely upon their parents. They must shift from acting like children who do not have to worry about where their food and clothing come from to acting like adults who feed and clothe others. Warmi mañay is thus an arena in which parents inform the joven and cholita of what living as a married couple means and press them to demonstrate proper respect for their parents.

If a woman is stolen from a fiesta, her parents will initially be critical of the young man and unwilling to agree to the match without setting certain conditions. The oldest generation of married couples in the community told me that they were afraid (*manchay*) of having acted without the approval of their parents and of what people in the community might say before their warmi mañay took place. Osebio and Aleja were in their late sixties in 1995. They were one of the few elderly couples who had a Catholic wedding as well as a warmi mañay. They told me, laughing at the memory, that after Osebio had "carried away" Aleja during a fiesta, they were frightened. Aleja hid in Osebio's family's house. They were scared, Osebio said, until his father went and straightened things out with her parents.

Osebio said, "Yes, [our parents] were making ch'allas . . . making offerings . . . My father went there to her house. He also went there to make us obey. He was going to inform them of what happened [to their daughter]. Then . . . umm . . . we were scared, we were really scared."

"But what about?" I asked.

"But they hadn't yet been making ch'allas for us! And we had not yet been made to obey. We had not yet been made to carry out our obligations! And then we all went to her house. That one, though," Osebio continued, indicating his wife with a nod of his head, "she would not go at first. She thought, 'My father will say no. I'm not going to go there.' But then her father said yes. Her father lent her."[3]

Although a woman's parents usually agree to "lend" their daughter eventually, they may at first refuse. A young woman's parents may kick out the young man's parents when they arrive to make amends. Aleja was not the only woman who was afraid to face her parents. Many other women in Sullk'ata remembered anxious moments wondering whether their parents would agree to let them marry the young men who had stolen them. Nora, who was in her mid-twenties and had already been married for ten years in 1996, recalled that her father refused to let her marry for a long time, making her husband's family return three times. She was just fifteen when she was stolen, and the young man who stole her was already in his twenties. Her father finally agreed to the match but warned that he would come and take her back himself if he found out she was mistreated in any way.

Although a certain degree of hostility is expected between the family of a young woman who is stolen and the family of a young man, eventually the two sets of parents agree. The term *mañay* refers to "what should be lent, that which should be requested" (Lira 1944:628); or something "which lacks a pair" (Gose 1994:135); or a prestation that "receives a delayed counter-prestation in kind" (Mannheim 1991b:91). Mañay indicates an unfinished cycle. Parents say that they will lend their daughter only after asserting their own dignity and the worth of their daughter and assuring themselves that their daughter will be treated well in the household of strangers (also see Carter 1977; Daza 1983:88; Valderrama y Escalante 1998).

Often the woman's parents choose the *padrinos de matrimonio* (godparents of the marriage, Sp.) as a condition for their approval. The godparents are ideally

After the betrothal ceremony, a relative relaxes. Until the bride's
parents have agreed to the match, adults are uneasy.

a mature married couple well respected in the community. They have the responsibility to help the young couple in their new life and especially to medi-
ate disputes. The godparents have specific responsibilities during the Catholic
wedding ceremony and the wedding fiesta. Once the young man's parents have
garnered the acceptance of the couple, the parents of the bride, the parents of
the groom, and the padrinos will all address each other as *comadre* and *compadre*. The young married couple will address the padrinos as *madrina* and *padrino* (godmother and godfather), and the godparents will call their godchildren *waway* (child). The event of warmi mañay thus formalizes a relationship

between the two sets of parents as well as between the young man and woman. The "exchange" occurs between the two families.

The potential for a young man's parents to be refused creates a great deal of anxiety among Sullk'atas. Until they reach an agreement, parents worry that other community members will gossip about them and their children who have run off together (also see Valderrama and Escalante 1998). For example, Roberto and Zenobia, who was from Kallpa, had run away together and lived in Santa Cruz for four years before returning to visit their families. Upon their first trip back to their natal communities, Roberto and his parents brought coca and alcohol to Zenobia's parents in order to make amends and ask that the children could marry. Roberto's mother, however, one of Ilena's cousins, first sought out Ilena to get her advice, because she was concerned that they would be refused. As it turned out, Zenobia's parents approved the match. Roberto's parents hired a small band and hosted a betrothal celebration in Zenobia's parents' home, to which the entire community of Kallpa was invited. Although such a large mañay is unusual, only after the warmi mañay do parents say that they have "done the right thing." The ritual shifts the relationship between their children into the social and moral universe of adults, making the relationship public rather than hidden. Through warmi mañay parents bring the actions of their children into the adult moral discourse of reciprocity and sociality and reassert the authority of parents and the ideal obedience of children.

Tantanakuy: *Living Together*

After a warmi mañay most Sullk'ata couples live with their husband's family for several months and up to several years. This period is called *tantanakuy* (to be together with each other) or *sirvinakuy* (to serve each other).[4] Some anthropologists have referred to tantanakuy as "trial marriage." The authority of parents is reinscribed during tantanakuy as the inexperienced adolescents are taught how to live as married adults. During this time the young man and woman also determine how compatible they are with each other under the supervision of the young man's parents. If they fight or do not work well together, the young couple may separate, with the woman returning to her parents' household. The period of tantanakuy is often challenging, especially for the young woman. The young people are dependent on the husband's parents for food and shelter. Although a young man will usually receive a bit of land from his father and the young woman will usually receive several sheep that she has raised since childhood, the transfer of this inheritance does not happen immediately. Until they live in their

When my husband learned to plow a field, men joked that he was a son-in-law (*tullqa*).

own house, care for their children, and produce the food and products necessary for subsistence, they are themselves considered children.

While living in the parents' household, the young people are obligated to help, typically following a gendered division of labor. A young woman is more subject to the demands of her in-laws daily than a young man is to his. A woman is expected to carry out tasks readily and cheerfully demonstrate her respect for her mother-in-law. Not all women acquiesce easily to the emotional, social, and economic demands of their mother-in-law or to the stress of living in a strange household and community.

A man, in contrast to his wife, works for his father, as he has since his childhood. As a son-in-law (*tullqa*) he may have relatively little to do with his affines. During August, when my husband learned how to plow a field prior to irrigation, the men joked that he was don Juliano's tullqa, because he was using Juliano's team of oxen and plowing his field. Most women simply laughed when I asked about their husbands working for or helping their fathers. Unless a woman expects to inherit land from her parents, a man has little reason to return to his wife's community to help her parents with planting or harvesting.[5]

Even after the young man and woman move out of the household compound of the husband's parents, if they remain in the community (and especially if the husband is the youngest son), they continue to help the parents with daily and seasonal tasks. For example, Felicia and Imilio lived with Imilio's parents for six years and moved out only after the birth of their fourth child, when their single room became too crowded. Three years later, Felicia still went to cook at the hearth of her *suegra* (mother-in-law, Sp.) or sent her oldest daughter (who was at that time about ten years old) to spend the night with her grandparents, helping them prepare evening and morning meals and doing chores when she returned from school. Imilio assisted his father in planting fields and in several other agricultural tasks.

The exchanges of alcohol and coca between parents consolidate their agreement to the marriage of their children. Many other exchanges follow, as the daughter-in-law moves to her husband's natal household and gives her labor in exchange for food and as both change their understandings of themselves from adolescent to adult. As Gary Urton (1985:260) noted several years ago, the period of tantanakuy in the Andean communities of Peru with which he was familiar required "developing new and different forms of behavior and . . . receiving from other people in the village confirmation of one's new status through signs of respect, adult terms of address, etc." This is also true for Sullk'atas. The rituals and the everyday interactions that follow a warmi suway are the performative means by which the young people begin to establish themselves as individual adults and as a married couple, even as they are treated as children.

While the novios live together, they prepare for a Catholic ceremony and community fiesta, the final ritual events of the marriage process (Van Vleet 1999:294–299). Currently neither the younger generation of Sullk'atas just married (or about to be married) nor their parents consider warmi mañay sufficient to legitimize a marriage. The community fiesta is in many ways the culminating ritual of marriage and integrates a couple into an array of affective, social, and economic relationships. Preparing for the wedding fiesta often requires years of work as the young man and woman struggle to accumulate the money and the social and economic relationships needed to provide food, corn beer, and entertainment for their natal communities and any other people who might attend. Many young couples will return to the city to earn money to pay for the Catholic ceremony and wedding fiesta. But the novios also must spend a significant amount of time in the rural community to establish the relationships of exchange necessary for accomplishing a fiesta.

From Individual to "Compassionate Companion"

"A Little Piece of Paper"

The significance of the Catholic ceremony and fiesta is indicated in part by the willingness of Sullk'atas to respect the additional preconditions for a Catholic wedding that have been required of them since the 1980s. In 1982 an international group of Catholic nuns established a mission in a town, just a few hours' walk from Kallpa. Viewing Sullk'atas and other communities as incompletely missionized, the sisters attempted to correct erroneous beliefs and practices by teaching "the meanings of the sacraments of the Catholic Church," instituting biweekly masses in a community church, and ministering to the youth of the region. The nuns built a house for themselves and a medical clinic, a church, and a public secondary school for the community. In addition to increasing many children's access to education beyond primary school, the nuns also influenced the curriculum of the school by teaching courses themselves. For a time a sister from the Philippines taught English classes, and the sisters from Montreal, Canada, taught French and religion classes. The nuns also began teaching classes on marriage and baptism, following a general curriculum set out by the Catholic Church. Soon afterward the regional priest began requiring evidence that people had attended the classes before agreeing to perform baptisms or marriages.

Nicolás and Remedios were among the first Sullk'atas for whom the marriage course was required. This fact emerged in the context of an interview about wedding practices, from which I present only a short excerpt.[6] The question that preceded Nicolás' statement about the wedding courses was not about the classes at all. Instead Dario, who was assisting, asked about the clothing the young man and woman wore to their wedding in order to prompt discussion of what the godparents of the wedding usually provided. He asked: "In order to enter into the church did you just wear your own clothes? Or maybe someone changed your clothes? Just how did you enter the church?"

Ignoring the direct question about clothing, Nicolás replied by discussing the "conditions" that the priest and the nuns had set on him and his wife in order to enter the church at all:

> In order to get married we had to pass courses in Pocoata. For three days and almost an entire week we took this course. "He will not marry you without passing the course," they said to us. "Without this knowledge from God, you would not get married, would you?" They told us that we would have to pass the course. For a week we took this course, in order to meet the sisters' conditions. And still after that, just then . . . um . . . luckily they gave us the little paper to validate us. That Saturday they gave it to us. With that paper, we crossed over to the Father priest. Only then did the priest recognize that we could marry. Without that bit of paper, they might have kicked us out of the church. Um, that is how we got married.[7]

Nicolás and Remedios married in 1985. His attention to the marriage class that he was required to pass ten years earlier indicates in part the impression that the Catholic priest and nuns made by imposing the class. It is that "little piece of paper" not the "knowledge from God" that Nicolás perceives as necessary to validate themselves as marriageable in the eyes of the Church.

In spite of Nicolás' consternation with the unexpected demands of the nuns, he and his wife passed the course. They needed that piece of paper to hand to the priest in exchange for a ceremony. As Catholics, they had to marry in the Church in order to sponsor their wedding fiesta. If they wanted to baptize their children in the future, they also needed to show another piece of paper—their Catholic marriage certificate. Andean religious practice is not a thin veneer of imported Spanish Catholicism overlaid upon an ancient (or Inca) cosmology— at least not in the experience of native Andeans themselves. The Catholicism of present-day Andean communities emerges from a long history of mission- izing that began in the colonial period with Spanish priests and administra- tors, whose Catholicism also looked very different from that of present-day North Americans (MacCormack 1991). Making libations to the "most heavenly father" and "most heavenly mother"—the Sun and Moon—at the beginning of each fiesta, or feasting a patron saint and a Catholic sacred mother on the same day "because they are married," or acquiring godchildren and compadres through baptisms, graduations, and marriages is what Catholics do in Sullk'ata experience. Sullk'atas are Catholics, and they explicitly contrast themselves and their religious practices with evangelical Protestants, who do not drink or dance.

In spite of the commitment of time and energy, Sullk'ata couples continued to pass these marriage courses throughout the 1980s and into the first years of the twenty-first century. The marriage classes usually take place over several days for four hours each day. Each person must complete agricultural and herd- ing tasks prior to the class or, alternatively, find someone willing to help them with the work. Because the Church of San Juan de Bautista in Pocoata is a re- gional church serving communities several hours away by foot, couples who want to be married may go to great effort simply to travel to the church or the nuns' mission to attend the required courses.

Catholic Marriage Classes in Sullk'ata

Requiring that couples take a course on marriage is typical in Catholic churches throughout Bolivia, and indeed throughout the world. In marriage classes the nuns follow a curriculum set out by the Church, reviewing the scriptures deemed most significant to marriage and attempting to educate people about their appropriate social roles, familial duties, and affective relationships with their spouses. The curriculum for the class taught in Sullk'ata is based on a small book written in Quechua and Spanish by the Catholic Diocese of Potosí (Equipo Pastoral 1989). In the classes that I observed, one of the nuns read the indicated Bible passages and led discussions of passages in Quechua. The classes were typically attended by more than one couple at a time, and the nuns drew responses from men and women who had varying levels of integration into Church and state institutions. To generate an exchange of ideas, the sisters passed around enlarged photocopies of the book's line drawings, depicting scenes between men and women in the rural Andes. They asked participants to describe what they thought was happening in the pictures. In this way the nuns initiated discussions of various scenarios and issues, including domestic violence, community involvement, hygiene, education, gendered work, and responsibility to the Church. They also discussed the characteristics of a "good husband" and a "good wife."

The curriculum of the marriage course emphasizes familial and affective ideologies and gendered and racial discourses that align with transnational Catholicism and companionate marriage and with Bolivian national politics. In early pages of the book readers are asked why a person might want to get married. On one page are the "common reasons" given by a native woman and man: "It's just our custom"; "Our parents obligated us to marry"; "We already have many children"; "We are already married in a civil ceremony"; "We have also gathered together the money that we need for a fiesta"; and "My wife has a lot of land and animals" (Equipo Pastoral 1989:6). Most Sullk'atas, like the unnamed voices in the book, say that they marry because marriage is customary and necessary to maintain a household. Some point out that they are undertaking a Catholic marriage because they work well together. Younger couples also said that they married in the Catholic Church because they wanted to be able to baptize their children. As the text continues, however, it is clear that these statements are just a starting point for what couples will be taught about why a person should marry.

The notion stressed in the courses taught by the nuns is that couples should not marry because of custom or for any reason other than that the husband loves (*munakuy*) the wife and the wife loves the husband. Love is the most important thing in the life of a married couple. The book outlines what love means and what the affective stance between the husband and wife should be from the perspective of the Church.

Have compassion (feel pity) for each other.

Help each other in all of your work.

Love each other as human beings.

Care for and do not abandon the other if he or she becomes sick.

Be together in sorrow as well as in happiness.

Repent to each other; do not believe another more.

If one person sins or offends the other, forgive each other.[8]

That married partners should love one another is a commonplace notion in the United States. Sullk'atas also say that they love and care for each other; older couples use the Quechua term *munakuy,* which reflects the reciprocal action of the verb. Younger couples tend to use the Spanish term *cariño* (affection) or sometimes *amor* (love), but most couples would not admit that they felt affection for their partner before marriage. Most Sullk'atas do not say that they married because they "fell in love."

Recent scholarship on marriage describes the ways in which companionate marriage and "love" are recent historical developments. During the 1920s and 1930s the term "companionate marriage" appeared in marriage manuals and popular health literature in the United States and Western Europe and was used to reference marriage based on friendship and sexual familiarity. As Jennifer Hirsch (2003:10–11) notes, by the end of the twentieth century the idea that mutual sexual pleasure and emotional intimacy are at the core of the marital relationships had become "a sort of native theory of kinship on an increasingly global scale." Although sexual intimacy is not discussed in either the text or the classes in Sullk'ata, the overt emphasis on emotional attachment between partners is striking. Not only is "love" the most important aspect of a marriage, but in explaining what love entails the teachers refer to other facets of affective closeness: compassion/pity, sorrow, happiness, repentance, and forgiveness. Far from emphasizing passion and mutual sexual pleasure, the manual invokes a sense of the importance of the couple as a unit and the potential fragility of bonds between spouses, who must have compassion for and trust each other.

The emphasis on emotional attachment is reinforced with specific behavioral injunctions: to talk rather than fight, to educate children in the public schools, to participate as adults in the community, nation, and Church. One of the most prominent features both of the classes conducted by the nuns and of the book itself is the emphasis placed on talking rather than fighting and the detrimental effects of drunkenness on marital relationships. In marriage classes the nuns repeatedly stress that women and men are equally valued and have dignity, that a husband should not hit his wife or think of himself as superior to his wife, and that drinking and drunkenness are not paths to a closer relationship with God or to a harmonious relationship with one's spouse.

Within the book this message emerges clearly in the interrelationship of text and pictures. The text emphasizes that "men and women are the same," although "some men believe that they have more rights than women do" (Equipo Pastoral 1989:21). The picture accompanying the text shows a woman on her knees, reeling backward, her hat flying, from the open-handed hit that her husband has given her. In the background are children crying and pots tipped over on the ground. A few pages later a series of pictures depicts the "bad" ways and the "good" ways to live as a family. In the five negative images, two pictures show men going about drunk and waving bottles; a third shows a woman being kicked by her husband, who has a bottle in his hand; and a fourth represents children abandoned and crying from hunger. The final negative picture depicts a man walking with his arm around a woman, holding a cup, with another woman following in the background. This series of pictures is contrasted to those representing the right ways to live as a family: a husband and wife work together in the fields, a woman bathes her child, a father leans down to assist a child who is writing at a table, and a man (contrary to Andean social norms) hands bread to his family.

The overwhelming emphasis on the negative aspects of drinking in part reflects the social reality in which foreign and national missionaries find themselves. In the Andes both men and women drink during fiestas but rarely or never drink outside of fiestas and other rituals. Women tend to drink less than men because they are responsible for caring for their children, feeding their families, and herding their sheep even during fiestas that last for several days. Some men and women drink to unconsciousness, a state of alterity associated with the dead and thus with fertility. Although drunkenness is considered crucial to the success of the fiesta, even Sullk'atas recognize that people are far more likely to express conflict and to become violent when drunk.[9] Of course, the increase in incidents of violence that occurs during fiestas troubles the sisters. The explicit association between drinking and recognizing a sacred landscape—the Sun and the Moon, the mountains, the furrow, and the sheep's corral—also disturbs them. The nuns encourage Sullk'atas to drink "just a cup" of corn beer or alcohol, as they do themselves. One sister told me that they always attend the wedding fiesta if they are invited but only drink one little cup, sipping the drink slowly, refusing the two wooden bowls (*turu wasus*) offered to them, and ignoring the rounds of whispered invocations, in order to serve as an example to others.

One after another, participants at a fiesta are handed two bowls of corn beer. Each takes his turn making a libation and drinking the entire contents of both bowls. (Photo by Lawrence Kovacs)

From the perspective of many Sullk'atas, however, the positive examples of family life are only possible in the context of maintaining relationships of reciprocity with human and supernatural beings through exchanges of labor, food, and alcohol. In rural Andean areas drinking and getting drunk are integral aspects of Catholic practice, in contrast to the religious practices of evangelical Protestants. Moreover, the manner in which one drinks—usually from two cups or bowls rather than just one—is also significant. Guests at a wedding fiesta are always offered two wooden bowls carved with a team of oxen, from which to offer a ch'alla and drink. Drinking from two bowls conceptually links drinking, the fertility of the earth, the virility of oxen, and the complementarity of a married couple and parallels other dualisms in the symbolics of Andean weddings, as I discuss below. Drinking from these two bowls during the wedding fiesta, and later in life during other fiestas, reinforces relationships with human and supernatural beings and the cycling of energy through the bodies of people, animals, plants, the earth, and the heavens.

By explicitly critiquing the practices of drinking in terms of the importance of the family, Catholic missionaries attempt to shape intimate affective and moral relationships, especially the relationship between spouses. The nuns' message of human value and dignity, the painfulness of a loved one's violence, and the necessity for compassion and caring cannot be disregarded (I discuss violence between affines further in the next chapter). Yet by highlighting drinking and drunkenness among native Andeans and the violence of physical abuse and abandonment, the Catholic pedagogy about marriage overlays transnational discourses of gender and human rights with racial discourses of "Indianness." In the Andes drunkenness and violence are stereotypically identified as specifically Indian problems that the more "civilized" urban populations do not encounter. Moreover, the emphasis on violence between husbands and wives may obscure the conflict, and sometimes physical violence, that erupts among women.

Sullk'atas are aware of these stereotypes and may attempt to distance themselves from violence. At the end of an interview on marriage, I thanked Celedonio and Sonia, who had spent the previous hour relating the events of their Catholic wedding ceremony and fiesta in 1989. They responded to my thanks in a formal way. Celedonio replied first, emphasizing to me that they did not fight; and Sonia followed immediately, elaborating on and representing their marriage relationship in a slightly different way.

CELEDONIO: That's the way ... We married each other and from the time even before that, when we lived together, we have never known how to fight with each other. We do not know how to hit each other. Others do ... But we, we don't know about that. From friendship [amistad, Sp.], love [amor, Sp.], we love each other [munanakuy]. We weren't forced to love each other.

SONIA: My mother used to tell me ... "Not one or the other, neither husband or wife should take advantage of the other," saying that she used to advise me. "For what reason is that [person] taking advantage?" she would say to me. We were seriously scolded. Me? I don't know how to take advantage of anyone, no way, not me. And now, I also know to respect the knowledge of what God Our Father says. When she scolded me, saying that to me, I grabbed onto it. Perhaps he also travels like that to those others [other women] . . . Men take advantage of one and then another . . . "Which one would he go to?" my mother used to say.

Celedonio's final statement integrates the behavioral emphasis on not fighting with the idea that he and his wife married because of love. He spends much of the year in Santa Cruz, working on a large farm run by Japanese immigrants. He uses first Spanish terms (*amistad* and *amor*) and then the Quechua term (*munanakuy*) to express that he and Sonia love each other. The Quechua term specifically integrates a notion of reciprocal feeling or action through the suffix -*naku,* which is added to the verb *munay* (to want, to like, to love). His reply intertwines both local ideals and perhaps more urban ideologies of marriage that emphasize friendship. Sonia's words, in contrast, emphasize that a husband and wife should not take advantage of each other. She stresses her mother's reprimand that a husband and wife should help each other. She does not address the issue of violence or claim love or friendship as the basis of the marital relationship. Highlighting the ideals and alluding to the realities (her husband's possible adultery) of her married life, she indicates that—although she does not take advantage of anyone—she is not so sure of her husband's actions as he travels here and there.

From Multiple Exchanges to Indebtedness

One morning in August 1995 Marianela and her husband entered the courtyard, knelt down, grabbed my hands, and invited my husband and me to the wedding of their daughter. The day before, with little fanfare, the wedding party had walked to Pocoata for the Catholic ceremony. On this day of the fiesta Marianela and her husband went to every house in the community and invited each married couple to the wedding fiesta in the nearby Sullk'ata community of Ranisupi.

In contrast to the discourse of obedience, which revolves around the relationship and exchanges between the novios and their parents, and in contrast to the discourse of compassionate companionship, which emphasizes the married couple as a isolable unit, the community celebration legitimates and produces moral and affective bonds that extend beyond the two individuals who marry. Through the preparations for the fiesta and the fiesta itself, Sullk'ata couples are integrated into a dense network of social and economic relationships. During the course of the wedding fiesta, labor, food, money, and other commodities circulate among people. These exchanges during the fiesta constitute another discourse on marriage, one through which a husband and wife solidify their

Men set large ceramic pots into the ground and women stir boiling water into ground corn, the beginning of a process that will eventually produce hundreds of liters of corn beer.

position as adults in the moral economy of Sullk'ata. The wedding fiesta alters the newly married couple's positionality and affective stance toward each other, toward community members, and toward the supernatural world by entangling them in debt.

A Wedding in Sullk'ata

Typically taking place in the community of the groom, wedding fiestas occur almost exclusively in August and September. Although I regretted that I did not know about the church ceremony in time to attend, Marianela and others reassured me that the fiesta was the more significant event. In spite of the efforts of the Catholic priest and nuns, few community members bother to attend the wedding ceremony. Unless people are immediate family members or somehow directly involved with the ceremony as a godparent or witness, they do not make the trip to Pocoata but continue doing the everyday tasks of herding sheep or working in the fields. Almost every adult will attend at least one day of the wedding fiesta, which usually begins the day after the church ceremony.

On the first day of the fiesta I walked to the community of Ranisupi with Fidelia, an older woman with two married daughters of her own. We followed the footpath that led out of Kallpa, south and slightly east toward the mountains, walking for over an hour. Once we arrived in Ranisupi, we descended the steep bank of the creek and climbed back up again several times as the path wound through houses and fields before angling toward the mountains. Finally we saw a house with flags flying from long poles in the stiff breeze. As we neared we could hear a band playing and a celebration clearly in progress. In front of and inside the house the Ranisupiños drank and made ch'allas and sang and danced. A small group of musicians played drums and the accordion.

Instead of entering the house, however, Fidelia veered off to the right, staying outside of the courtyard wall. I followed close behind as she crossed a ditch and made her way to an area across from the house where the men and women from Kallpa were already sitting on the ground, lined up against a wall in the shade. Upon our arrival we were asked to make libations with *aqha* (corn beer). The aqha was taken from a huge earthenware jar decorated with leaves from pepper and eucalyptus trees and served in *turu wasus*. Fidelia made cha'llas first; and after drinking both full bowls, she handed them back to the server. He refilled the bowls and offered me the pair of turu wasus so that I might make ch'allas and drink.

Soon after making my libations, I realized that—in contrast to the air of celebration emanating from the groom's household—the bride's family, even her entire natal community, had an air of loss and solemnity. Someone pointed out

Kallpa women watch the celebration at the groom's house across the way.

to me the bride's brother, who was crying as he drank corn beer. "A brother always cries. No one ever likes to lose a sister. It is always painful," my compadre told me.

All of a sudden the bride and groom arrived at the house with their padrino, the godfather of their marriage. They had been with their godparents all morning, making libations for them. The couple ran up to the house where the Ranisupiños were celebrating. Occasionally the newly married couple would run down the hill, past the Kallpaños, to welcome guests who arrived from Ranisupi. In a frenzy of thanks, the novios would kneel down and kiss the hands of their guests; then, hugging them by the elbows, they would lead them up the hill to the house. The novios did not acknowledge the presence of the Kallpaños.

The first movement of Kallpaños across the gully into the house of the groom's family came late in the afternoon. All morning long, as Kallpaños made libations for the couple, the middle-aged woman Celestina stirred a huge pot of *lawa* (a porridge made of ground corn, salt, and spicy red peppers). When the lawa was finally ready, Celestina made ch'allas around the food. She served it out into large basins, putting hot rocks pulled from the fire into each one.[10] Kallpa women then carried the basins of soup across the gully to the house of the groom, leaving the soup with the female relatives of the groom to feed the Ranisupiños. A while later the groom's community sent the basins back to the Kallpaños, now filled with "dry food" for the Kallpaños to eat: noodles, boiled potatoes, and ch'uñu with a spicy sauce. The Ranisupiños ate the wet lawa that the Kallpaños had cooked, and the K'allpaños ate the dry food that the Ranisupiños had cooked.

Finally, after everyone had eaten, the musicians danced over to the Kallpaños from the house, playing a lively tune. Four men picked up a mirrored wardrobe (a gift, I was told, from the bride's brother), two others carried a bed frame, and another man held up the big caldron in which the lawa had been cooked. Raising these gifts high over their heads, the men danced down the gully and over to the groom's house, with many other men and women from Kallpa following. In a line, they danced up the path to the house and then entered the courtyard with the gifts.

Leaving the gifts in the middle of the courtyard, the men and women returned across the gully to the Kallpaños. Finally, all of the people from the Kallpa side danced over to the house with the rest of their gifts: big plastic bowls, pails, washtubs, a clock that plays music at each hour, dishes, and glasses. As the Kallpaños arrived at the house, the bride and groom welcomed each person, moving through the crowd, kissing hands and hugging shoulders. Not until the end of the day, after the physical and material exchange of food and gifts, did the bride

Kallpaños cross to the groom's house carrying gifts. The tall poles holding the *arku* (gifts from the groom's sister) are visible in the background.

and groom welcome the Kallpaños. Only then did the Kallpaños enter the house and sit down in the courtyard with the Ranisupiños.

Affect and Duality on the First Day

The oppositions performed on the first day of the wedding fiesta—between Kallpaños and Ranisupiños, wet food and dry food, outside and inside, men and women, happy and solemn—are linked to broad conceptual understandings of a universe in which uniting opposing principles or contrasting elements generates equilibrium and energy. Tristan Platt (1986:244–246) has argued that the concept of *yanantin* underlies much of Andean cosmology and everyday and ritual practice, including the relationship between husbands and wives. Quechua speakers use the term *yanantin* to refer to pairs or mirror images: body parts that occur in pairs (eyes, hands, ears, legs, breasts, testicles), twins, a team of oxen (*yunta*, Sp.), ch'allas that are almost always made in pairs, and qhari-warmi (married couples). The term *yanantin* is made up of the stem *yana-* (from *yanapay*, to help) and the suffix *-ntin*.[11] According to Gose (1994:135), the meaning of *yanantin* "might be 'helper and helped united to form a single category' . . . much as yanapa (help) is ayni without a strict calculation of labour debts and credits." A more literal translation might be that certain things, "by virtue of their complementarity (*yana*), make up a whole" (Mannheim, personal communication, 1999). Yanantin is in many ways an affective ideal indexing a mode of being in a marital relationship and in the Andean universe.

During the fiesta, the overlapping dual oppositions reinforce a sense of complementarity between husband and wife in which each is necessary to the other in establishing and maintaining a household (e.g., Allen 2002; Harris 1978, 1981; Isbell 1977). Yet a singular focus on the conjugal pair obscures the opposition between communities, collectivities that play fundamental roles in the social, economic, and political life of the married couple. During the fiesta, for example, the bride and groom sit with their parents and godparents in an E-shaped structure (*ramada*) built within the courtyard of the groom's house. Made from the branches of eucalyptus trees, the ramada resembles a booth divided in two parts. The novio sits with his father and father-in-law and godfather on the right side of the structure, divided by a wall of ponchos and pepper tree leaves from the novia and her mother and mother-in-law and godmother, who sit on the left (also see Platt 1986: 244). The symbolic opposition most clearly represented in this structure is that between husband and wife (and between men and women), with the opposition between the communities receding into the background.

Yet, far more than the ideal symmetry of husband and wife or the complementary opposition between man and woman, the members of the bride's community emphasized maintaining a distinction between the two communities on the first day of the wedding fiesta. As one Kallpa man stressed to me, "The Kallpaños are like one finger. They come together and sit together and then leave together." When I asked if the bride and groom were also like one finger, he shrugged his shoulders and grudgingly agreed, saying that the husband and wife should also come together to the fiesta. But it is more important, he reiterated, that the community is one unit. Even after the Kallpaños sat down in the courtyard of the house, the sense of opposition persisted. Not only did the members of two communities sit in different areas of the courtyard, but they also refused to talk and dance with each other. At one point a man from Ranisupi approached my husband and me and tried to talk to us. After a few moments the woman sitting next to me, who was from Kallpa, said, "Leave us alone, don't talk to us, you're from the other side. Don't talk, they're Kallpaños. They're with us." He finally turned away, properly chastened, to respect the ritual separation of the communities.

In Andean cosmology and ritual practice, the competition of opposing forces generates energy that is circulated throughout the universe. During a wedding fiesta, the communities of the bride and groom not only are distinguished by eating different foods, sitting in different places, and expressing different feel-

Kallpa men discuss additional prestations next to a wardrobe, given to the couple from the bride's brother.

ings but also in a sense compete with each other. The gifts given to the married couple are distinguished, and accounted for, according to gendered and affinal dual oppositions. Married couples, who attend the fiesta as guests, give gifts separately: each man or woman arrives at the fiesta with a gift or a cash donation. The amount of money or the value of the gift is accounted for within each community. The Kallpaños painstakingly wrote out two separate lists—one noting the name of each man and the thing given and the other noting the name of each woman and the thing given. The counting and listing of the money and other commodities given by the men and women of Kallpa was pervaded by a sense of urgency, as the counters shouted for additional prestations of money. The Kallpaños' gifts would be compared to those of the Ranisupiños—and the Kallpaños did not want to fall behind.

When people marry, the wedding fiesta generates wealth (in money and commodities) through the competition between the two communities. Specific kinds of affective and economic orientations among people are implicitly and explicitly expressed through dualism and competition. Dual opposition alone does not describe the meanings that people derive from exchanges or the array of exchanges taking place in the arena of the wedding fiesta. For example, the dualism of eyes in the human body or of husband and wife or of opposing ayllus is refracted by the multiplicity of eyes of the potato.[12] The eyes of the potato are closely associated with fertility; each eye when planted in the earth produces multiple potatoes. Money—or more specifically silver and other minerals—grows in clusters under the earth, just like potatoes (Harris 1989, 1995). Sullk'atas make ch'allas, asking for the fertility and productivity of animals, fields, and money. When someone buys a ten-liter can of cane alcohol to resell in smaller quantities, the money that is earned as profit is understood to be fertile. Sullk'atas also closely associate mirrors and shiny coins with the process of multiplication. By bringing attention to the modes of exchange and the things exchanged, we may more clearly comprehend the ways in which the circulation of commodities (including money) shapes the affective and economic relationship of the newly married couple with each other and with many other individuals and collectivities.

Accounting for Things on the Second Day

On the second day of the fiesta the tenor of exchanges shifts from a competition between the communities to an accounting of what the newly married couple received. Designated people list and total up all the money and commodities and announce the amount so that the couple and their community members know what was received. The ritualized distance and separation of the two communities partially recede to the background, reinforcing the naturalness of the bond of the married couple and the integration of the couple into the broader community and ayllu.

The events of the second day of the wedding in Ranisupi revolved around collecting and accounting for "gifts" given to the married couple. Almost every married adult that I spoke with emphasized the importance of this practice. For example, when Isidoro and Rosa told me about their wedding fiesta in an interview in May 1996, they emphasized that *all* of the things they received were counted and valued. Not only did respected men from the community announce the value of these gifts to the entire crowd of people gathered, but Isidoro and Rosa had to kneel down to have the huge bundles of things tied to their backs. They were then made to stand and walk around the crowded courtyard. When I saw this ritual during wedding fiestas in 1996, the bride and groom—invariably exhausted and drunk from their obligations to make libations—were bent double with the weight of the bundles; they would fall to their hands and knees only to be helped up again.

Sullk'atas give and receive three categories of things: *arku, regalu* (*regalo*, Sp.) and *aumentu* (*aumento*, Sp.).[13] To trace their differences, I include an excerpt from Isidoro and Rosa's interview in which each of these categories is named. I should note that this interview was conducted with Dario acting as an assistant. He is a compadre of Isidoro and Rosa, the godfather of one of their children. Dario actively participated in the interviewing of Isidoro; he asked very directed questions that prompted Isidoro and Rosa to describe specific details of the wedding.[14] The excerpt thus highlights Dario's own perceptions of which aspects of the fiesta were most significant as much as those of Isidoro or Rosa. In the excerpt Isidoro answers a query from Dario about whether aumentu were given on the second day of their wedding fiesta and, if so, who began them. Isidoro then continues to talk about other kinds of things given:

ISIDORO: My padrino began the aumentu and my madrina began it at the woman's altar. Yes, there was an altar prepared for the women and another altar for the men . . . After that, our entire family went up to put down an aumentu. That day, throughout the whole day, there were arku, and there were regalus—gifts—shirts, skirts, sweaters . . . there was everything there . . . plates, cups, spoons . . .

ROSA: From the women there was a cow.

ISIDORO: From the women there was a cow. Yes, there was a cow. And from her mother there was a bed. My compadre, that one, he arrived with carrying cloths, three carrying cloths, or four, right? There were four carrying cloths: one hand-woven and three from La Paz.

ROSA: Unh hunh.

DARIO: That day, Sunday, was it all giving aumentu late into the night? Throughout the afternoon weren't people putting aumentu at the altar and weren't there people who counted it? In some weddings, they say they name an accountant, who receives it all . . . In the afternoon did he count the money?

Isidoro and Dario then discussed the counting of aumentu and arku. Rosa remembered the names of the men who accounted for their value. Dario asked whether or not a written list was made of everything the married couple had received from each wedding guest. Then Isidoro turned again to the question of the accounting:

ISIDORO: The next day, still later in the afternoon, not Sunday but Monday, in the afternoon they made us carry it on our backs . . . We continued giving meat, soup, corn beer, when people gave us the regalus. Yes, then the evening came. When evening fell, the people finished cutting the things from the arku. There were almost forty-something arku. There were more, right? Maybe there were sixty . . .

DARIO: When they had finished the whole arku, weren't there also regalus? Didn't you, when the regalus were all counted, didn't you perhaps total them up? How much money might they have entered? How much might it be worth? Those gifts, didn't you total them up?

ISIDORO: He totaled it up. The total was 600, umm . . . and a fraction: 600 . . . 630 or 628, maybe? All of it, he said. Money. Then clothes, and with the clothes, how much might it have been . . . ? But there were two huge bundles. There were two huge bundles! I was not able to carry that bundle on my back. They lifted it onto my back. They made me carry it on my back. It weighed me down to the ground, and I wasn't able to get up again, it was so heavy.

DARIO: Did the counter tell the community what the total was? Was he saying that the huge amount of money is for the year, or something like that?

ISIDORO: The counter advised them. The entire community heard . . . The community knew the entire amount.

Sullk'atas usually attempt to hide their access to material wealth from each other in order to avoid envy. During weddings, however, the recipients of the cash and commodities—the groom and bride—are not permitted to hide either the things themselves, which are displayed and written down in lists, or their total value. Everything is counted by a third party and is written down, which makes the giving public and official. The total value of the aumentu and the arku is announced, and the groom and bride are made to carry all of the things on their backs, so that the people of both families and communities know what that couple has gained during the wedding fiesta.

It was clear to me from my conversations with Sullk'atas and my observations of wedding fiestas that the accounting of things received was a significant part of the wedding fiesta. I was not, however, initially aware of the different kinds of things given and accounted for. Aumentu, I knew, was typically a monetary prestation given to supplement other prestations. I had first heard of arku when, months earlier, I interviewed Gregoria about her wedding and the things she and her husband, Sebastián, received. Not knowing of the category arku, I asked, "Then . . . did they give you gifts [regalus]?" Gregoria stressed that she did not receive any gifts at all.

"Hmm give . . . that time, at that time they did not give gifts [regalus]," replied Gregoria.

"There weren't any?"

Gregoria then explained: "There was just the arku . . . There used to be just the arku; there weren't any regalus. At that time, there weren't any. And now the arku has shirts! Also all of these." She pointed to a few plastic bowls, stacked neatly next to her stove: "These bowls are ones that were given to my Angélica, to my daughter-in-law . . . That younger one [my second son's wife] also received everything—even pails, a lot of pails. In my time there weren't any regalus. Yes, there were just balls of hand-spun yarn and wool that were given. There was just an arku with yarn, definitely not any gifts. Now they have regalus."

Confused by the term *arku,* I then switched tactics to ask about things that I suspected they had received, such as land and sheep. Although I did not use the term *regalu,* I did use the verb *quy* (to give). Gregoria reiterated over and over that when she and her husband were married (in 1951, according to the parish records) no one "gave" her anything. Nor did they receive any gifts (regalus). It was clear, however, that Gregoria and her husband received some *things:* hand-spun yarn to make her husband a poncho, a cow, and a small amount of money. The yarn and wool and a little money were part of the arku, Gregoria asserted. The cow was given to her husband, not to her, as his inheritance.[15] Gregoria was not the only older Sullk'ata who stated that she did not receive gifts. Although the grandmothers remembered receiving only hand-spun yarn, women and men who were married in the 1980s and 1990s commented upon the huge bundles of gifts that they had received.

I initially suspected that the difference between regalu and arku was categorical, a distinction between manufactured products bought in the marketplace and subsistence products like wool and yarn. "Gifts" or regalus were a relatively recent phenomenon in Sullk'ata weddings. Guests at the weddings that I attended brought many regalus, and most of those were commodities like clothing and dishes, buckets, and bedframes. However, there were also arku at the weddings I attended. The poles that I had taken for flags as I walked to Ranisupi the first day of that wedding were—I was informed by my Kallpa companions—the long poles of the arku. On top of each pole, made from a eucalyptus tree sapling, a frame had been fabricated. A woman's blouse and sweater with two plates sewn in strategic locations topped one frame. Other frames held men's pants, carrying cloths, plates, and dishes. Thus the arku also held many commodities as well as hand-spun yarn and sometimes money.

I eventually began to understand the distinctions between arku, aumentu, and regalu as less about the type of things given than about the mode of exchanging and the social expectations and affective meanings that inhere in those exchanges. Arku, I learned, is given by the sisters of the groom and may include

Women married before 1980 remember receiving only hand-spun yarn (*qaytu*), and a little money, at their weddings.

hand-spun yarn and manufactured articles, especially clothing but also plates and bowls and money. Arku indicate a specific relationship between giver and receiver and a particular kind of debt and future obligation. Olivia Harris (1989) notes that arku are understood to be part of a cycle of prestations. Given to the cross-sex siblings of the sponsor of a fiesta in the nearby ayllu of Laymi, arku in some ways "reward those who take their turn to feast their neighbours and their divine guardians" (Harris 1989:245). Sullk'ata wedding arku might similarly be thought of as a prestation, part of a cycle of giving and receiving that is ideally maintained throughout the life of the person or the married couple. The arku has an inherent obligation for a counterprestation.

Aumentu, given on the first day of the wedding fiesta and on subsequent days, is typically in the form of money and considered to be something *in addition to* another prestation, to augment that which has already been given. Aumentu is given in a competitive way on the first day, but more generally is understood to generate wealth. Aumentu, like arku, is carefully accounted for by Sullk'atas during the wedding fiesta.

Regalus are typically manufactured items and are given by people who come to the wedding. Regalus do not require a formal counterprestation, however. Although the total monetary value of everything that has been collected is announced to all of those gathered, regalus are often counted separately from the arku and aumentu. Offering regalus is understood by Sullk'atas as an expression of affection, particularly reserved for children, godchildren, compadres, and friends. Regalus are things that a person might buy to gratify individual desires for commodities rather than to consolidate wealth.[16]

Accounting for these things in different ways in the context of the fiesta has implications not only for the economic and material relationships but also for the affective relationships among Sullk'atas. Because arku and aumentu are part of a wider cycle of giving and receiving, a substantial proportion of that wealth generated during a wedding fiesta is actually viewed as debt. The concept of debt has close associations with fertility, not through a metaphorical relation with "giving birth" (as with profits) but through a metaphorical relationship with "manure," which is also *manu* (Harris 1989:248).[17] To be in debt to others is a precondition to production and reproduction. *Mañay*, as discussed earlier, means "to lend or loan" or "to request the return of something one has lent" (Morató and Morató 1993:190) and is the term used to describe the ritual of "betrothal" after a woman has been "stolen" or "carried away." It also refers to one cup of corn beer being given rather than a pair of cups (as when a person gives an aumentu and receives one cup). *Mañay* is semantically related to two other Quechua verbs: *manuy*, "to lend, loan, or give on credit consumable . . . goods" (Morató and Morató 1993:189), and *manukuy*, "to borrow or ask for the loan of consumable . . . goods" (ibid.). The couple receives money, and other commodities, during the wedding and in the future will give arku and aumentu to others. The accounting of these prestations helps the married couple know how to discharge their debts in the future.

The wedding fiesta also requires that the couple ask others to work for them in ayni and thus puts the bride and groom in the position of having to return labor to others in the future. For example, the couple solicits the labor of the young man's entire community in order to make hundreds of liters of corn beer. The corn beer not only is used to make libations for the couple during the wedding but is given to people in exchange for the gifts they bring. The novios require other people's help (material and spiritual) while at the same time—by sponsoring the fiesta—providing to ayllu members the stuff with which offerings are made to the forces of the universe. Although even as children Sullk'atas may begin to develop relationships of ayni, the most significant relationships—especially for women—are those established after marriage, after a woman takes up residence in her husband's community.

The commodities and labor received by a couple may help them begin their life together but also integrate them into the community of adults through the receipt of gifts which require an eventual return. Obligations cannot be understood only as "rules to be followed" or social requirements without affective content. The obligations created through accepting commodities, labor, and products during a wedding might be understood in terms of the more general emphasis on cycling in the Andean universe. By making libations and offerings, for example, Sullk'atas understand themselves to be "feeding" supernatural beings. But feeding is the proper behavior, the assumed common sense of everyday actions and interactions. "You naturally expect that other human beings will feed you, *but you do not offer food to visitors in order that they should reciprocate.* Similarly, humans must feed the devils to assuage their voracious hunger; but their eating the food does not guarantee food or prosperity to their worshippers" (Harris 1989:263; my emphasis). Feeding is simply what one does; as a married couple, as adults, Sullk'atas feed others.

Far more than the transgressive behavior of adolescents, the stingy behavior of adults may cause comment in a community. When people become adults (that is, when they are married), have children, farm ayllu land, and take on cargos (like the wedding fiesta), their actions are scrutinized, and they are held to account. The actions of adults, who have established relationships of exchange that extend beyond the partnership of the couple, have consequences in terms of their relationships with other adults in the community and with the supernatural forces that affect people more generally.

Conclusion

The nature and the meanings of the exchanges—of words, ideas, or things—that I have described in this chapter inhere in the quality of the actions and the interactions of the various individuals and collectivities, who bring different understandings, desires, fears, and life experiences into an arena of interaction. The three discourses are interlaced with each other and bespeak a multitude of exchanges through which the meanings of marriage are produced. Even before the wedding fiesta, differently configured groups play fundamental roles in the social, economic, and political relations of the couple. The husband's parents, who teach them "how to be a married couple," provide the initial point of integration of a young woman into a new community. Other people in the community (children and adults) shift their habitual modes of interacting in order to acknowledge the adult status of the couple. Whether or not the husband and wife remain in the rural community, they rely upon community members to help them provide a wedding feast and fiesta. In part, the wedding fiesta is a statement of already having accumulated those important relationships of ayni, a statement of having become an adult.

Moreover, when couples host others during the fiesta that follows a Catholic wedding they become further enmeshed in ties of mutual support and obligation as they take on a debt—a load—by accepting the things that are offered to them. The emphasis in the wedding fiesta on the circulation of goods and labor through ayni is interlaced with the circulation of goods in a global economy. The shifts in labor and work patterns since the mid-1980s have brought Sullk'ata youth into closer contact with urban ideas of modernity and with global markets. A huge increase in availability of foreign goods in Bolivia, especially from China and Mexico, followed the liberalization of the Bolivian economy in the 1980s. The influx of money created by the cocaine economy also affected rural as well as urban regions. Not only do people buy regalus and include manufactured goods in addition to yarn in their arku, but many more young couples than in previous generations can afford the expense of hosting the members of their natal communities for the three days of a Catholic wedding and fiesta. Desires for things do not simply reflect the impact of global markets on marriages.

At another level, Sullk'atas consider the wedding fiesta, with its emphasis on giving and receiving in cycles, to be associated with the wedding classes. A more recent dimension of Catholic practice, the "exchange" that is made with the Catholic Church (going to classes in return for a piece of paper), enables the creation of additional social relations through compadrazgo and affinity. The Catholic missionaries' emphasis on the husband and wife as a unit aligns with more "modern" conceptions of family and marriage that young people are exposed to in other contexts such as public school. The emphasis on companionship and compassion does not necessarily contradict the recommendations and scoldings given to the novios during the warmi mañay or the symbolic dualism in Sullk'ata wedding symbolism.

Aspects of these discourses may also be experienced as contradictory, of course, but ideals and admonitions or commodities—whether plastic bowls or the Catholic wedding ceremony itself—also take on meanings as they circulate among people.[18] Ideologies of gender and family that emphasize the "modern" Catholic married couple may undermine aspects of the moral and affective bonds legitimated and produced through warmi mañay and the wedding fiesta (which stress the novios' obligations to other people in the ayllu). Admonitions to talk and not to fight may be welcomed but viewed as contradictory when voiced alongside recommendations to remain sober. Thus certain kinds of relationships are created through various exchanges, but what a married couple *is*—or how to understand the process of "becoming a married couple"—cannot be assumed. Sullk'atas take up variable aspects of these discourses, maintaining and transforming the meanings and experience of marriage even as an individual internalizes, enacts, and articulates them in particular contexts.

SEVEN

"Now My Daughter Is Alone"

Violence and the Ambiguities of Affinity

IN LATE DECEMBER 1995 the Ley contra Violencia Familiar (Ley 1674) or Law against Family Violence was signed by President Gonzalo Sánchez de Lozada. By the time I left Bolivia in July 1996 the law had been advertised for months. Broadcast in Quechua from the popular Llallagua radio station Pío Doce, the most dramatic of the two commercials began with a woman screaming and crying and a man yelling in the background. As I remember it, moments later the calm voice of a male doctor spoke over the crying: "I have seen many women come to the clinic with injuries from domestic violence. Now, with the Law against Family Violence, women are protected from this." Part of the attempts by the national government, and national and international nongovernmental organizations, to publicize and inform even marginal citizens of the new law, the commercials also reflect the ways in which domestic violence is increasingly part of the public discourse in Bolivia. The hegemonic discourses about domestic violence, and the law itself, emphasize social relationships that only partly coincide with the social and material realities of Sullk'atas. Most significantly, the assumption that domestic violence emerges solely from a relationship of power asymmetry between men and women obscures the significance of those relationships that extend beyond the married couple.

Marriage creates multiple bonds of intimacy and hierarchy among individuals.

In this chapter I explore various events of domestic violence in order to deepen understanding of the relatedness of affines or in-laws. Almost every instance of physical abuse that I know about from my fieldwork in 1995 and 1996 involves women and their affines. Violence erupted between women and their husbands, mothers-in-law, and sisters-in-law (especially their husbands' brothers' wives). Although violence between husbands and wives is more frequent and more readily acknowledged among Sullk'atas, physical violence among women is not uncommon. Many women in Sullk'ata, for example, recount stories of the violence of their mothers-in-law. The unequal relationship of power between *swiras* (mothers-in-law or *suegras,* Sp.) and *qhachunis* (daughters-in-law) is not unique to Sullk'ata. Anthropologists have noted the subordinate position of qhachunis in other regions of Bolivia and elsewhere in the Andes.[1] Although scholars have closely examined conflict between spouses in the Andes, they have directed little attention to the violence among women affines or the overlapping discourses that sustain asymmetries of power among affines, both women and men.[2]

In this chapter I explore instances of conflict among husbands and wives, mothers-in-law and daughters-in-law, and sisters-in-law as material and emotional ways in which individuals construe relatedness. I complicate understandings of gender and kinship by focusing on Sullk'ata women as perpetrators as well as victims of abuse who are caught up in webs of broader structural relationships. The ways in which women negotiate potentially violent situations or react to the physical abuse of an affine vary according to the contingencies of the situation, the life histories of individuals, and the more general social and historical contexts in which violence takes place.[3] Moreover, the meanings attached to any event of violence emerge not only in what is said but also in the interstices of that which remains unspoken.

Much of my understanding of domestic violence in Sullk'ata is refracted through informal conversations with Sullk'ata women. They usually initiated these discussions of violence, and I was asked on more than one occasion whether my husband hit me, if we fought, or if he had another wife in the city. My positionalities as an anthropologist and feminist, a gringa from the United States, and a married yet childless woman living apart from her husband and far from her family are not inconsequential to what Sullk'atas told me about affinal violence and to the assumptions I made about incidents of violence or how I have come to understand violence as linked to affinity in Sullk'ata.

Local Discourses of Violence and Affinity

As in other Andean regions, many women in Sullk'ata discuss violence openly in everyday gossip or during fiestas, typically recounting an affine's abuse to other women.[4] In their talk about particular events of abuse, women simultaneously normalize and criticize the violence of affines. Both men and women normalize affinal violence by pointing out the drunken state of the abuser or by claiming that violence is "just custom" (*kustumbrilla;* or *costumbre,* Sp.). The notion that affinal violence is customary indicates the relative lack of an explicit metadiscourse on violence.[5] The violence of affines, and particularly that of spouses, is also marked. For example, women and men joke and make innuendos linking violence, heterosexuality, and sexual reproduction. At the same time, women resist affinal violence by lamenting and complaining about affinal violence not only to other women but also to local and state authorities. Women sometimes fight back, abandon abusive spouses, or refuse to work for or live with their mothers-in-law. In local discourses of domestic violence there is a doubled distinction: people normalize violence but also point out instances of violence and recognize both the power and vulnerability of women. Attention to the crosscutting axes of these local discourses indicates the complexities of the lives, relationships, and stories of women, who clearly suffer from abuse but are not simply powerless in relation to their affines.

The Case of Claudina and Her Daughter-in-law

One of the first instances of violence between affines that I heard about was between a mother-in-law and daughter-in-law. I did not witness the incident, but my comadre Ilena did. She told me about it that evening as I sat preparing a meal with her. At the time I had been living with Ilena and her family for over six months, cooking and eating evening meals with them, often assisting with agricultural work, and accompanying Ilena to community work projects and fiestas. Along with Ilena and several other women, I had just spent the past few days helping Claudina and her husband with the work of sponsoring one of the largest and most financially demanding fiestas in the community. The fiesta required the sponsors to pay the fee, food, and lodging for a marching band of fifteen to twenty men, mobilize a troupe to perform one of the national dances of Bolivia, and host the drinking and dancing of community members, which would last a week. We peeled potatoes and ch'uñu, made soup and corn beer, carried water, and washed dishes. On the eve of the fiesta Claudina and her husband, who were both in their late fifties, awaited the arrival of their children, who were all married adults. Finally, as Claudina started berating herself as a "bad ritual sponsor," the children arrived on a large truck. Claudina wept with relief as they began unloading additional crates of food, bottles of beer, costumes for the dances, and even soda pop. The fiesta was a huge success; but on the final day Claudina accused one of her qhachunis of failing to collect eggs or assist with cooking that day's midday meal. Angry and drunk, Claudina hit her daughter-in-law in the eye.

Claudina's explanation for hitting her daughter-in-law—that she had failed to cook—is the most common explanation given in Sullk'ata for a woman being hit, whether by her husband or by her mother-in-law. Cooking and serving food indexes not only gender identity but also adulthood and specific kinship re-lationships with other household members.[6] In the context of everyday life in the Andes, the primary task of a married woman in the household is cooking. Cooking may be understood as a locus of power for a wife, in control of the consumption and distribution of subsistence products. When a daughter-in-law lives with her husband's family, one of her main tasks is cooking for the house-hold. Although the mother-in-law typically serves the food, emphasizing her role in allocating household resources, the daughter-in-law demonstrates her proficiency, obedience, and care for the sustenance of the household by cook-ing. The everyday aesthetics (Desjarlais 1992:65–71), attitude, and efficiency with which a daughter-in-law cooks are practically and symbolically associated with the way in which she will contribute to the reproduction of and become inte-grated into her new household and community.[7] Though not outside a system of gender, then, cooking and violence are also laminated on relationships and discourses of kinship.

Claudina's daughter-in-law and son were no longer living in her household. The daughter-in-law was already well established as a *warmi* (adult woman and wife) with six children of her own (one of whom was soon to be married), a household in another community, and extensive labor exchange relationships in both communities. When Claudina's son heard about the conflict that day, he supported his wife rather than his mother in the dispute. The daughter-in-law and son returned home with their children the next morning.

Five months later, when I asked Claudina about the incident, she told me that her son and daughter-in-law had not yet returned to visit, refusing to come even for Carnival, when families throughout Bolivia return home, sometimes travel-ing great distances to celebrate and bless natal households and communities.

Normalizing and Contesting the Violence of Affines

Sullk'ata women, like others in the Andes and elsewhere, may challenge the abuse of their affines, as did Claudina's daughter-in-law. Women may fight back physically or more commonly inflict pain through other means, as in Weis-mantel's (1988:181–182) description of a woman who offered bowl after bowl of food to her abusive husband, who was obliged to eat in spite of his hangover.[8] A

Sullk'ata woman may simply leave her in-laws and return home to her parents, especially if her marriage has not yet been formalized by a civil or religious wedding ceremony and community fiesta. Although I know one woman who moved out of the house that she shared with her husband after many years of marriage due to the severity of his beatings, most women do not have the financial, material, or emotional resources to live alone.

In extreme situations, women go to their godparents or to state authorities to complain formally about affinal violence. For Sullk'atas, the godparents who helped sponsor the marriage (*padrinos de matrimonio*, Sp.) are considered the most appropriate people to arbitrate a disagreement between affines (see also Carter 1977:198). Andean scholars of various regions and periods have noted that native Andean women as well as women of Spanish descent have historically appealed to the colonial and republican state authorities in instances of domestic violence.[9] By going to a judge or to the police, however, a woman puts herself into a potentially contradictory position, having to take on non-native Andean notions of family, gender, and femininity (Harvey 1993:135) as well as racial and class stereotypes and language, literacy, and financial barriers. During my residence in the community, three women notified the police or the judge of a spouse's violence, and a fourth woman threatened to turn her sister-in-law in to the police because of physical violence. In one instance the police put the husband in the provincial jail until his mother was able to collect enough money to bail him out. The young woman returned to her parents' home, as her marital relationship was not yet solidified by either a civil or a religious ceremony.

Although a woman will typically recount an affine's abuse to other women, Sullk'atas silence more far-reaching deliberations about violence through discourses of drunkenness and custom. Both men and women normalize affinal violence by pointing out the drunken state of the abuser. As Claudina told me her version of the story months after she had hit her daughter-in-law, she reiterated how drunk she had been at the time. Women and men alike make libations and drink with their affines. As already noted, most women do not reach the same state of extreme inebriation as many men do because they are responsible for cooking for their families, herding sheep (a daily necessity), and taking care of their drunken male kin—usually their husbands and sons (Harvey 1994:85). The sponsors of a fiesta, however, are expected to become drunk. Quechua speakers conceive of drunkenness as an altered state, and people cannot be held responsible for their actions when they are drunk.[10] In some instances of violence the disclaimer of drunkenness does not go uncontested; nonetheless, all of the violence among affines in Sullk'ata that I know of occurred during the feast days of the annual ritual calendar or other ritual contexts in which people were drunk.

The discourse of drunkenness is also intertwined with a discourse of custom through which violence is simultaneously publicly disclosed and pushed to the margins of public attention. At times the normalization of violence through a discourse of custom is implicit, as when Ilena told me about the incident of violence between Claudina and her daughter-in-law. She said that she regretted the incident had ever occurred: Ilena had work-exchange relationships with both the mother-in-law and the daughter-in-law involved in the dispute. She did not directly criticize Claudina's actions, however. Instead, she recounted stories of her own mother-in-law's violence and ended: "I suffered badly. I lived there for five years, and I had to do everything."

"Did you and your swira get mad at each other?" I asked.

"Yes," she said.

"What did your husband do?"

"He went back to his mother. He should have been with me. She really hated me." Ilena positions Claudina's actions within a more general context of affinal relationships and affinal violence among women. Older women in particular told me stories of their swiras and the difficult years that they had endured living in the households of their in-laws. Although women emphasized the painfulness of their experiences, they did not suggest that their experiences were exceptional.

At times the discourse of custom is far more explicit. The gap between my own sensibilities and those of the women I had come to know, and the overlapping perception of the painfulness of violence, became most apparent to me during the week of Carnival in 1996 when Máxima was hit by her husband. Over several months I had become close to Máxima and her husband, both of whom were probably in their late sixties. I visited with them each week and often watched Máxima as she worked on her weaving. In the following excerpt from my fieldnotes of 28 February 1996, the discourse of custom is intertwined with a context of ritual drinking.

When Máxima walked through the back gate, I was already sitting in the shade. For the first time during the whole week of Carnival, the men of the community had taken the wall in the bright sun. Roberta was sitting on the ground, talking with Nicolasa, whose moon-shaped face was wet with tears. Roberta's red sweater was faded in spots to an orange and her apron billowed out in front of her. Máxima sat down on the other side of Nicolasa and greeted everyone. Roberta barely acknowledged her, though they are comadres. After a few moments, Máxima came over to me. "My husband hit me . . . Am I still black on the side of my face?" she said, starting to cry.

"When did he hit you?" I asked.

"When was it?" she asked herself.

"Was he drunk?" I asked. Then I answered the question for myself: Of course, everyone has been drunk the past week. Why wouldn't he be drunk?

Her left eye was a purplish red around the edges, especially in the corner by her nose. The side of her face by her temple and below was purple and black, though not very swollen, and the skin wasn't broken.

"When are you going to Sucre?" she asked me. "I want to go to Sucre. I will tell my sons what he did. He kicked me." She confessed that she had no one to tell. Her mother and father were dead. Her children were all far away. "My brothers, they are with my husband. I would not tell them," she went on. I glanced at Roberta (who was sitting right next to us). Her head was turned in the other direction, though I thought she could hear Máxima quite plainly. Máxima's husband sat on the ledge with the other men, his elbows on his knees, his head up but only his eyes moving as he looked around the patio. "I did not know who to tell. But I want to go to Sucre. [My son's] wife has another baby, a boy. I would like to see him. When will you go?" she asked me again.

I said I had been thinking that I would go to La Paz to see my husband, but I told her that I would accompany her to Sucre instead. I shook my head and looked at her face . . . Later in the evening, I cried, thinking that this is what people think my husband does to me: hits me when he's drunk or angry, pushes me around yelling. Máxima had said to me, "I called but no one came, *ni qhari ni warmi,* not a man or a woman."

"You have to understand it is the custom here," said Roberta when I asked her if she'd heard what her comadre Máxima had said. "It's the custom. When men are drunk they scold and hit their women."

"Does [your husband] hit you?"

"Yes," she said. "It's the same with [my husband]."

At the time Roberta's reaction surprised me: I knew her and her husband well and did not think of their relationship as abusive. Nor did I think of domestic violence in Sullk'ata as customary. The disjunctures between my attitude and those of my Sullk'ata companions in part reflect the ways in which my own deep-seated cultural assumptions—about love in marriage and the stigma associated with being a victim of abuse—became entangled with their very different sets of assumptions and material conditions through the contingencies of field-work.[11] Máxima's complaints about her husband's abuse were not out of place in the public context of the fiesta. Women and men sometimes cried and laughed in quick succession during fiestas, often airing concerns or complaints on various matters to the assembled audience of community members. I empathized with Máxima and through her story caught a glimpse of the painfulness of a loved one's abuse. Roberta, in contrast, displayed only indifference to Máxima's story, reflecting the more typical Sullk'ata reaction to spousal abuse in the context of drinking. Moreover, Roberta's explicit statement to me that violence is custom challenged me to acknowledge that Sullk'atas have proper and improper ways of doing and talking about violence as well as accepted ways of being in relationships with kin and nonkin, with human and supernatural beings.

Thus, although women in Sullk'ata recognize some degree of variation among individuals (with some more inclined to violence than others), the more pervasive notion is that violence is associated with particular states (such as drunkenness) and positionalities (such as affinity). In Sullk'ata affinal violence is custom when people are drunk, as Roberta states, but violence between affines is decidedly *not* considered to be custom when people are sober. The one incident of violence that I heard of between a husband and wife that occurred when both were sober was met with horrified exclamations and discussion of the man's improper upbringing. Although criticism of an affine's actions and expressions of pain may be intertwined with the details of personal circumstances and normalizing discourses in people's talk about violence, the general notion that affines may use violence is rarely challenged by Sullk'atas. Máxima, as it turned out, did not go with me to Sucre to tell her sons of their father's violence; she told me that she could find no one to herd her sheep while she was gone.

Sexuality and Violence: Marking the Violence of Husbands

Sullk'ata women tend to emphasize the violence of their husbands more than the violence of their women affines. This emphasis may indicate the greater frequency of abuse by husbands. The underscoring of spousal abuse might also reflect the greater potential for harm that a husband's violence inflicts, because of his physical strength or the social and economic consequences that ensue from the conflict. Although either a woman or a man may dissolve a partnership with relative ease early in the relationship, separation is infrequent after a series of marriage rituals and the birth of children. The intensity and significance of the relationship between a husband and wife tend to increase over time. In contrast, the significance of the relationship between a mother-in-law and daughter-in-law tends to lessen over time as a woman establishes her own household, family, and labor exchange relationships with other women.

It is just as significant that both women and men in Sullk'ata have access to a greater range of public discourses, from sexual jokes and ethnic stereotypes to representations promulgated by the media, giving voice to men's violence against women. In local discourses the conceptual links between drunkenness and fertility in Andean cosmology are extended to the married couple. In Sullk'ata both physical violence and sexual activity are generally understood to occur when men and women are drunk during fiestas. As noted, marriages in Sullk'ata are typically initiated by a young man "stealing a woman" during a fiesta when the young man and woman are drunk. In many parts of the Andes during the wedding rituals that follow a young woman is formally warned about her husband's potential for drunken violence.[12] Yet it is in relation to those times of drunkenness, during the Catholic feast days of the agricultural calendar, that Sullk'ata women remember giving birth as well as getting pregnant.

The emphasis on sexuality and violence in the context of spousal relationships also emerges in the joking and sexual innuendo that typically occurs among same-gender groups in Sullk'ata. For example, men attach affinal as well as sexual meanings to eating (*mikhuy*) and cooking (*wayk'uy*).[13] One common sexual joke is to say, "Do you want to eat meat? I will feed you meat" (also see Harris 1994:53). In their joking and teasing of each other, Sullk'ata men also ask, "Does your wife cook [*wayk'uy*] well?" Or they say to a married man who is childless that his wife does not "know how to cook." Women and men in Sullk'ata also use the term "cooking" to describe pregnancy and, more specifically, the maturation and development of the fetus (see also Arnold and Yapita 1996). Cooking is thus not just about sex but about sexual reproduction in the context of marriage. A husband may imply that his wife has failed to uphold the sexual and reproductive obligations of affinity when he alleges that his wife has not cooked for him.

The relationship between eating, affinity, and sexuality is also evident in the referential content of some Andean folk stories. Harris (1994:53–55) describes a story told throughout the region of a condor (likened to the son-in-law) who offers meat to a young woman, carrying her away to his nest so that she may eat. On arrival, the young woman finds that the meat is raw; she refuses to eat it, escaping to the home of a grandmother, who hides her in a large pot. The story ends with the grandmother lifting the lid of the pot to tell the young woman she is safe and finding nothing but bones. Although additional meanings are undoubtedly layered upon the symbolic, eating meat may be interpreted as having sex in this story. The meat is raw, which indicates that the sexuality occurs out-side of marriage and is thus unacceptable to the young woman. Yet the story also indicates that she must enter into a relationship with a wild being and eat raw meat—get married—so that she is not reduced to dry bones, a symbol of old age and infertility, before her time (Harris 1994:54).

I never heard women in Sullk'ata use "cooking" as a sexual innuendo, but women did use the verb "to hit" (*maqay*) in suggestive joking. One of the first times a Sullk'ata woman asked me if my husband hit me, the community was preparing corn beer for a wedding. Several women carried water back and forth, back and forth, while others oversaw the mixing of the milled sprouted corn and boiling water that would be fermented into beer. We carried water for hours, stopping about halfway in each ten-minute walk to the house to rest in the shade thrown onto the road by the adobe walls of another household compound. When the woman asked me if my husband hit me, I replied, "No, he doesn't." I asked if her husband hit her, and she said, "No."

"Do men hit their wives here?" I asked.

"Well, no," one woman answered.

"Well, some do and some don't," said another woman.

And then another woman asked, "Your husband doesn't hit you?"

"No. Does yours hit you?"

"Oh, yes," she said, to the uproarious laughter of the women.

I did not get the joke until months later when I was chatting with a young woman, a teenager I hoped would work for me as an assistant. After a few mo-ments of conversation, she asked me if I had any children, although by then it was well known that I did not. And then she asked, "Why don't you and your husband have any children?" Having no ready answer, I simply said, "Because." *Mana maqasunkichu,* she replied, laughing. "Doesn't he hit you?"

Women at once talk and cry about the pain of physical violence inflicted on them by their husbands and joke about the sexuality of hitting, and the vio-lence of sex, which points to a complicated relationship between sexuality, af-finity, and violence in Sullk'ata. Violence between native Andean spouses is also easily stereotyped, however.[14] For example, after describing to me an instance of violence between an indigenous couple, an urban Bolivian woman who spoke fluent Spanish and Quechua said disparagingly, "If he doesn't hit you, he doesn't love you." A similar version, "The more you hit me, the more I love you" (*Más me pegas, más te quiero,* Sp.), is commonly reported in Peru by urban mestizos to describe Quechua-speaking campesinos in a derogatory way (Mannheim, per-sonal communication, 1996). Yet as Harris argues for a nearby Aymara-speaking region of northern Potosí: "Women do not justify their husbands' violence on the grounds that it is an expression of love, in the commonly reported cliché. Their view is that of the saying quoted by Jorge Sánchez Parga: 'of course he beats me, that's how husbands are' (*ha de pegar, marido es pues*)" (Harris 1994:48; Sánchez Parga 1990:38). Thus assumptions of the racial or ethnic otherness of native Andeans embedded in the cliché may overlie and obscure the lived realities and complexities of Sullk'ata relationships of gender, sexuality, and affinity.

Likewise, in media representations and development discourses in Bolivia men's violence against women is emphasized, based on national and transnational ideologies of gender hierarchy that do not take account of local categories of power (Spedding 1997b:61–62). According to the text of the law, *any* family member, male or female, adult or child, is protected against the abuse of another family or household member (as long as the abuse is reported within twenty-four hours). The literature on the issue of domestic violence emphasizes that the rights of women and children against domestic violence are human rights.[15] Few Sullk'atas would have had access to the printed materials, which were published in Spanish by the Bolivian Ministry of Human Development and the international nongovernmental organization UNICEF, but many Sullk'atas heard the radio announcements described above. These announcements partly obscured the extent of the law's protective power by representing domestic violence as a man's abuse of a woman and by leaving implicit from whom a woman may be protected.

The explicit emphasis on gender difference and sexuality in these various discourses blurs the significance of affinity to the emergence of violence between spouses and simultaneously conceals the violence that occurs among women in Sullk'ata. Sullk'ata women's emphasis on the violence of husbands as opposed to other men indicates that affinity is a significant aspect of spousal violence. For Sullk'atas, a husband occupies a unique positionality in relation to the woman to whom he is married. Not just any man may hit a woman in Sullk'ata: violence between unrelated men and women is almost unheard of, and relationships characterized by gender difference but not affinity (for example, adult brothers and sisters or comadres and compadres) are marked more by an exaggerated politeness than by violence or aggression. The relationship of affinity between spouses is indicated by the violence itself, as Harvey (1994:84–85) has argued, and through the layers of intertexts around violence that support acceptable explanations, jokes, folktales, and narratives of personal experiences. Moreover, the similar explanations and justifications given by husbands and mothers-in-law in Sullk'ata for hitting a woman and the overlapping discourses of drunkenness and custom that normalize affinal violence suggest that gender difference is not a sufficient category of analysis for domestic violence in the region.

Swiras and Qhachunis: Reading Affinity among Women

The relationship between affines in Sullk'ata is inflected by gendered and racialized asymmetries of power. At the same time, affinity is itself a category of power and shapes hierarchies, including gender. Thus further analysis of kinship relationships, in particular relationships among women affines, is necessary to understand the power hierarchies that structure those relationships and the ways in which conflict emerges in the networks of interactions among kin. In this section I explore the ways in which affinity is enacted between mothers-in-law and daughters-in-law. I focus on two interrelated aspects of the power asymmetry between women affines—asymmetrical exchanges of labor and competing ideals of affection and respect—to demonstrate the salience of affinity for understanding domestic violence and the salience of differences among women for understanding kinship in the Andes. Relationships between swiras and qhachunis are not, however, isolated from other kinship relationships or wider discourses of identity and power. Thus I also draw into the discussion an analysis of kinship relationships among parents and children and draw from the discussion some implications for understanding violence among sisters-in-law.

Becoming Kin

The affective and economic relationship between a mother-in-law and daughter-in-law is intertwined with the structural relationship and more general system of values that shapes relationships between parents and children. Daughters-in-law are only partially integrated into their husbands' families, however, and may never become "true kin" (*parientes legítimos,* Sp.).[16] Thus, for the woman's family, a recently married daughter or sister is understood to have a difficult time living with her in-laws, far from her family. On the first night of the Fiesta for the Virgin of Rosario, for example, Anacleta sat on a church bench sobbing as people lit candles. "Now my daughter is alone," she wailed. I was confused at first, for I had attended her daughter's wedding only two months before. I thought that maybe her daughter's husband had died, but that was not the cause of her daughter's aloneness or of Anacleta's pain and sadness. Anacleta made me understand that her daughter was alone because she had no close kin, no true kin, in her husband's community.

A new daughter-in-law is understood to be from somewhere else and to be constitutionally different from her affines. As discussed in Chapter 3, people who eat the same food are quite literally understood to be composed of the same flesh (see also Weismantel 1995:694–695). When she marries, not only does a woman move away from the network of kin with whom she grew up, but she also moves away from the material sources through which her body developed and the familiar pantheon of sacred places. When a man and woman marry, the husband's family celebrates the addition of a daughter-in-law but also has the burden of incorporating a stranger into the household. The process of integrating a qhachuni into her husband's kin network takes place only over an extended period. Kinship relationships are forged between a qhachuni and her affines through the same daily interactions and practices—feeding, eating, and working together—that create relatedness and hierarchy among parents and children. During the time she lives in her mother-in-law's household, a qhachuni is dependent on her affines for food and shelter and is positioned as a child who is morally obligated to work because she is fed. As Cecelia, a middled-aged woman who still lives with her husband in the household compound that her parents-in-law built, said to me, "Where else would we have lived? We had nothing when we married. No animals, no land, no house, no pots or bowls or spoons."

Moreover, because of the gender division of labor, the swira is initially the qhachuni's main locus of integration into the household and community. A qhachuni may spend more time with her swira than with her husband. Although the qhachuni is expected to address her swira as "my mother" while the swira addresses her as "my child," no automatic intimacy is expected between mothers-in-law and daughters-in-law. According to Sullk'atas, it is the qhachuni's responsibility to develop a relationship of goodwill or affection with her swira. Similarly, during a wedding ceremony in a native Andean community in rural Peru, the bride's mother warns her daughter that as a new bride she must gain the favor of her affines:

> You have to be lively . . . You have to look around you with affection . . .
> You have to make yourself fond of them. You have to respect them be-
> cause they are able to accuse you: She is in a heap! She just sits there! She
> doesn't do anything! . . . Now that you are going to begin your life in the
> house of your mother-in-law, your mother-in-law has to be your best
> friend. You owe her; you have to tell yourself to consult her, and she, as a
> mature woman, is going to put her words, her life experience, into your
> head. In this way, you must undertake the road of life. (Valderrama and
> Escalante 1997:167; my translation)

The qhachuni is expected to respect her mother-in-law's authority and to take orders from her. Through her facility in the kitchen, her willingness to work, her obedience, and her ability to be sociable and lively, a new daughter-in-law is encouraged to win the approval of her swira.

A daughter-in-law who gives of her own labor power and does not receive labor from her swira is put into the subordinated role of a child, yet she is not simply a child. She also partakes of the positionality of an adult who is not kin, especially early in her marriage. By marrying and moving out of her natal household, a young woman is becoming an adult, a process that is further solidified after the birth of her first child. Yet, while living in her mother-in-law's household, a qhachuni may not easily extract herself from labor obligations to her mother-in-law. A daughter-in-law is especially vulnerable to the criticism and potential abuse of her swira if she does not yet have children of her own. Nevertheless, a qhachuni may contribute labor to her in-laws' household with an expectation of an eventual return of equivalent labor or products, as in more reciprocal forms of labor such as ayni.

Ambiguities of Power

In their daily interactions mothers- and daughters-in-law negotiate the disjunctures in their economic and affective relationships. Because the relationship between swira and qhachuni partakes of, but does not completely mesh with, the relationship between parents and children, the hierarchies of affinity are ambiguous, and affinity may become an arena for rapprochement or potential conflict. Among affines the very lack of control in an already ambiguous relationship may trigger an outburst of violence in an attempt to resolve the ambiguity and reestablish harmonious kinship relationships (see also Harvey 1991, 1994:76–77). A daughter-in-law may directly challenge her swira's violence or her claims to authority by pointing out that the swira is not true kin. Although a daughter-in-law who does not show her affines respect is criticized, even hit, she is not said to become a condemned soul at death, as is a disrespectful child.

The ambiguity and potential for negotiation in kinship categories and the uneven overlap between categories of hierarchy among affines are recognized by Sullk'atas, who mobilize various discourses to negotiate positionality and power. Daughters-in-law also explicitly bring attention to their ambiguous position by highlighting their aloneness in times of distress. Women recognize that in their affines' community they have little recourse; there is no one, really, to protect their interests. A mother-in-law's abuse may be curbed by her son (as in the case of Claudina's daughter-in-law), or a husband's abuse may be lessened by the presence and intervention of his parents (e.g., Harvey 1994:77). Whether or not a husband or swira will support a woman is not clear-cut, however, as indicated by Ilena's claim that her husband often sided with his mother in disputes.

The ambiguities of affinity also extend to relationships among kin more generally and shape the contingencies of actions and interactions among people. Although Harris (1994:54) notes that in the nearby region of Laymi, Bolivia, a woman's brothers will beat her husband in return for his violence to her, in Sullk'ata a brother may not support his sister. A brother's protection rests not only on his knowledge of the event of violence but also on the contingencies of his relationship with his sister's husband. A brother may, for example, participate in work networks, be linked by relationships of compadrazgo, or rent land from his sister's husband. As Máxima expressed in an example above, her brothers were "with her husband"; she would not tell them of his violence but instead would go to her sons. Thus, even after a woman has lived in a community many years and established her own household and family, she may still cry about "being alone," without a mother and father, whether or not her true kin are alive.[17]

Although younger women in particular often told me that they lived with their swiras out of affection, older women frequently criticized the moral character of their swiras. On one occasion I brought a tape of regional Andean songs to the kitchen where Aurelia, her daughter, and I were preparing dinner. The song "My Good Little Mother-in-Law" ("K'acha Swiritay") was transformed when Aurelia sang "my evil little mother-in-law" (saqra swiritay) over the refrain. When she was newly married, Aurelia lived for five years with her swira before moving to her own household. But even after many years of living in separate households, Aurelia's mother-in-law continued to cause her aggravation. Although a qhachuni is expected to act respectfully toward her mother-in-law, the daughter-in-law gradually develops a greater position of power as she consolidates her relationship with her husband, establishes kinship bonds with her children, and develops labor-exchange relationships with other women. Once she has her own household, a daughter-in-law's obligations to and relationship with her swira are reconfigured.

Moreover, because the affinal relationship between swira and qhachuni also intersects with other relationships of power and identity, a qhachuni may contest the asymmetry of her relationship with her mother-in-law through national and transnational discourses of class and ethnicity, family, and gender. Discourses of progress, which emphasize the relative status of speaking Spanish, having access to commodities, and being educated, sometimes allow younger women to stake out a ground of superiority. Additionally, some young qhachunis simply refuse to live with their swiras for more than a few months after marriage. During my stay in Sullk'ata in 1995–1996, the two most recently married women in the community refused to live with their swiras at all. Their initial years of marriage, prior to a religious ceremony, were spent with their spouses in Bolivian cities, earning money. When the young couples returned to live in the rural community, they built houses of their own. At the time of my fieldwork both husbands had migrated for wage work and remained absent for months at a time. Even so, each young woman would eat and sleep in her own house with her baby. Although each daughter-in-law would herd her mother-in-law's sheep daily, they both declined to cook for their affines. As one woman told me: "There are still too many people at my swira's house. It is a lot of work to cook. Here I cook quickly, just for me and my baby on that gas stove."

Refusing to live with her affines may enhance a daughter-in-law's status within the terms of national urban discourses and may lessen her obligations to her swira, but it may also have other consequences. For both of these young married women, the alternative to living with in-laws was to live alone, a choice considered unsociable and somewhat odd by many Sullk'atas. Moreover, living in the rural community or in a city without having undertaken the more traditional obligations of a daughter-in-law may increase a woman's isolation and her vulnerability to her husband's violence, even as she is less constrained by her swira's demands. A swira may also reverse national discourses of ethnicity and class that stigmatize native Andeans and instead disparage a qhachuni who is "beautiful" and "white," who does not know how to work or to be sociable with other women (Valderrama and Escalante 1997:167). Thus women in Sullk'ata, both swiras and qhachunis, draw on personal experiences and local and national discourses of ethnicity, class, gender, and family to normalize violence, to contest affinal authority actively, and to mark their negotiations for positionings of power. As much as a qhachuni may profess to be alone or highlight her ability, plans, and desires to live in the city and earn money or claim her status as a warmi, while she lives in the campo she is not outside a hierarchical though ambiguous network of relationships among kin.

The Entanglements of Kinship

Not only do relationships between mothers-in-law and daughters-in-law partake of the power hierarchy established between parents and children, but they are also influenced by the differential expectations, obligations, and potential rewards of multiple other relationships. A focus on the binary relationships between mothers- and daughters-in-law, though perhaps necessary as a heuristic device, ultimately falls short of the contradictions and negotiations of related-ness as it is lived in everyday interactions. In Sullk'ata networks of economic, social, and political relationships entangle individuals, cutting across and ex-tending beyond any particular household.

In this section I trace the trajectories of unequal exchanges and ambiguous hierarchies through two instances of violence. Both incidents involve my co-madre Ilena and her affines and occurred during the time I lived in Sullk'ata. The two events, the first between Ilena and her sister-in-law and the second be-tween Ilena and her husband already described in Chapter 1, were separated by a period of six months. Initially I did not perceive the events as related. I would argue now, however, that the tensions between Ilena and her sister-in-law and between Ilena and her husband are inextricably intertwined on multiple levels: the interactions of individuals, the structural relationships among the siblings and affines of the same generation, and the more general social and economic context of Sullk'ata. I first describe the instance of violence between Ilena and her sister-in-law and focus analytically on the network of kinship relationships and individual interactions that radiate outward from that event.[18]

The physical conflict between Ilena and her sister-in-law (her husband's brother's wife) occurred during the New Year's celebration in January 1996. My description of the event is pieced together from multiple eyewitness accounts. Apparently, late in the evening when both women were drunk, Ilena's sister-in-law berated her for having borrowed an ox a few months earlier without prop-erly asking permission. Ilena defended herself and her husband, Marcelino, by pointing out that they had borrowed the ox to plow her husband's father's field, not Marcelino's field. Ilena suggested that her sister-in-law should be thankful that she and Marcelino did so much work for the elderly parents of their hus-bands. Then her sister-in-law punched Ilena, grazing her cheek. Ilena returned the punch and bloodied her sister-in-law's nose. The next day Ilena's sister-in-law asked me if I had seen what happened. I told her that I had not. She replied that when she awakened that morning with blood on her face and apron, she needed her husband to tell her what had happened. For days afterward Ilena's sister-in-law threatened to turn her in to the police. Ilena's husband's brother dissuaded his wife. Although Ilena's sister-in-law eventually dropped discus-sion of the matter, the ill-will between them continued to simmer just below the surface.

The overlapping and intersecting obligations of kinship provide a textured ground from which to interpret this event. First, like the relationship of affinity between mothers- and daughters-in-law, relationships among siblings and in-laws of the same generation are characterized by ambiguities of hierarchy and affect. As I have already mentioned, sisters-in-law stand in a highly ambiguous relationship with each other. Sisters-in-law are not usually true kin and do not typically create the material and affective relations of kin through their daily practices, as mothers-in-law and daughters-in-law attempt to do. Although a young man and his wife will typically live in his parents' household along with unmarried siblings, it is uncommon for more than one married brother to live in the household at any time. Thus the wives of brothers do not work, eat, or share space with each other in their mother-in-law's household.

Moreover, the relationship between sisters-in-law is shaped by the respective relationship between their spouses. Although brothers are ideally close companions, the potential for ambiguity and disruption in the kinship hierarchy between brothers is high, as I have already discussed. In particular, the negotiation and competition around land inheritance and the obligations to work and care for parents that fall unevenly on older and younger brothers and their wives create tensions that extend beyond any singular household as siblings perceive inequalities in a context of scarcity. Because of these structural factors, brothers and their wives living in the same community rarely develop labor exchange relationships or relationships of ritual kinship, although brothers and sisters and their respective spouses, and sisters and their husbands, often do. There is little camaraderie among the wives of brothers unless they come from the same natal community.

From this perspective, the dispute between Ilena and her sister-in-law over borrowing the ox is part of more complicated negotiations around unequal labor obligations that are linked to the economically and politically significant issues of inheritance and the distribution of power and authority within and between generations. Ilena emphasized that she did more work for her affines than her sister-in-law did. Ilena's husband, Marcelino, was the youngest son of aging parents. She and her husband routinely assisted his elderly parents with agricultural tasks, especially plowing and planting fields and herding sheep. Her husband's older brother and wife (with whom she had the dispute) also lived in the community, but they did not assist with caring for the parents. Although Ilena expressed frustration at the additional obligations that she shouldered, herding her mother-in-law's sheep also allowed Ilena to make an implicit future claim on the sheep. Similarly, by plowing his father's field, Marcelino was reiterating an inheritance claim to that land, even though he plowed with his brother's ox. Ilena's sister-in-law scolded Ilena (rather than Marcelino, who actually did the plowing), which reflects both the gendered constraints on activities and interactions among Sullk'atas and the ways in which conflicts may spill over into multiple other relationships.

During the months following the fight between Ilena and her sister-in-law, a growing divide developed between Ilena and her affines. Her sister-in-law refused to greet Ilena. In February and March of that year Ilena voiced her suspicions that her sister-in-law was circulating malicious gossip about her to other women in the community with whom she exchanged labor. In May her brother-in-law scolded Ilena while her husband was absent, working in the city of Cochabamba. In June 1996, during the final week of my fieldwork in the community, Ilena was scolded and hit by her husband. Her husband was drunk, having stayed up all night at the wake of a community member. He accused her of infidelity as he hit her.

The next day Ilena went to the godmother of her marriage and then to the judge in the nearest town. Ilena complained to the judge about the malicious gossip of people in the community that in her view had caused her husband's violence. By voicing her concerns about gossip and envy, Ilena pointed toward the structural relationships of rivalry and competition among siblings and in-laws of the same generation (see Nash 1993:67–68). She did not explicitly name her sister-in-law but grounded the moment of conflict with her husband in a specific history of interactions with her own affines that I have partially described above.

The conflicts between Ilena and her affines, both her husband and her sister-in-law, are also embedded in a more general social and economic context. Most households cannot survive solely on wage or subsistence labor, and continuing access to land requires working that land. Thus husbands who work in urban areas depend on the labor of their wives in rural communities for subsistence production. This has consequences that extend beyond the relationship between spouses to relationships among same-generation affines. First, married men who migrate seasonally depend on their kin and compadres to watch out for and support their families. Yet, in these months prior to the instance of violence between Ilena and Marcelino, the structural ambiguities of the relationship among affines developed into a more critical rupture. His wife, his brother, his brother's wife, and their respective children were no longer speaking with each other when Marcelino returned from the city. From this perspective, Marcelino's violence was not simply about the control of Ilena's sexuality or his altered state of drunkenness. His violence also resonated with the ambiguities of relationships that require the physical presence of individuals to reinforce the intimacies and hierarchies of relatedness and with the vulnerabilities of husbands who require, yet cannot control, the labor power of their wives in a context of more general economic instability and shifting social conditions.

Second, because of the ways in which kin and nonkin relationships in

Sullk'ata are interwoven, the strain on the relationship between Ilena and her sister-in-law also extended to relationships among women more generally in the community. Particularly in regions such as this, where men seasonally migrate and children go to school, women like Ilena increasingly depend on labor-exchange relationships with other women to carry out the agricultural requirements of a subsistence economy. Although Ilena and her sister-in-law did not exchange labor with each other, the physical conflict between them, as well as the continuing tensions, negatively affected other networks of interaction and everyday relationships that Ilena depended on. Relationships among women are inflected by ideals of communality; a woman's emotional, social, political, and economic well-being is in part balanced on the state of those relationships. The instance of violence between Ilena and her sister-in-law and Ilena's reaction to her husband's violence exemplify the ways in which the ambiguities of hierarchy among affines may be refracted through the everyday interactions among other individuals.

Inevitably conflicts and compromises radiate outward because the associations among people overlie each other. Rather than being isolated events that serve as examples of static structures of kinship, then, these events of violence may be understood as "busy intersections" (Rosaldo 1989:20–21) of intertwined but ongoing and lived relationships among individuals. The conflicts between Ilena and her affines are embedded in the general social and economic context of Sullk'ata, the structural asymmetries that shape the daily practices of sisters-in-law, siblings, and spouses, and the more specific history of interactions among particular individuals. By drawing attention to the conflicts among affines, and to the intricate negotiations for positioning and power among differently situated individuals, a more complicated understanding of kinship and affinity in Sullk'ata emerges, alongside a rethinking of domestic violence.

Reflecting on Violence and Kinship

The first time that Ilena and I heard the radio announcement about Bolivia's domestic violence law, she said to me, "Who would go to a judge? My husband is a good man." Differently positioned individuals may interpret a law in different ways. Even in the shadow of an event, an affine's violence may seem less problematic than living without that person or being cut off from the network of encompassing social, economic, affective, and political relationships in Sullk'ata. Women may not be prepared to denounce their abusers. They may not have alternative places to live or means of economic and emotional support, envision life outside of marriage as a viable possibility, or trust the adequacy of the state's protection. The varying constraints under which women and men live and the material, social, and political options that they may access or mobilize are thus crucial to understanding the implications of conflict in the people's lives.

Attention to the discourses and practices of violence involving husbands and wives, mothers-in-law and daughters-in-law, and sisters-in-law in Sullk'ata demonstrates that gender discourses and hierarchies alone do not adequately explain the ways in which domestic violence emerges among Sullk'atas. Although gender hierarchy is not an inconsequential aspect of domestic violence, kinship obligations and ambiguities of hierarchy significantly shape the ways in which relationships are negotiated. These obligations and ambiguities create the conditions for the emergence of conflict among individuals, especially those related through marriage. Thus the violence among women, though not as frequently acknowledged as violence between husbands and wives, is crucial to a more general understanding of domestic violence in the Andes. The violence among women also highlights the ways in which relatedness is at once intimate and antagonistic.

By locating conflict in a network of negotiated yet hierarchical relationships among kin, both violence and relatedness may be understood as extending beyond the walls of a singular household, affecting and affected by wider relationships of power. Husbands and wives, mothers-in-law and daughters-in-law, and sisters-in-law who may or may not reside in the same household are bound by the obligations, opportunities, and expectations of affinity and relatedness more generally. As exemplified by the conflicts among Ilena and her affines, various instances of violence and multiple households may be layered over each other. From this perspective, a narrow definition of domestic violence that only incorporates violence between married couples or individuals living within the same household obscures the instances of violence among women affines, the particular histories of events, and the discourses of power that make violence possible in Sullk'ata. Rather than existing in a distinct category (something other than domestic violence), violence between affines in Sullk'ata requires more complicated and expansive notions of both "the domestic" and "domestic violence."

Assumptions about who may be a perpetrator or victim of domestic violence, what actions constitute domestic violence, and whether violence is acceptable or not are intimately tied to unequal relations of power. Expanding the boundaries of the domestic might enable more integrative interpretations of domestic violence that occurs within and across generations, in Sullk'ata and elsewhere. In many localities, including Bolivia, legal definitions of domestic abuse incorporate notions of heterosexuality and residency into the formalization of who is protected from whom. Law enforcement and judicial systems, as well as the individuals involved in specific events of violence, may see certain abuses as more or less legitimate, limiting who might claim to be abused or gain assistance and constraining how abuse might be interpreted against wider asymmetries.[19]

The analysis of affinity in Sullk'ata also raises the question of how the emotional and material realities of embodied individuals are intertwined in other social and cultural contexts. For example, many people in Sullk'ata, as elsewhere, implicitly or explicitly associate domestic violence with sexually intimate, marital, or romantic relationships. In Sullk'ata, however, people typically recognize the economic aspects of these intimate partnerships. The obligations, expectations, and affective ideals intertwined with a daughter-in-law's labor are particularly important to household power dynamics. From this perspective, both affinity and violence are embedded in an array of economic and social relationships. It is necessary to rethink the complex realities of relatedness in situated localities in order to reassess both the contingencies and the analytical frames through which relatedness and domestic violence are understood.

EIGHT

Conclusion

Reflections on the Dialogical Production of Relatedness

IN THIS ETHNOGRAPHY I have described the everyday discourses, both violent and sociable, through which relatedness is constituted in a small region in Bolivia. Attention to Sullk'ata narratives and practices illuminates the ideals of sociality and, at the same time, the complex practicalities of relatedness as *lived*. Most Sullk'atas do not, for example, assume a universal (biological) connection between family members or romantic love as the affective foundation of marriage but embed relatedness into broader understandings of the cyclicity of the universe. At the same time, Sullk'atas collude with and contest multiple identities and hierarchies as they navigate their relationships with each other. Within the constraints of interactions and in broader social contexts, they actively participate in the construction of affective social relations and social reality more generally. Taking the perspective that relatedness emerges through dialogical interactions, I have attempted to convey both the disputes and dissensions among individuals and to illuminate the pervasive sensibilities of sociality in Sullk'ata.

Of course, a book that focuses on the intimate and hierarchical relationships of a people for an audience of readers unfamiliar with that region also makes some claims to broader implications. In the following pages I reconsider the questions that I articulated in the introductory chapter of this ethnography. How do we understand sociality in everyday life—the unremarkable and passionate as well as the antagonistic and harmonious? How do we make sense of the ways in which violence emerges in spite of ideals of closeness and conviviality? What might stories, and the act of telling stories, say about everyday life and social relationships? How do we represent others, recognizing both the structured configurations and the contingencies of their lives? Refracted through the ethnographic details of Sullk'ata, three themes surface: the essential and emergent quality of relatedness, the practice of narrating meaningful sociality, and the hierarchy of intimate relationships. Braided together, these three strands of ethnographic and analytical exploration illuminate kinship and gender beyond the borders of Sullk'ata.

Relatedness as Essential and Emergent

In Sullk'ata, relatedness is not so much an essentialized "fact" as a process *essential* to and emergent in the everyday lives of individuals. Relatedness is essential to the lives of Sullk'atas because the sensibilities of relatedness organize many of the practicalities of daily life and shape relationships of power and value. Relatedness is emergent because the social, affective, and material bonds of relatedness are not simply predictable from the intentions or genealogies of individuals, the histories of interaction of various social actors, or even the social and historical discourses in which people are enmeshed. Relatedness occurs in process: the connections of sociality are transformed through habitual activities and talk among individuals and, at the same time, constrained by structured discourses.

One of the ways in which I have illustrated the essential character of relatedness is by locating relatedness in the broader conceptual context of ayni. The "common sense" of a universe that operates cyclically—and of cycles of giving and receiving that are not necessarily evenly balanced—is the unremarkable background of Sullk'ata relatedness. Variations on the theme of ayni illuminate the complexities of relationships among Sullk'atas: the strength of ties and the expressed sorrows of parents and children; the inscription of hegemonic values of labor exchange among women; and the production of affective bonds between husbands and wives that tie married couples back into the circulation of energy through the ayllu. While my elaboration of the conceptual significance of ayni for Sullk'ata relatedness has challenged any simplistic notion of an isolated or hermetically sealed culture, I have also used ayni as a gate-keeping device, one quite common in anthropological scholarship on the Andes. By integrating the diverse experiences of individuals into this frame, I expand the definition of ayni beyond an exchange of labor, challenge the assumption that exchanges among kin are inherently egalitarian, and demonstrate that Sullk'ata relatedness provides alternative renderings—sometimes contradictory, sometimes mutually reinforcing—of kinship.

By exploring the ways in which Sullk'atas ground relatedness in ayni rather than in sexual reproduction, I bring attention to the specific parameters of kinship in another place. A Sullk'ata child eats food grown in his father's chakra, cooked in his mother's pot, and served by his mother's hand; he shares a bed with his parents or siblings, breathing in the warmth generated by bodies in a small room; he helps his parents by gently unearthing potatoes, herding sheep, carrying water, and collecting fuel for the fire; and, as he grows, he increasingly contributes to the circulation of food and energy in the universe by giving as well as receiving care. As previous examples have illustrated, even the categories of "mother" and "father" require constant reiteration. Ayni also permeates the multiple events of a marriage process, as the novios begin to share food, work, and close physical proximity and as the members of their communities offer the arku, aumentu, and regalus that will weigh the novios down until they carry out their obligations in future fiestas. As much as Sullk'atas and other native Andeans mobilize discourses of birth and blood, the strengths and fragilities of relationships are comprehensible through the conceptual frame and continuous practice of ayni more than through that of genetic connection.

Although the significance of habitual practices for the process of constituting kinship bonds has been discussed in other Andean contexts, this ethnography has placed the discourses and practices of relatedness at the center. Of course, the degree to which relatedness is essential to social and material relationships in other Andean contexts requires further exploration. Additionally, in-depth research examining the system of compadrazgo in Andean societies in the twenty-first century (particularly the on-the-ground relationships among compadres and between godparents and godchildren) would enhance understanding of the concept of relatedness in Sullk'ata and elsewhere. Recognizing relatedness in Sullk'ata as an emergent aspect of social life is also suggestive of further research into the discourses and practices of "raising children" or child fosterage. As increasing numbers of campesinos migrate to urban centers and to other countries such as Spain, leaving their children in the care of family members, compadres, and friends, the significance and meanings of fostering may be transformed in the twenty-first century. Understanding relatedness in the Andes, finally, also requires increased attention to the agency and identity of children, who, like adults, negotiate relationships of caring and companionship, migrate in search of economic and political security, and claim belonging in a variety of collectivities.

Understanding Sullk'ata relatedness also illuminates questions of kinship and gender more generally. A reader might see Sullk'ata notions of relatedness as quaint, misguided, or simply incorrect, in spite of my best efforts to the contrary. Yet increasingly diverse practices (local, national, and transnational adoption and fostering, *in vitro* fertilization, sperm and egg donation, divorce and remarriage, and surrogate motherhood, among others) have challenged the assuredness with which people might claim that children "are" sons and daughters because of their biological or genetic relationships to particular adults. In recent years scholars have described the diverse ways of producing kinship in North America and elsewhere in the world, challenged the naturalness of a (woman's) reproductive body, and demonstrated that even the scientific "facts" of reproduction are cultural and partial (for example, Franklin and McKinnon 2001). Thus this ethnography of Sullk'ata relatedness is but one case of many in which human beings employ a diverse set of conceptions and actions to create families and to make sense of "family."

Narrating Sociality

Further, considering the emergent nature of relatedness in Sullka'ta highlights the ways in which kinship is lived by and through social actors and challenges us to expand our analyses of how social relationships, like kinship, acquire shape and character in a process of constant formation. In the pages of this book, I have explored relatedness as embodied and linguistic performances that act upon the situation at hand as well as dispositions created through habitual actions and implicated in Sullk'atas' sense of the world. Sullk'atas use stories—about themselves and others—to navigate relationships, transforming relatedness in the process. Sullk'atas also negotiate the social and material parameters of relatedness through emotional and social discourses, such as llakikuy or envidia, and through particular kinds of events, such as the ritual scolding of novios. Understanding relatedness in Sullk'ata requires attention to multiple discourses, talk *and* actions, that do not necessarily refer to kinship.

Taking seriously the talk, and specifically the storytelling, of Sullk'atas, I develop a framework for analyzing relatedness as produced in the dialogical interactions of social actors. Sullk'atas engage in a wide variety of narrative practices, and I have used the "texts" of informal conversations, folktales, personal narratives, and interviews as sites for understanding the creation and negotiation of social relationships. Sullk'atas also employ multiple levels of dialogue within their stories, embedding citations, alluding to other stories or events, relying on an interlocutor to add questions or comments. Who tells the story and to whom; how, when, and where the story is told; whether the plot is transparent or unresolved; what moral stance the interlocutors take toward the characters, events, and each other: these dimensions have an impact on the form, meanings, and social force of Sullk'ata narratives. From this perspective, the meanings of a text are not limited to the referential content of what is said or the intention of the speaker. Narratives are intimately linked to the context in which they arise and productive of social relationships themselves. Thus individuals may come away from an interaction with various interpretations of events and relationships. Just as importantly, the very process of talk may create relatedness through the fusion of practices and performances among actors.

This book shows that by closely integrating narrative analysis with ethnographic study anthropologists may understand more fully both the social relationships that shape specific narrative events and the broader discursive frameworks that stories illuminate. Although both linguistic anthropologists and cultural anthropologists have fruitfully explored questions of gender and kinship, linguistic approaches have often failed to engage with broader cultural and social contexts. Instead, linguistic anthropologists have focused attention on the micropolitics of interaction of communicative events. In contrast, in spite of the recent attention to discursive analysis in cultural anthropology (e.g., Abu-Lughod 1993), cultural accounts do not always illustrate just how individual actions are productive of social relationships. This ethnography suggests that integrating an analysis of the micro-interactions among people with attention to the specific contexts in which these interactions take place will enable richer and more complicated understandings of the social and cultural parameters of people's lives.

Considering relatedness within a framework that takes seriously the joint production of talk and practice also has implications for the ways in which scholars might more thoroughly integrate embodiment into analyses of kinship and gender. Human beings have little choice but to live in and through bodies: the physicality of pregnancy or of sorrowing over a loved one's death is difficult to deny. Similarly, narrating a cautionary story about lik'ichiri, expressing affection, and internalizing respect or other appropriate modes of being in the world are corporeally enacted and take place within a network of relationships. As linguistic anthropologists have demonstrated, bodily presences and practices, though often not consciously mobilized, do have significant impact upon linguistic interactions and meanings (for example, Goodwin and Goodwin 2001; Hanks 1996). There is no position outside of culturally constituted and gendered bodies from which to describe relatedness, but our sociality as human beings is also corporeal. Relatedness may thus be seen as emerging in a field of relations among embodied individuals without reverting to an essentialism that ties women to a specific "biological nature" (of reproductive role or hormonal constitution).

Intimacy and Conflict

As I have illustrated throughout this ethnography, relatedness is not only about creating bonds of caring and commensality through sharing stories, food, or work. If we take into account the social world that always includes human (and even supernatural) beings engaged in relationships, then we also must acknowledge the ways in which discursive practices are always carried out through bodies that are embedded in a patterned network of prior actions and interactions. Sullk'atas perform relatedness in relation to structured relationships of power. Moreover, relatedness itself is political: the circulation of care, energy, and labor is as significant to the production of hierarchy as it is to the consolidation of intimacies in Sullk'ata. By bringing attention to the ideals of closeness, specific configurations of power, and the practical conflicts and concerns of everyday life in Sullk'ata, my analysis reinvigorates scholarship on kinship in the Andes.

Through my ethnographic research with Sullk'atas, I have found that the politics of relatedness is shaped by two major axes of conflict: one between brothers and the other between affines, specifically mothers-in-law and daughters-in-law. Brothers, though ideally close, often have relationships fraught with discord. The fragility or brittleness of those "biological" or blood ties between brothers stands in contrast to the flexibility and strength of bonds between parents and children. Although brothers are born in the same family, raised sleeping in the same bed, eating food cooked in the same pot, and working the same fields, they do not enter into cycles of exchange with each other. In contrast, the relationship between parents and children is typically produced through exchanges as parents feed children and as children reciprocate through working or carrying gifts back from the city. The hierarchies that characterize these paired relationships (of older and younger brothers or of parents and children) are often represented structurally as parallel. They are in fact materially, socially, and affectively distinct.

People engage in different configurations of power asymmetry, sometimes reinforcing and at other times contradicting each other. The second axis of hierarchy, highlighted in my account, is that between affines. Consideration of relationships between mothers-in-law and daughters-in-law in particular contributes to defining the parameters of affinity in Sullk'ata and brings attention to the simultaneity of camaraderie and conflict in relationships. Though growing up in different households and frequently in different communities, affines establish relatedness through feeding and eating and working together. In spite of ideals of reciprocity and respect between mothers-in-law and daughters-in-law, the ambivalences of the relationship are recognized in songs, stories, gossip, emotional displays, and physical violence. Similarly the ideals of complementarity and caring between marriage partners may be inflected with competition or antagonism as individuals navigate different material demands and obligations, social configurations, and structures of power.

Recognizing that the social and affective relationships of Sullk'atas are intimately intertwined with relationships of power has implications for an analysis of gender and of violence more generally. Considering the conflict among women affines in Sullk'ata demonstrates that gender relations and hierarchies are not just about the differences between homogeneous categories of men and women. Gender also extends to the relationships, practices, and interactions that constitute differences among men and differences among women, such that distinctive identities and positions of power are embedded in specific contexts. Individual relationships and even particular moments in relationships affect the ways in which people establish or recognize hierarchies and intimacies of relatedness. Women contend with the obligations, unequal exchanges, and ambiguities of affect in affinity; yet individuals also experience both gender and affinity in different ways, depending on age and generation, relationship with a spouse, access to resources such as wage work and education, and other factors. Just as gender is not necessarily the only or the primary axis of inequality that structures a woman's life at any particular moment, affinity is not the only or necessarily the primary axis of inequality that shapes the identity and experiences of a married individual. Nonetheless, attention to relationships among women and relationships among men is fundamental to understanding the ways in which power is deployed between women and men and to understanding the ways in which kinship, especially affinity, structures gender and gender hierarchies in the Andes.

This perspective also illuminates the ways in which violence emerges among those who are related. Violence in Sullk'ata is culturally embedded and reflects interpersonal negotiations for positioning and power in the context of multiple structured inequalities. In spite of the seemingly universal nature of domestic violence, violence, like kinship, requires complex and locally relevant modes of interpretation and understanding. By broadening the focus on domestic violence to incorporate the webs of power within which women and men find themselves or through which they might actively seek to alter their circumstances, this ethnography brings attention to kinship as lived by people who are sometimes in pain and through relationships that are sometimes fraught with uncertainties. These networks of relationships and the individual interactions that are implicated shape events and the ways in which interlocutors, including anthropologists, may interpret kinship or violence as lived interactions.

Making sense of violence and relatedness requires analysis of political and material hierarchies and everyday interactions as well as those ideals of sociality. As they negotiate relatedness, Sullk'atas identify with and claim belonging to a diverse set of collectivities. Sullk'atas also refigure discourses of national identity, citizenship, and modernization. If gendered and racial discourses of "progress" are implicated in the talk and practices of relatedness, then relatedness cannot be seen as isolated within a separate domestic domain. From this perspective, the living narrative of everyday interactions, even in marginal yet transnational communities, creates positioned subjectivities and imagined communities, turning on its head the assumed trajectory of influence between the national and local or the public and domestic. By considering the processes through which relatedness is performed in relation to other forms of power, I contribute to the understanding not only of kinship but also of diverse and dynamic forms of identifying with particular collectivities.

A Pause: Considering Contingencies

By integrating attention to situated manifestations of interpersonal conflict and broad material and political relationships, this ethnography refuses to reduce the strategic interactions and affective practices of individuals to static structures or biological givens. Relatedness, I argue, is negotiated, produced, and revised in interactions. Yet I have also reduced and reshaped the on-the-ground interactions of individuals in my retelling in order to paint a picture, evoke an image, and narrate a (perhaps too) coherent story about Sullk'ata lives and relationships. I thus pause to consider the contingencies of relationships. This reflection is prompted by two diverse sources, one an ethnographic account and theoretical discussion of political violence by E. Valentine Daniel (1996, 1997) and the other an email written in haste by one of my Bolivian godchildren to inform me of a tragedy. Each raises the question of how scholars might understand and represent the "recalcitrantly ambiguous character" of people's lives in spite of our attempts at coherence (Daniel 1997:358; see also Connolly 1987:151).

In his accounts of the bloody riots that took place in Sri Lanka in the 1980s, Daniel (1997:361) has argued that anthropologists should take seriously a genealogical method of representation. By genealogical, he does not mean the charts of triangles, circles, and single and double lines that anthropologists of an earlier generation used to trace the relationships of sexual reproduction and marriage among men and women of other cultures. A genealogical mode of representation, he writes, "is suspiciously alert to the voice of coherent narratives and their concerns and equally—but sympathetically—alert to those voices that are not in concordance with such narratives" (Daniel 1997:361). In turning toward post-structuralist critiques of any attempt to capture the exact essence of things (Foucault 1972), Daniel does not encourage a quest after a "hidden transcript" (Scott 1990) of the subaltern so much as issue a challenge to be open to those stories, claims, statements, or actions that seem to be tangential to the more expected ones.

Both the contingency of the material and emotional bonds of relatedness for Sullk'atas and the impossibility of coherently representing the entirety of those connections of relatedness are epitomized in an email message that I received from my goddaughter Marisa in September 2005. In the short message, which I have translated from Spanish, Marisa informs me of the sudden death of her father, my compadre, even as she actively attempts to reinforce her relationship with me. She writes:

Dear Madrina,
I am sorry to tell you of the tragedy that has occurred to us, but I feel the necessity to unburden myself with one of the most beloved people that I have in my life. Lamentably, we are orphans. We no longer have a father. I don't know how it happened, because until just one week ago I was in Spain. I heard the terrible news that my father fell from a cliff and hit his head on a rock. It was that which provoked his death. So immediately I went to Bolivia, wanting to see him one last time, but I did not arrive in time to be at the funeral. Now all of us find ourselves in a terrible confusion. Now we are all left to the care of my mother. I hope that you all are well, and I wish all the happiness in the world for each one of you. From a distance, I send each of you a kiss, and I will write to you again soon.
Love, Marisa

Although I have added punctuation to the message, Marisa's original email reads as if the story rushed out of her like water over a dam after a heavy rain. Beginning with the phrase "Lamentably, we are orphans" she continues for several lines with hardly a punctuation break, until she admits that the family find themselves "in a terrible confusion." Pulsing through the message are Marisa's anguish over her father's death, sorrow at having been absent from his funeral, and apprehension for her mother.

Shocked and saddened by Marisa's news, I replied to the message immediately. When I received no response, I called the cell phone number that my comadre had given me on my last visit to Bolivia. It was no longer in service. I had become used to these gaps in communication over the years, for the family did not own a computer or telephone line; but in this instance I especially regretted that I could not easily contact them. A few weeks later Marisa's sister called collect from Spain. She also gave me the news of her father's death and told me that she and her two brothers would be traveling to Bolivia. I realized that the entire family would be gathering in Kallpa in a few days for Todos Santos, to build an altar for Marcelino, to mourn and remember him. Enmeshed in the care of my then infant daughter, Sophia, I was not able to make a trip to Bolivia to visit my comadre and her children until nearly a year later, in August 2006.

A death points toward the strengths and contingencies of relatedness, the significance of caring for people's lives, and the impossibility of controlling the beginning or ending of a life (Rosaldo 1984). When I saw her, Ilena told me that on the night he died Marcelino had been making ch'allas in honor of the newly named community officials. Late that night he had walked home alone down a steep and rocky path and had probably lost his footing, tumbled down the embankment, and hit his head on a rock at the edge of the creek. A neighbor found his body the next morning when he passed by to let his oxen quench their thirst. In her brief account, Ilena indicated Marcelino's attempt to care for his family and contribute to their sustenance by maintaining relationships with human and supernatural beings as much as she alluded to his drunken state.

The constant yet ambiguous character of relatedness is of course evident even without the lens of tragic loss. Since 1998, for example, Ilena and Marcelino had often resided in different locales but continued to operate as an economic, social, and affective unit. He primarily lived in Kallpa, where he helped care for his aging parents and managed the subsistence agricultural production. She lived in the house in Cochabamba that Marcelino and his oldest sons had been in the process of constructing in 1996. There she cared for their younger children and a grandchild. While the children attended high school and university classes, she worked as a vendor of *refrescos* (Sp., nonalcoholic, homemade drinks) to earn a little money. Although Marcelino had envisioned the house in Cochabamba as a place for his oldest sons to take up residence once married, the oldest sons and then Marisa and her sister had migrated to Spain in search of work. If the collective efforts of Marisa and her siblings to return to Kallpa, in spite of great distance and expense, index the force of relatedness, Marisa's message also points toward the ways in which social and emotional bonds are fragmented and re-configured in more mundane ways. Marisa and three of her siblings rarely saw their father because they were so far away.

Marcelino's death more noticeably left an emotional gap in Ilena's life that she could not completely express but that had social and material consequences. His death made his children into "orphans," left to the care of only their mother. Ilena worried about how she would ever support her children on her own. After the funeral, she remained in Kallpa for several months to manage the agricultural production for the household. Some of her compadres helped her with the planting, but she also had to pay some neighbors to work for her. She could no longer draw upon Marcelino's ayni relationships, and her own ayni relationships had been weakened by her absence from the community. Although the oldest children returned briefly to Kallpa to mourn and remember Marcelino and to be with their mother and younger siblings, they soon returned to Spain. According to Ilena, before they left her children told her, "We don't want you lugging around those heavy pails of glasses and drinks anymore. It makes you too tired." The children in Spain, she hoped, would send money back to her to help support their younger siblings.

In many ways the contingencies of life are crucial to conceiving of relatedness as it is lived. In spite of all the ways in which individuals constitute relatedness in their actions and interactions, in a very real sense a representation of relatedness will always fall short. My compadre's death could barely be narrated by those related to him, due to both lack of information and depth of feeling. Yet in bringing this particular story to the forefront, other seemingly tangential details are obscured: that Marisa contacted me by email; that she had been working as a household companion for three elderly Spaniards before returning to Bolivia; that the adobe walls and concrete floors of the family's house in Cochabamba have been improved with plaster and paint, tile, and rugs. The very attempt at narrative elides the contingencies of life that are crucial to the bonds of caring and conflict among Ilena's family and among Sullk'atas more generally.

Affective Ethnography

In our everyday lives we listen and interact, participate and contemplate, draw information together into interpretations and leave some knowledge to the side. Sullk'atas told me stories—of the people who envied Ilena, of Javier's two mothers, of Julia and Wilberto running away from her brothers—to make sense of events and draw the contingencies of everyday life into particular frameworks. I have in turn used these stories and others to provide an image of Sullk'ata relatedness and of the key discourses and sensibilities through which Sullk'atas understand their world and navigate the significant social and affective relationships of their everyday lives. At the same time, acknowledging that the meanings of words are an emergent product of social interaction implies that multiple interpretations are probable, not simply possible. This is as true of an interaction while it is happening as it is true of a representation now frozen in print.

An ethnographer's role in the making of meaning requires an engagement that is inherently dialogical, although the published product, an ethnography, does not have the fluidity of a social interaction or even a performed narrative. Considering the partiality of representation and the transformative potential of refracting stories through different voices, oral historian Della Pollock (2006:89) writes of a practice she calls "listening out loud," in which one social actor re-creates an informal interview through "improvised retellings, scenic description, poetic transcription and public rehearsal." I have told stories based upon my observations and experiences, conversations and interviews, and transcriptions and translations in order to provide an image of Sullk'ata relatedness. The stories in this book are not word-for-word renditions of Sullk'ata voices but are, in a sense, another (kind of) performance, refracted through my own understandings and engagement with Sullk'atas.

Attending to another person's story and evoking a sense of those stories and lives bespeak the engagement of ethnographic practice in and out of the field. The engagement of ethnographic practice is affective and social, but it is not isolated from relationships of power. One of the primary ways in which I gained an understanding of Sullk'atas was through interacting with individuals on a daily basis. At least in part the embodied interactions of people create affective content that is intertwined with the referential content of any conversation. However, the stories that I listened to and those that were silenced in my presence, and the stories that I retell and those that I obscure, are shaped by several overlapping discourses of power. Sullk'atas categorized me as an educated white woman; as a married woman with no children; as an individual wealthy enough to travel; as a citizen of the United States, a country whose policies and practices position Bolivia as politically, socially, and economically inferior. Although some Sullk'atas identified me as a comadre and friend—and although empathy, warmth, and trust are part of ethnographic engagement—this book also bespeaks a relative economy of power and intimacy in the production of knowledge. The form of interaction cannot be extracted from the content of what is said; thus the intimacies and power asymmetries of any interaction are also productive of meanings.

An ethnographer draws upon a different range of experiences and conceptions than do those with whom she interacts in the field. As any particular interaction is in process (and later in the processes of transcribing taped conversations and interviews and writing and revising interpretations as ethnography), the theories and relationships of those around her inflect the ethnographer's retelling. Although Sullk'atas are not engaged in an ethnographic project, they do construct theories about their lives, the events in which they are caught up, their pasts and their futures, and the people with whom they interact. Barbara Christian (1987), in an essay about race and the production of theory, has argued that subaltern people have often theorized in various forms. "[O]ur theorizing (and I intentionally use the verb rather than the noun) is often in narrative forms," she writes, "in the stories we create, in riddles and proverbs, in the play with language, since dynamic rather than fixed ideas seem more to our liking. How else have we managed to survive with such spiritedness the assault on our bodies, social institutions, countries, our very humanity?" (Christian 1987:52). Christian's words resonate with my understanding of the theorizing that Sullk'atas do, the theories that emerge in conversations and stories, in weaving, and in weddings.

Theorizing from subjugated positionalities may promise more adequate transformational accounts of the world but is not innocent or exempt from critical examination. Expanding our conceptions of theorizing that others do and of how theorizing takes place in the commonplace events of fieldwork is crucial to an engaged anthropology. How we do ethnographic and linguistic research, what counts as credible evidence, the power relationships that structure those hierarchies of credibility, and how we anthropologists position ourselves within the discipline (among other disciplines in a broader academic context and in a global economy) are issues implicit in an analysis that crosses cultural boundaries and international borders.

To understand relatedness, and to understand the place of relatedness in dynamic relationships that converge in the domestic arena yet extend beyond it, requires detailed analysis of spoken and unspoken meanings, the micropolitics of interactions, and historical structurings of power in particular places at specific moments. Drawing on multiple forms of evidence, I have tried to portray the inconsistencies and contradictions, the complexities and the subtleties, of social and affective relationships and interactions among Sullk'atas. By integrating linguistic and cultural approaches to the analysis of these clues, I have developed an analytical frame for interpreting experiences and discursive practices as located in a network of interactions among people, as simultaneously corporeal and cultural, and as affecting not only the politics of a particular situation but also the broader politics of social life.

Chapter 5 Narrative Transcriptions in Quechua and in English

Story Told by Seferina in Conversation (See Intertext III in Chapter 5)

SEFERINA: Chay enamoradonchá wañurqa ah.

KRISTINA: Wañurqachu?

SEFERINA: Ah, chaytaq wañusqa a.

KRISTINA: Ahh.

SEFERINA: Chanta imillaman,

Imilla SINchi waqasqa puriq nin.

Chanta rikurisqa nin almaqa.

Chaymanta "Ja-jaku ripusunchis," nisqa.

Imillata mana jawjatasqachu.

"Jawjataway a!" nisqa.

KRISTINA: Í.

SEFERINA: Mana jawjatasqachu.

Chaymanta rillankupunichá, rillankupunichá.

"Lago kasqa," nin, "qhucha."

KRISTINA: Í.

SEFERINA: Arí.

Chanta [yawning] wakiq kanchá chay qhucha kantuspiqa wasisqa.

KRISTINA: Unh.

SEFERINA: Un.

KRISTINA: Chay wasiqa karqa uj qhuchaneqpichu.

SEFERINA: Arí.

Nin "Ñaq'ararimusaq, wayk'upusun arí," nispa nisqa.

Imillaqa risqa, nin, nak'arariq.

"Wayk'ukusun," nispa, "wasita."

Chaymanta alqu

Awu^{uuuuu}aw$_{auwauwau}$ awau^{uuuuuuu}auwauw$_{auwauwaw}$!

Awullaaqan nin alquqa!

KRISTINA: Uuuum!

SEFERINA: Chaymanta alqu awullasqa nin.

"Chayman," chay wasiyuq nin.

"Su ^{Suuun}sa$_{siii}$p$_{aaas}$!"

"Ima," nispa, "ayataq qhatiy yachanchiri?"

"Ayllaqa, arrii!" nispa nisqa.

Almaqa, arí!

"Imapaq almaqa qhatiy yachanki?" nispa nisqa.

Sumaq sipas nin aaa!

KRISTINA: Uuuum.

SEFERINA: Un. "Kunan ama sunsachu kay!

Uuum chay lagota ñawpaq pasachinki.

Chay lagota, chay qhutata ukhutaqa, [inaudible] . . . saqrañatawan espejotawan saq'ikuy," nisqa.

KRISTINA: Í.

SEFERINA: Chaymanta imillaqa librakamusqa ayamantaqa.

Arí, chay qhucha kantuta mana pasanchu.

Nilla atinchu nisqa.

Almaqa ñak'asqanpi nin.

KRISTINA: Umm.

SEFERINA: Condenadochá.

Chay condenadoqa waqanchá pero,

[Seferina begins singing.]

"Qhapallayta qupuway hukumwarum.

Qhapallayta qupuway hukumwarum."

Qhuchatataq [inaudible] jamuntaqchá, rintaqchá.

KRISTINA: Auhuum.

SEFERINA: Chaymanta imilla jampusqa chay wasiyuqman.

Chay chayamusqa.

"AwueLIta!" nin.

"Qaqaumita chaya chayasqa," nin chay wasiyuq.

Jinata ayllatapis qhatiy yachaq imillas ninchá! Arí!

KRISTINA: Ayy!

SEFERINA: Enamoradoschá kaq kanku peru.

KRISTINA: Í.

SEFERINA: Chanta qulqita urqumusqa nispachá tatanpaq chayman rin.

Chanta imataq. Tatallantaq wañuchisqa nin chay joventaqa.

Nispa parlaq karqa.

KRISTINA: Arí?

SEFERINA: Ajina kwintu karqa.

Story Told by Dario, Formally Solicited

i

A long time ago there were two lovers.

He was so in love with a young woman.

That woman he wanted.

And his father did not like her, they say.

The father did not want to give the young man money, or anything,

so that he might earn a living with the young woman.

So the lovers left and went to another place.

They lived there.

With that girl the young man lived.

ii

Night was coming on.

He went to his father's house, for money.

Arriving at that house,

He stole money from his father.

He stole food . . . corn, potatoes, whatever.

He went there, and from that house he stole.

Another time he just had to carry away some food.

Another time he just carried food away so that they could cook.

Already they finished it all up, all that food.
Yet again he came, the young man
Stealing from his father.
He arrived just like the last time.
He stole corn, potatoes, whatever they didn't have.
And he just carried it away.

iii

His father said, "Aaaw, food is missing from here.
Who could have carried it off?
Did you sell it?" he said to his wife.
"I didn't sell it," she said.
"Food is missing. And who took it from here?"
"For what . . . ?" [she said.]

Already another night.
Again his son carried food away.
And again he just carried it from his father's house.
He returned [to where they lived].

Already, even the next day, more food was lost
And he could see just by looking that food was lost.
"All right then," he said to his wife. "And there is more food that is just missing."
"What can we do? Why would someone carry it away?"
"Little by little it is definitely lost," he said.
"Yeah, *carajo,* maybe a thief carried it."

iv

He waited for him then
With a machete.
The thief arrived.
It was just his son.
But he did not recognize him in the DARK.
He spied on him.
Once with the ax he gave it to the thief.
Once . . . with the machete he gave it . . .

"I killed the thief!" said the man to his wife.
"This one is the thief," he said. "I killed him."

"Bring me a candle. Let's look," he said.
"Oooh nooo. . . . my child, it's my child!
It's not a thief," he was saying as he cried. "He was ours!"

Crying, they went and buried him.
They [went] to the cemetery.
They put him into the ground.
Covered with dirt.

v

That girl was probably waiting for him.
He didn't arrive very quickly.

He exited from the cemetery, that man's son.
Dead, he still left.
He left the cemetery to go to his girl.
And then he arrived at the place where his woman waited.

"Why didn't you come back quickly?" [she said.]
"Oh, I am hurting. My neck is hurting me," he said.
He would not show her his neck.
[He walked with his shirt pulled up around his neck.]

"Let's go. Let's return," he said.
"Let's go away," she said.
They went away, they say.

vi

They arrived at someone's house.
Then "Missus, please let me in," s/he said.
(What, what could her name have been? Maybe doña Rosa.)
"Open up!" s/he said.
"All right, come in, sleep" [the woman answered.]

Then the man did not want to enter.

He did not want to enter.

"No, I will sleep just outside," he said.

Then the woman said, "Let's go, we will sleep in the house."

"You just sleep inside. I will just sleep on the patio.

No way, Aunt, would I sleep inside the house. I will sleep on the patio."

"All right then," she agreed, saying, "He sleeps outside."

"You come inside now to the house," she said [to the girl].

The woman entered the house.

The girl entered the house too.

vii

Night came upon them.

The woman who owned the house said, "There it is."

With a candle, like a flame.

"It's making a light," she said.

"Like an *alma,* a soul. Exactly like a soul."

Entering,

The woman with the house got the young woman up out of bed.

(What could her name have been?)

"Your husband is not well.

He is an alma. He is a condenado," she said.

"He is definitely a condenado, a condemned soul."

And then . . .

"Now what am I going to do, Aunt?"

"Now, my child, with this mirror [inaudible]," she said.

"With this brush you will go."

She gave her a mirror and a brush.

"Now to the water, hurry, you must cross really quickly," she said.

"Pass by the lake with the mirror.

First, throw out the brush," she said.

"All right, already he will pass by farther behind.

He will follow,

And then you will just throw out the mirror," she said.

viii

Then the girl first threw out the brush.
A brush, a brush she tossed out.
Right then she passed the lake.
Right then she threw out the mirror.
The mirror she has thrown away.

She escaped to a church, to the father priest.
To the priest she arrived.
To the locked-up church.
"Father! Father! A condemned soul is coming after me," she was saying.
"That's all right, all right, I will meet him," he said.
"Enter my house. Go inside."
The girl beat the condenado to the house.

ix

The priest waited by the door.
Then the condenado arrived.
"Would you please give me a little water, yes ayyqq, a little water, water, please give me
    a little water."
And the priest offered him a little water.
Again, "Please give me," he said.
Again he just offered him.
Another time.
"I will go in now," said the priest.

In God's name he castigated the condenado.
God, Holy Spirit [making the sign of the cross over the condenado].
"Now you are saved."
He sent the boy.
He was sent away.

Then coming to the ground, the boy finally died.
He was finished, the condenado.
He died another time from the priest.
He buried [the body], he burned the alma . . .

He was finished off.
He returned, going up to the sky like a wind.

Just then the priest said to the woman,
"Now you are freed my child.
The condenado has returned to heaven.
You are now able to return, my child."

x

Just lately, then, the girl came back here finally.
The other had already gone to heaven.
He finally returned to the high sky
And was no longer a condenado.
The condenado had already returned.

The priest castigated him.
With God's words he was saved.
The condenado is no longer a condenado. He returned.
The woman also came and was saved. She was freed.

I think the condenado would have wanted to eat [her].
That lover, she caused the lover to become a condenado.
He got killed because of a woman.
Because of a woman, a girl.

That is a little one.

Chapter 6 Interview Transcriptions in Quechua

1. Dario's Question and Nicolás' Response (See the section "A Little Piece of Paper" in Chapter 6)

DARIO: Iglesiaman yaykunaykichispaq p'achan-p'achantinchu yaykurqankichis o sinoqa pichus kambiasurqachis. Imaynaylla yaykurqankichis chayra.

NICOLÁS: Kasarakunaykupaq cursillustaraq pasarqayku [Pocoata]. Kinsa diyataq kasi simanataraq pasarqayku cursillusta. Mana kasarakunqachu mana cursillu pasaspaqa. Mana Diusmanta yachaspaqa mana kasarakuwaqchischu niwarqayku. Cursillusta pasanayku tiyan niwarqayku. Madrecita jina condicionpi cursillusta si- manataraq pasayku. Chaymantaraq recien . . . a . . . valetajina papelituta quwayku. Chay sabadonpaq qupuwayku. Chaywantaq padreman chimpayku. Recien . . . un . . . padreqa valechiwayku. Mana chay mana kharqumuwaykumanchá karqa. Un . . . ajinata kasarakurqayku.

2. Celedonio and Sonia's Responses Summing Up Their Marriage (See the section "Catholic Marriage Practices in Sullk'ata" in Chapter 6):

CELEDONIO: Ajinalla . . . Nuqayku kasarakurqayku desde tantakusqaykumantapa- cha mana maqanakuyta yachaykuchu mana maqanaykuchu yachaykuchu. Wakin kanku qanchus ninkuta jap'ichikuspa munanakunku llikllas ninkuta khichuranku munananrayku. Nuqaykuqa pero mana chayta yachaykuchu. Por amistad amor munanakuyku. Mana a la fuerzachu munanakuyku.

SONIA: Nuqaqta mamay niwaq . . . Mana uqtapis ni uqtapis qharitapis ni warmitapis enganañachu nispa niwaq. Ima chay enganañakuna nispa niwaq. Graveta rimawaq kayku. Chay ni pitaq engañay yachanichu ni nipuni nuqaqa. Kunitanqa tata diyuspis yachan nispa awantakuy yachani. Rimawaqtinqa jinata nispa niwaq jap'ikuni. Paychá jinatapis purin ni chaykunastaqa . . . Qharisqa uqtataq uqtataq engañan . . . Mayqinman risunman nispa niwaq mamaysi.

3. Isidoro, Rosa, and Dario's Discussion about Counting Regalu, Arku, and Aumentu (See the section "Accounting for Things on the Second Day" in Chapter 6)

ISIDORO: Padrinoy qallarirqa madrinaytaq qallarirqa warmimisaman arí. Warmi misa waq wakikun qhari misa waq wakikun arí. Entonces padrinoy qallarirqa chaymanta tukuy phamiliayku chayman aumentuta churarqa. Chay diyaqa arku diyantin karqa regalus.

DARIO: Diyan dominguta.

ISIDORO: Regalus . . . camisas, puleras, chumpas, y inawas tukuy ima karqa platos, cupas, cucharas . . .

ROSA: Warmi runamanta uq waka karqa.

ISIDORO: Warmi runamanta uq waka karqa. Arí waka karqa y kama paypata karqa mamanmanta. Compadriy chaypacha chayamullarqataq chay lliklla kinsa llikllas tawa karqa, í?

ROSA: Ah.

ISIDORO: Tawa llikllas karqa. Uq awasqa llikllaq kinsataq paceñas. Arí.

DARIO: Chay diya diya dominguta aumentupura ch'isillanku.

ISIDORO: Arí.

DARIO: Tardellaqtinqa nichu chay qulqita karqa aumenta churasqa misapi chaytaq pitaq yuparqa? Wakin matrimoniospiqa contado nisqa sutiyuq uq recibotakuq . . . tardita yupakurqachu qulqi? . . . Chay dumingu tardeta nichu qulqi yupankun sumaq pantiqllapi ima? Chay nichu qanman q'ipirichirqasunku?

ISIDORO: Niraq q'ayantinraq. Q'ayantin tardiraq dumingu lunes tarderaq q'ipirichirqayku . . . Regalusman sigue k'ankata qullarqaykupuni piladosta ima. Sigue qullaykupuni. Arí . . . chaymanta tardekapun tardemanta ruthuyta tukukapun. Casi arku karqa, cuarentachu ima karqa. Astawan karqa í . . . seisenta karqa . . .

DARIO: Y chay arku tukuy tukukapun regaluspis tiyan. Nichu chay regaluta tuku-

kuyta mayk'aqchus? Qulqi yaykumurqa mayk'aqchus valornin chay regaluspata
nichu totalizarqanku? Ni mayqin contador . . .

ISIDORO: Totalizakurqa totalizarqa seiscientos . . . unn . . . de fraccion karqa.
Seiscientos . . . seisientos treintachu veintecincochus. Tukuy nin. Qulqi. Chanta
ropastaq mayk'aqmanchá . . . Piru iskay pitulla karqa iskay pitulla karqa. Chayta
mana q'ipiriyta atirqanichu aysariwarqanku. Arí. Q'ipikuchikuni qunqurisqa-
manta manaña jatariyta atinichu.

DARIO: Chay totalizakuqtin contador uyarqachu comunidadman? Kay chhika qulqi
kasqan watapaq uq hinawan nispa.

ISIDORO: Willarqa. Tukuy comunidad uyarirqa . . . Wakapis totalizakurqa enteron.
Mashka valorniyuqchu wakapis karqa. Chay enteronta comunidadqa yacharqa.

Chapter 1

1. A *madrina* is a godmother. In this case, Ilena went to the godmother of her marriage, a highly appropriate person to consult about her marital dispute.

2. Drunkenness is understood as an altered state, in which a person is not responsible for his or her actions or words. See Harvey 1991; Saignes 1993.

3. Early works on women, gender, and the relationship between nature and culture include Collier and Yanagisako 1987; Comaroff 1987; MacCormack and Strathern 1980; Ortner and Whitehead 1981; Reiter 1975; Rosaldo 1980b; and Rubin 1975.

4. Anthropologists hotly debated the specific associations of genealogical (read "biological" or "genetic") relationships, kinship terms, and on-the-ground social relationships for several years. Among many others, see Fortes 1969; Gellner 1987; Josselin de Jong 1952; Lévi-Strauss 1963; Leach 1968; Malinowski 1963; Scheffler 1991; Schneider 1968, 1972, 1984; and Weismantel 1995. See also Van Vleet 1999:128–134.

5. The concept of gender has sometimes been constructed along an opposition between sex as biological (that particular collection of chromosomes, organs, and hormones) and gender as the culturally specific elaboration of the raw materials of sex. This formulation has been criticized because the biological body is retained as an

essentialized base upon which the superstructure of social and cultural ideologies is built. Sex—and biology—is also constructed (Butler 1990, 1993; Grosz 1994).

6. Abu-Lughod 1990a, 1993; Anzaldúa 1990; Butler 1993; Collins 1990, 2004; di Leonardo 1991; Gutmann 1996; Haraway 1991; Hirsch 2003; Kulick 1998; Mohanty 1984; Spivak 1988; Stephenson 1999; Stoler 1991; Suleri 1992; Yanagisako and Delany 1995; and Weismantel 2001.

7. By situating the practices and performances of individuals in specific cultural discourses and political economies, anthropologists have reinvigorated kinship studies. Among others, see Abu-Lughod 1986, 1993; Ahearn 2001a; Blackwood 2000, 2005; Carsten 2000, 2004; Franklin and McKinnon 2001; Glenn et al. 1994; J. Hirsch 2003; S. Hirsch 1998; Martinez-Alier 1989; Pollock 1999; Ragoné 1994; Rebhun 1999; Scheper-Hughes 1992; Trawick 1990; Weismantel 1995; Weston 1991, 2001; and Yanagisako and Delany 1995.

8. More recent discussions (Blackwood 2005; Borneman 1996; Carsten 2000, 2004; Weston 2001) point to the ways in which even the "new kinship studies" tend to retain a focus on reproduction and marriage—and thus reproduce assumptions of heterosexuality as the basis of relatedness.

9. Bronislaw Malinowski (1963) promoted the notion that the emotional ties that develop over the long and intimate association of family members would be the same for Australian aborigines as for East Londoners. He emphasized the universality of the biological relationship and those emotional bonds as a strategy to refute nineteenth-century evolutionary perspectives on the family. Anthropologists later refuted Malinowski's universalist claims and examined kinship terminologies, marriage practices, and domestic organization as a way of illuminating the diversity of kinship systems worldwide.

10. Prior to the 1980s, when anthropologists directed attention to the conjuncture of emotion and kinship, they often linked particular kinship positions to specific behavioral templates. For structuralist renditions of this, see, for example, Buchler and Selby 1968; Evans-Pritchard 1951; and Leach 1968, 1977. For recent discussions of emotion that incorporate attention to kinship and personhood, see, among others, Hirsch 2002; Lutz 1988; Lutz and White 1986; Overing and Passes 2000; Rebhun 1999; Rosaldo 1980a; Scheper-Hughes 1992; Tapias 2006a, 2006b; and Trawick 1990.

11. Among others, see Bakhtin 1981; Bauman and Briggs 1990; Duranti and Goodwin 1992; Goffman 1981; Hanks 1990, 1996; Howard-Malverde 1997; Irvine 1996; Kristeva 1980, 1993; Ochs and Capps 2001; Tedlock and Mannheim 1995; Urban 1991; and Williams 1977.

12. See Mannheim and Van Vleet 1998 for a more extensive discussion of the four levels of dialogue in Southern Quechua narrative. For a debate on the relative signifi-

cance of "big" and "small" stories, see Bamberg 2006; Freeman 2006; and Georgako-poulou 2006.

13. On the articulation of subsistence agriculture, market production, and migra-tion, see, for example, Collins 1986, 1988; Godoy 1986; Godoy and DeFranco 1992; Harris 1981, 1995; Langer 1989; Larson and Harris 1995; and Mayer 1984, 2002.

14. See, among others, Allen 2002; Arnold 1992; Bastien 1978; Bouysse-Cassagne 1986; Bouysse-Cassagne and Harris 1987; Earls 1969; Gose 1994; Harris 1978, 1980; Harvey 1993, 1994; Isbell 1978, 1997; and Platt 1986.

15. Sullk'atas built public primary schools in each community in the mid-1950s. A public high school near the provincial town of Pocoata was built in the mid-1960s; few Sullk'atas attended. In the mid-1980s a second regional high school was con-structed with assistance from the Catholic missionary nuns. Sullk'atas also send their children to school in Bolivian cities.

16. The literature on an ethnographer's "positionality," especially her relationships with interlocutors in—and out of—the field, is now quite large (for example, Fricke 2006; García 2000; Jacobs-Huey 2002; Narayan 1993; and Robertson 2002).

Chapter 2

1. On place and identity (including race, class, ethnicity, and gender) in the Andes, see Abercrombie 1991, 1998; Albó 1979; Alonso 1994; Bigenho 2002; Canessa 2005b; Flores Galindo 1988; Goldstein 2004; Goodale 2006; Howard-Malverde 1997; Lagos 1994, 1993; Salman and Zoomers 2003; Seligmann 1993; and Weismantel 2001.

2. I have also been influenced by Doreen Massey's (1994:154) conception of place as "a constellation of social relations, meeting and weaving together at a particular locus." Among many other influential texts on anthropology, place, and power, see Alonso 1994; Appadurai 1991, 1992; Blunt and Rose 1994; Coronil 1996; Fabian 1983; Feld and Basso 1996; and Trouillot 1991.

3. On households and the uneven overlap between family and household in the Andes, see Allen 2002; Arnold 1997; Bolton and Mayer 1977; Collins 1986, 1988; Ham-ilton 1998; Harris 1981, 1985; Mayer 1977, 1984, 2002; Paulson 1996; and Weismantel 1988, 1995.

4. *Mink'a* is a type of reciprocity in which people exchange nonidentical prod-ucts or labor, such as when one woman herds another's sheep in exchange for the milk. It may also refer to a large work party. *Yanapay* (literally "to help") is work for one's family and compadres, which is not accounted for but is done out of affection (*cariño*, Sp.).

5. On the relationship between husbands and wives within the household, see, for

example, Arnold 1992; Hamilton 1998; Harris 1978, 1981; Harvey 1994; Mayer 2002; and Spedding 1997b.

6. The sixteenth-century Spaniards who encountered the diverse ethnic groups of the Andes defined the ayllu as "kinsmen, family, royal lineage, moiety, kindred, extended family, nation, and exogamic, endogamic, ethnic and occupational group" (Godoy 1986:723). The structure and meanings of ayllus have altered over time (for example, Allen 2002:207–218). Modern ayllus in Bolivia are characterized by nucleated settlements, communal landholdings, rotational political and administrative offices, land redistribution, and, until quite recently, rural tax collection (Gelles 1995; Godoy 1986). On the sociopolitical structure and historical contingencies of the ayllu, see also Albó 1979; Bouysse-Cassagne 1986; Harris 1985, 1986; Klein 1993; and Platt 1982, 1986.

7. Anthropologists Tristan Platt (e.g., 1982) and Olivia Harris (e.g., 1985) have used the maximal ayllu names to refer to the people with whom they worked, the Machas and Laymis, respectively. I have not done so because of the linguistic and cultural diversity within Pukwata ayllu and because of the ways the people I worked with self-identified, primarily as Sullk'atas but also as campesinos or Bolivianos.

8. The oldest Kallpas remembered an annual migration to the valley lands owned by their families, herding their sheep for three days across mountains and dangerous river crossings, in order to plant corn. They no longer undertake this migration. Instead Kallpas plant corn just outside the community and migrate to urban areas for wage work.

9. In the 1960s the Bolivian government, with monetary and technical aid from the United States, encouraged migration to the Chapare, inadvertently setting the stage for the boom in coca production. Andreas and Sharpe 1992; Léons and Sanabria 1997; Sanabria 1993.

10. See Albó 1979; Godoy 1986; Klein 2003; Nash 1992, 1993; and Platt 1982, 1987 for discussions of the relationship between the state, campesinos, and taxation.

11. Protests over the privatization of water and of natural gas reserves since 2000 and against Lozada's plan to develop natural gas fields, which led his ouster from the presidency in 2003 during his second term of office, demonstrate the broad-based context. In December 2005 Evo Morales, a former coca farmer and organizer, ascended to the presidency after a wave of popular protests. See Albro 2006; Goodale 2006; Olivera 2004; and Postero 2005 on the recent history of Bolivian protests.

12. Lozada's government also instituted a number of reforms designed to decentralize government funding. For discussion of the Popular Participation laws and how they coincided with neoliberal reforms, see Klein 2003 and Salman and Zoomers 2003.

13. Most of the time I lived in the community we addressed each other as "doña

Ilena" and "doña Kristina," maintaining a level of formality that was replicated in my relations with most other members of the community. In June 1996 I sponsored a mass for Ilena's daughter. Ilena and I then began addressing each other as *comadre* (co-mother). Ilena's daughter calls me *madrina* (godmother), and I call her *waway* (my child). In spite of ideals of equality, the relationship of compadrazgo can also involve hierarchy and patronage (Albro 2001; Ossio 1984).

14. See Arnold 1992; Harris 1978, 1981; Harvey 1994; Mayer 2002; and Spedding 1997b; and especially Hamilton 1998 for discussion of Andean households in which men are not the "head."

15. In spite of their attention to racialized discourses of progress, Sullk'atas do not mobilize an extensive racial lexicon. They do not, for example, readily refer to the provincial or urban elite of Bolivia using the terms *criollo* or *mestizo* as in other regions of the Andes. See Van Vleet 2003b for discussion of a girl's attempt to protest when her teacher called her *india*. On race and gender in the Andes, see Canessa 2005b; de la Cadena 1995; and Weismantel 1997, 2001.

16. On education, see Luykx 1999; Stephenson 1999; and Canessa 2004; on migration to urban areas for work, see Gill 1994 and Paerregaard 1997; on consumption of commodities and mass media, see Bigenho 2002; Colloredo-Mansfeld 1999; and Goodale 2006; and on mandatory military service, see Canessa 2005a and Gill 1997. See also Canessa 2005b and Salman and Zoomers 2003.

17. For examples of Andean moral discourse at a variety of historical moments, see Guaman Poma de Ayala 1987; Harvey 1991; Mannheim 1991a:20; and Mannheim and Van Vleet 1998.

18. Mannheim 1991b:90; see also Alberti and Mayer 1974:21; Paerregaard 1997:88.

19. Earls argues that the power and authority wielded by *mistis* or "westernized Peruvians" is of the same kind as the power of the mountain forces: "Both mistis and Wamanis are *munaniyuq* . . . to the Quechua peasantry" (Earls 1969:67). Earls translates *munaniyuq* as "powerful ones," but a more literal translation of the Quechua would be "those whose being is to want."

Chapter 3

1. Bourdieu probably draws the notion of habitus from Marcel Mauss (1935, 1979), who uses the term in an essay on the person in which he suggests that all human beings have a sense of spiritual and corporeal individuality. See also Csordas 1990: 7–11.

2. Silveria used the verb tense that refers to both the present and recent past: "I am/was his mother" (*Paypata maman kani*).

3. On children and childbirth in the Andes, see, for example, Arnold and Yapita

1996; Bolin 2006; Bourque 1994; Bourque and Warren 1981:87–96; Canessa 2000; Morgan 1997; and Weismantel 1988.

4. Male midwives are common in the region, following the pattern of husbands assisting their wives in labor and acting as healers and diviners (*yatiri,* Ay.).

5. Interpreting Sullk'ata conceptions of birth and reproduction as an array of exotic cultural beliefs set against a standard of sexual reproduction as biological "facts" fails to recognize the ways in which sexual reproduction and scientific authority are integral aspects of cultural belief in the United States. See, among many others, Franklin and McKinnon 2001; Martin 1987, 1991; Morgan 1997.

6. On Spanish notions of blood, see Martinez-Alier 1989 and Lavrin 1989. On notions of blood and kinship in the United States, see Franklin and McKinnon 2001; Schneider 1968, 1984; Weston 1991, 2001; and Yanagisako and Delany 1995.

7. Bouysse-Cassagne and Harris 1987; Earls and Silverblatt 1976; Harris 1982; Isbell 1978, 1997; Zuidema 1978.

8. Isbell 1977, 1997; Mannheim 1998a:397–401; Earls and Silverblatt 1976; Mannheim and Van Vleet 1998.

9. On feeding and eating in the Andes, see especially Weismantel 1995, 1988 and Harvey 1998; see also Allen 2002; Bastien 1978; Bolton 1977; and Crandon Malamud 1991. On the importance of "substance" in anthropological discussions of kinship, see Carsten 1995; Franklin and McKinnon 2001; and Peletz 1995.

10. In recent years more Bolivians have migrated to Spain in search of work, and children have been left in the care of others. See Leinaweaver 2005a, 2005b, 2007 for important analyses of the circulation of children in Ayachucho, Peru, and Weismantel 1995 for discussion of adoption in Ecuador. On adoption in other regions, see, for example, Cardoso 1984; Carroll 1970; Franklin and McKinnon 2001; Glenn et al. 1994; Howell 2001; Modell 1994, 2001; Ragoné 1994; Stack 1997; and Trawick 1990.

11. Teresa also sometimes calls Nelson "grandfather" (*abuelo,* Sp.). Although Teresa's older sister quipped, "She calls him that because his hair is white," Nelson is in fact Faustino's uncle as well as his brother-in-law. By addressing him as *abuelo,* Teresa recognizes the generational difference between the two men and explicitly positions Faustino as her father.

12. I use the term "horizon" to complicate metaphors of base and superstructure. "Horizon" evokes both the sense that relations have an ideal or desired aspect (Trawick 1990) and the implication of a mediating zone (between earth and sky, nature and culture, biological and social) that is both a line of distinction and a zone of indeterminacy.

13. A structural model of hierarchy in the Andes was developed by R. Tom Zuidema and Ulpiano Quispe (1968), based in part on the ethnohistorical sources of

Santa Cruz Pachacuti Yamqui, who described Inca cosmology in 1613, and of Juan Pérez Bocanegra, who represented Inca kinship. See MacCormack 1991:322–331 for a photograph and detailed analysis of Pachacuti Yamqui's work. The model has been elaborated by several Andean scholars, including Arnold 1992; Astvaldsson 1998; and Earls 1969. Significantly, Astvaldsson 1998 incorporates women into the structural representation of political organization and recognizes the ways in which affinal relationships are overlaid upon descent in the Andes.

14. Each year in Sullk'ata different individuals, usually married men, hold one of four ranked positions. Every man is obligated to serve in each position once in his lifetime. Although women are not formally initiated as authorities, a man usually must be married to hold office. If he loses his wife during his term of office, another woman (typically a mother or sister) must serve in her place. On political organization in the Andes, see, for example, Abercrombie 1998; Gose 1994; and Rasnake 1988.

15. Allen 2002; Arnold 1997; Arnold and Yapita 1996, 1997; Astvaldsson 1998; Harris 1978, 1980; Isbell 1978, 1997.

16. One exception is the schoolteacher, who may reprimand other people's children, drawing authority from the state.

17. The category of compadrazgo also overlaps that of relatedness, especially affinity (Ossio 1992), and is an area of future research. Sullk'atas formalize relationships with their siblings, as well as other unrelated people, through compadrazgo. I was integrated into the community through compadrazgo as well as daily practices. Compadrazgo has been little studied in Bolivia, but see Albro 2001 and Leinaweaver 2005b.

Chapter 4

1. Analyses of emotion as culturally constituted challenge North American folk assumptions of emotion as personal, interior, and irrational, yet "natural" for all human beings. See, for example, Abu-Lughod 1986; Ahearn 2001a; Desjarlais 1992; Lutz 1988; Lutz and Abu-Lughod 1990; Lutz and White 1986; Lyon 1995; Myers 1979; Rebhun 1999; M. Rosaldo 1980a, 1984; R. Rosaldo 1984; Tapias 2006a, 2006b; and Wikan 1990. See Reddy 2001 for a critique of the discursive approach of Abu-Lughod and Lutz 1990.

2. I follow Abu-Lughod and Lutz 1990:9 in using the general premise of Foucault 1972:49 that discourses are "practices that systematically form the objects of which they speak." I extend their argument by highlighting the dialogical aspect of talk.

3. The stem *lik'i* is "fat" in Aymara ("grasa" in Bertonio 1956:195), and the term *lik'ichiri* is probably a linguistic retention among Sullk'atas who have shifted from

speaking Aymara to Quechua over the past several generations. The more common Quechua term for beings who take fat and blood from others is *ñak'aq*, the agentive form of the Quechua verb "to butcher by cutting the throat." Other Quechua terms for these beings are *phistaku* and *kharikhari*, and the Spanish translation is typically *degollador* (butcherer). On lik'ichiri, see, among others, Canessa 2000; Liffman 1977; Mannheim and Van Vleet 1998; Morote Best 1952; Mróz 1992; Stern 1987; Szeminski 1987; Taussig 1987:238–241; and Weismantel 1997, 2001.

4. Anthropological discussions of emotion have elided the multifaceted and simultaneous processes of communication (Besnier 1990; Brenneis 1990; Irvine 1990). An emphasis on emotion vocabulary, or the lexical approach (e.g., Lutz 1988; Rosaldo 1980a), illuminates discourse *about* emotion and the ways in which discourses about emotion operate. The expressive approach focuses on discourse *as* emotion or the enactment or representation of particular feelings, placing more emphasis on pragmatic, prosodic, and other communicative devices. These two aspects are integrally related: "Language is about something, does something, and is something in itself; the content and conduct of emotional communication are integrally related" (Brenneis 1990:114). See also Besnier 1993, 1990; and Brenneis 1987.

5. Parts of this story were previously published in Mannheim and Van Vleet 1998:328–329. Based on a tape-recording of the conversation and fieldnotes, I have included the nonverbal details of the interaction as well as my translation of the spoken words. The narrative appears in the same order in which it was spoken in conversation.

6. See Weismantel 2001 for a discussion of lik'ichiri and sexual exploitation.

7. For example, Canessa 2000; Mróz 1992; Taussig 1987; and Weismantel 1997, 2001.

8. On death in the Andes, see, for example, Allen 2002; Bourque 1994; Carter 1968; Crain 1991; Gose 1994; Harris 1982; and Van Vleet 1999.

9. Sullk'atas map these social and moral distinctions onto places (such as city and campo), as I describe in Chapter 2. Lorenzo and María's story also implies, however, that the geographical spaces *in between* "here" and "there" are dangerous. They warn me explicitly not to sleep *on the bus*. Although they would prefer one of their sons to come back to Sullk'ata, Lorenzo and María know that a city may become a place where relatedness is maintained. Unless a person is traveling with someone who knows and cares for her, she is most vulnerable when she traverses the expanses between those places of relative security, where people care for them and they care for others.

10. I use this example cautiously. The mutual associations of affect and the "domestic" are at once evocative (playing on cultural assumptions of how and when and where affective bonds are developed) and problematic if distinctly bounded cate-

gories such as internal and external, natural and cultural, female and male, and body and mind are maintained.

11. Several anthropologists have challenged the assumed duality of body and mind and have coined alternative terms (e.g., "embodied thoughts" in M. Rosaldo 1984 and "body thoughts" in Strathern 1996). As Thomas Csordas (1990:37) notes, even Michelle Rosaldo's (1984:143) understanding of emotion as embodied thoughts "precludes the question of how thought in the strict sense is itself embodied."

12. The story did not follow a single plotline leading to a resolution; but as Elinor Ochs and Lisa Capps (2001) point out, the lack of a coherent plot is not atypical of narratives that emerge in conversation. On this characteristic in Quechua narratives, see Allen 2002; Howard-Malverde 1990; and Mannheim and Van Vleet 1998.

13. Embedded text, including poetic subtleties and reported speech, shapes the meanings of a narrative in different ways across cultures and languages. See Ahearn 2001a; Besnier 1993; Brenneis 1982; Hill 1995; Hirsch 1998; Howard-Malverde 1989, 1990; Hymes 1981; Irvine 1996; Mannheim and Van Vleet 1998; Nuckolls 1996; Tedlock 1983; Urban 1984, 1991.

Chapter 5

1. Julia used the term *qusachakuy* to refer to her newly married state. *Qusachakuy* and *warmichakuy* are verbs constructed through the addition of suffixes to the nominal roots of "husband" (*qusa*) and "wife" (*warmi*). A literal translation would be "to be made to have a husband" or "to be made to have a wife." When Ilena asked me since when I had a husband (*Maykaqmanta qusachakunki?*), I interpreted her question to mean how long had I been married or how many years had passed since my wedding. An interpretation closer to her meaning would probably be "How long have you two been [living] together?" Sullk'atas use a different term, *kasarakuy* (from the Spanish *casar,* "to marry"), to refer to a wedding ceremony in the Catholic Church. Throughout this chapter I use the term "marriage" in the sense that Sullk'atas use it: marriages among Sullk'atas begin when a woman starts living with a man, often years before the couple has had a civil or religious wedding ceremony.

2. I shied away from asking young unmarried men about the practice, uncertain how questions from a(n allegedly) married woman would be interpreted. Jaime Daza's (1983) discussion of courtship and marriage among Quechua speakers in Cochabamba indicates the significance of the researcher's positionality. This study, by a native Quechua speaker, is based upon interviews and conversations with young men, who were far more straightforward in their discussions of warmi suway than were the single women or the adult married couples I interviewed.

3. For recent examples of ethnographies on marriage that highlight individual

practices, see Abu-Lughod 1993; Ahearn 2001a; J. Hirsch 2003; S. Hirsch 1998; and Rebhun 1999.

4. The souls of women who have died are remembered on Easter. This is the only fiesta in which women are the sponsors rather than a married couple.

5. For a more detailed description of the eve of Carnival, see Van Vleet 1999:225–229.

6. Daza 1983:77 argues that drunkenness is one of the parameters of suway as a social institution. See also Harvey 1994; Harris 1994; Isbell 1978; and Millones and Pratt 1989.

7. Earls 1971:91; Gose 1994:222; Isbell and Fernández 1977:44.

8. See Bolin 1998; Femenías 2005; and Weismantel 2001 on cross-dressing in the Andes.

9. For the link between high voices and the supernatural, see Salomon and Urioste 1991.

10. On inversion in Carnival, see, for example, Bakhtin 1968; Limón 1989; Parker 1991; and Turner 1969, 1986.

11. See, for example, Allen 1983; Arnold and Yapita 1996; Earls 1969; Harris 1994; Mannheim and Van Vleet 1998; and Urton 1985.

12. Allen 1983 and Urton 1985 argue that in the central Peruvian Andes adolescents occupy an ambiguous position between worlds and are likened to bears. Boys between nine and eighteen also represent bears in *ukuku* dances. Descriptions of these dances have a striking resemblance to Carnival dancing in Sullk'ata. For example, Gary Urton (1985:270–271) writes: "Ukuku dancers are boisterous creatures; they speak in high falsetto voices (like adolescents, whose voices are on the verge of changing), are often sarcastic, and make liberal use of sexual innuendo; all these forms of speech are completely contrary to normal adult dialogue . . . Their dances are often extremely aggressive; two or three ukukus will often hurl themselves at one another, trying to throw each other down."

13. Women, in contrast to men, are able to survive in the community without being married. Parents are often happy to have a daughter remain in the household to help them as they grow old. Brothers may assist women with agricultural tasks. A child is welcomed into the family and community. By feeding her child, a woman becomes an adult even when she does not marry.

14. A version of the Lovers' Story as told by Seferina was originally published in Mannheim and Van Vleet 1998. I include the Quechua transcription of this story in Appendix A, along with a longer, formally solicited version in English. Following Hymes (1980, 1981), I present this narrative in poetic form, with line breaks corresponding to pauses in speaking and emphasizing patterned repetition in the story. Emphasis is indicated by capitalization and pitch changes by words rising and fall-

ing in the text. See McDowell 1974 on the contrast between performed and reported stories.

15. See Weismantel 1997 and 2001 for a discussion of the phistaku as a sexualized and racialized being.

16. See Hopkins 1982; Mannheim 1998a; and Mannheim and Van Vleet 1998 for other stories that include the flooding of a lake and the moral transgressions of human beings.

17. See Dedenbach-Salazar Sáenz 1997; Mannheim 1986; and Mannheim and Van Vleet 1998 on evidentials in Quechua. See also Hanks 1996 on social and grammatical authority among the Maya.

18. Distinctions between "capture marriage," arranged marriage, "love" marriage, and elopement have been described for certain regions of the world (e.g., Ahearn 2001a). In spite of a long emphasis on kinship in the Andean ethnography, little information exists that would allow the creation of a typology of marriages. Neither Carter 1977 nor Bolton 1977 indicates a distinction between capture marriage and elopement.

19. See, for example, Canessa 2005a, 2005b; Gill 1997; and Weismantel 2001.

20. On polleras, consumption, and identity near Ayacucho, Peru, see Femenías 2005.

21. On women's property and inheritance, see Arnold and Yapita 1997; Bolton and Mayer 1977; Daza 1983; Isbell 1997; and Valderrama and Escalante 1998.

Chapter 6

1. On marriage in the Andes, see, for example, Arnold 1998; Bolin 1998; Bolton 1977; Carter 1977; Daza 1983; Harris 1986; Isbell 1978; Platt 1986:244; Urton 1985; and Valderrama and Escalante 1998.

2. See extended descriptions of the recommendations given to novios in Carter 1977:187–188 and Valderrama and Escalante 1998: 300–311. During the wedding fiesta, the rimanakuy may include godparents and other married adults and both sets of parents.

3. Initially I failed to understand why Osebio and Aleja had been afraid. In part my understanding of their story was colored by my perceptions of the young couples who had recently married. Neither of the young women who were stolen from Kallpa during Carnival, for example, talked about being fearful in the same way that Osebio remembered. Younger women may simply have been unwilling to express their anxieties about their transgressions, their potential obligations, or the expressed hostility between their families. There may also be gaps between what can be recognized and voiced years after the fact and what remains unspoken while still in the shadow of the

event. Alternatively, young people, especially those who have lived in cities and been exposed to more urban and western notions of "love," family, and gender, may have a greater sense of distance from the values and obligations of the local community.

4. Tantanakuy is old and widespread in the Andes, with antecedents in marriage practices among Andean peoples prior to the colonization of the Andes by the Spanish. See Daza 1983; Harris 1986, 1994; and Ossio 1984, 1992 for discussion of contemporary examples and colonial sources. The ethnohistorical accounts tend to emphasize the ritual service that a son-in-law provides for his wife's parents, by bringing wood and thatch or by assisting in the burial of his parents-in-law (Ossio 1992). See also Carter 1977:177 and Price 1965:319-320.

5. The classic distinction between "wife-givers" and "wife-takers" emphasizes the relationship between groups (Leach 1968, 1977; Lévi-Strauss 1969). For the Andes, most have emphasized the ascendancy of "wife-givers" over "wife-takers," following from a pattern of alliance in which the Inca gave women to men in regions that they had conquered (for example, Harris 1986:268-269, 1994; Saignes 1993; Zuidema 1964). The men then had to work in mink'a, providing tribute to the Inca. In the absence of this conquering power, Sullk'ata men seem to recognize little authority or obligation to work for affines. Here, however, I emphasize the relationships between individuals, not the relationships between groups.

6. I hired Dario as an assistant near the end of my fieldwork to help me interview additional people, especially men, about marriage practices. I had already conducted several interviews, had countless informal conversations, and observed several weddings on my own. Before beginning the interviews, I discussed with Dario the open-ended questions that I wanted to explore. In the interviews, however, Dario asked very specific questions, leading his interlocutors down the path of what he saw as most significant for an outsider to know about weddings. Although I now see ways in which these content-rich interviews indicate some important aspects of "native theories" of marriage, at the time I did not perceive the interviews as going well. After a week of working together in the campo, I told Dario that we had completed what we needed to accomplish. In addition to my frustration with the interviewing process, a good deal of gossip began circulating about my relationships with Dario: Why were we walking off together to different Sullk'ata communities? What were we doing in my room? How did I know him? What did my husband know of his visit? Having presented myself as a respectable married woman, I was hesitant to be the object of so much speculation.

7. See Appendix B for the Quechua versions of all Chapter 6 interview transcriptions.

8. The Quechua reads as follows: "purajmanta khuyanakuy; tukuy llak'anaspi yanapakuy; runa jina munakuy; ujnin onqosqa kajtin, mana unjin saqerparinanchu

tian; imatapis uj saqerparinan tian, ujnin kusisqa kananpaj; llakiypipis, kusiypipis, kuska kananku tian; purajmanta respetanakunanku tian, mana uj aswan creekunanchu tian; ujnin faltajtin, ofendejtin ujninta, perdonakumanku tian" (Equipo Pastoral 1989:10).

9. Harris 1994; Harvey 1991, 1993, 1994. See also Chapter 7.

10. This soup is made and served in the same way when a new house is built and roofed.

11. The suffix *-ntin* is "inclusive in nature, with implications of totality, spatial inclusion of one thing in another, or identification of two elements as members of the same category" (Solá and Cusihuamán 1978, cited in Platt 1986:245).

12. Arnold 1998; Harris 1989, 1995; Isbell 1978, 1997.

13. Carter 1977:196 notes that Aymara speakers in the region of Lake Titicaca accounted for three different categories of things during a wedding: *wayqʼa* (a tray of fruit and bread); *ayni* (produce or some manufactured item); and *arku* (money).

14. See note 6 above.

15. Sebastián's father was a laborer on the finca and died when Sebastián was a child. Sebastián's mother gave him a cow as his inheritance. When, many years later, his mother's second husband died, Sebastián and Gregoria buried him and later waited for his soul during the fiestas of Todos Santos and Carnival. Because he acted in the place of a son, Sebastián was given his "stepfather's" land as an inheritance by the community. Prior to this he rented land from Gregoria's brother. (See Ossio 1992 and Harris 1985 for other descriptions of this particular relationship between a woman's husband and her brother.) Gregoria herded sheep from her parent's house sometime after the wedding fiesta, but these were not a "wedding gift." Sullkʼata women often give a lamb to each of their daughters. The child comes to own all of that animal's offspring. The sheep were Gregoria's own, which had been combined with her mother's flock since she was a little girl.

16. Arku prestations may be used to buy movable wealth, especially livestock (and particularly bulls), but should not, according to Laymis, be used to purchase items for personal consumption, such as oranges or bread or sweets. This is the case because converting arku to livestock "contributes to long-term recycling" of wealth, fertility, and energy in the ayllu, whereas "gratification through individual consumption is potentially incompatible with this aim" (Harris 1989:245).

17. Harris (1989) derives this relationship for Aymara speakers both through association of the word for manure (*manu* or *wanu*) with the Spanish word *guano* (the potassium-rich bird deposits on the western coast of Peru) and through Ludovico Bertonio's *Vocabulario* (1956), in which "debt" and "loan" are both given as *manu*, with the second root as *mira* (or Sp. *logro*, profit); with the related phrase *mira warmi* or fertile woman.

18. Among many examples, see Appadurai 1986, 1991; Canessa 2005a; Crain 1996; Harris 1989, 1995; Parry and Bloch 1989; Sallnow 1987, 1989; and Taussig 1980, 1987.

Chapter 7

1. See, for example, de la Cadena 1991, 1997; Harvey 1994, 1998; and Weismantel 1988:174 on the relationship between mother-in-laws and daughter-in-laws. I use *qhachuni* and *swira* interchangeably here with "daughter-in-law" and "mother-in-law." Because of a long history of language contact in the Andean region (Mannheim 1991b, 1992), some words may be etymologically Spanish yet integrated into Quechua pronunciation and grammar. Among the lexical terms borrowed from Spanish into Quechua are kin terms, including those for mother-in-law and father-in-law (*suegra* and *suegro*, Sp.), which I have chosen to represent according to their Quechua pronunciations. The use of these terms in Quechua does not necessarily have the same semantic value as the use of the terms in Spanish. For discussion of the difficulties of translation of kin terms in contact zones, see Collins 1983.

2. For analyses of spousal abuse in the Andes, see Harris 1994 and Harvey 1994. Harris 1994 emphasizes symbolic as well as material foundations for domestic violence between spouses, exploring gender and masculinity as well as diverse contexts and types of violence in the Andes. Harvey 1994 argues that the relationship of affinity, in addition to sexual difference, is significant to violence between spouses. See Allen 2002; Bolin 1998; Canessa 2005a; Carter 1977; Cereceda 1978; Daza 1983; Hopkins 1982; Millones and Pratt 1989; Platt 1987:97, 111; and Starn 1999:173–183 for discussions of violence in Andean courtship practices and between married partners. Hamilton 1998:195–197 describes ideologies of collaboration and nonviolence in Chancaló, Ecuador. See Hünefeldt 1997, 2000 and Christiansen 2004 for discussions of gendered and affinal conflict in nineteenth-century Peru.

3. Affinal violence for Sullk'atas is in part shaped by a social and historical context that includes state-sponsored violent repression of miners, campesinos, and cocagrowers; regional conflicts between native Andean ethnic groups over land; traditional ritual battles; strife among community members; and the physical punishment sometimes used to reinforce hierarchy between parents and children. Little has been written on the relationship between state-sponsored violence and domestic violence in the Andes, but see Goldstein 2004; Nash 1993:77; and Starn 1999:155–191. For an excellent analysis of spousal abuse in the local context, including regional violence between ethnic groups, see Harris 1994. On the relationship between ethnicity, ritual battles (*tinkuy*), and courtship practices in the Andes, see Allen 2002:154–162; Bolin 1998; Bouysse-Cassagne and Harris 1987; Cereceda 1978; Harris 1994; Har-

alcol: cane alcohol

alma: spirit of the dead; soul

alma wasi: house where someone has recently died

apay: to carry (an inanimate object)

apu: ancestor, mountain, (male) supernatural force

aqha: corn beer

arku: gifts given by groom's sisters

aumentu: monetary prestation given in addition to another prestation

aya: spirit of the dead; soul

ayni: labor exchange; reciprocity

campesino: peasant, rurally based native Andean

cariño: affection

chicha: corn beer

cholita: used interchangeably with *sipas,* young unmarried woman; also market
woman

ch'uñu: freeze-dried whole potatoes

comadres: "co-mothers," spiritual kin

compadrazgo: ritual kinship

compadres: "co-parents," spiritual kin

condenado: condemned soul

costumbre: custom

envidia: envy

joven: youth, teenager (usually refers to a young man)

kasarakuy: to marry (indicates a Catholic ceremony with a community fiesta)

kwintu: folk story

lik'ichiri: being who steals the life force of others

llakikuy: to sorrow or feel sadness

mañay: to lend

maqay: to hit

marido/a: spouse

mayores: married adults

mikhuy: to eat

mink'a: work done in an unequivalent exchange

munakuy: to love

mut'i: snack of boiled corn and peas

novios: bride and groom, unmarried couple

oka: a small, sweet tuber

padrinos: godparents

papa wayk'u: potatoes boiled in their skins

parientes legítimos: "true kin"

partero/a: midwife

pollera: full skirt worn by native Andean women

pusay: to carry (an animate object)

qaytu: hand-spun yarn

qhachuni: daughter-in-law

qhariwarmi: married couple, literally man-wife/woman

qusawarmi: married couple, literally husband-wife/woman

quy: to give

regalu: gift given without explicit obligation

sullk'a: younger sibling

suway: to steal

swira: mother-in-law

tantanakuy: to live together before civil or church marriage

tullqa: son-in-law

turu wasu: wooden bowl with a team of oxen carved in the center

urqu: mountain, male supernatural force

uyway: to raise a child

waqay: to cry

warmi: woman, wife

warmi mañay: betrothal ceremony; literally, to lend a woman

warmi suway: to steal a woman

wawa: child

wawachakuy: to make a child into a son or daughter; adoption

yanantin: mirrored pairs

yunta: team of oxen

Abercrombie, Thomas. 1998. Pathways of Memory and Power: Ethnography and History among an Andean People. Madison: University of Wisconsin Press.

———. 1991. To be Indian, to be Bolivian: "Ethnic" and "national" discourses of identity. *In* Nation States and Indians in Latin America, Greg Urban and Joel Sherzer, eds., pp. 95–130. Austin: University of Texas Press.

Abu-Lughod, Lila. 1993. Writing Women's Worlds: Bedouin Stories. Berkeley: University of California Press.

———. 1990a. The romance of resistance: Tracing transformations of power through Bedouin women. American Ethnologist 17: 41–55.

———. 1990b. Shifting politics of Bedouin love poetry. *In* Language and the Politics of Emotion, Catherine A. Lutz and Lila Abu-Lughod, eds., pp. 24–45. Cambridge: Cambridge University Press.

———. 1986. Veiled Sentiments: Honor and Poetry in a Bedouin Society. Berkeley: University of California Press.

Abu-Lughod, Lila, and Catherine Lutz. 1990. Introduction: Emotion, discourse, and the politics of everyday life. *In* Language and the Politics of Emotion, Catherine A. Lutz and Lila Abu-Lughod, eds., pp. 1–23. New York: Cambridge University Press.

Ahearn, Laura. 2001a. Invitations to Love: Literacy, Love Letters and Social Change in Nepal. Ann Arbor: University of Michigan Press.

———. 2001b. Language and agency. Annual Review of Anthropology 30: 109–137.

Alberti, Giorgio, and Enrique Mayer, eds. 1974. Reciprocidad e intercambio en los Andes Peruanos. Lima: Instituto de Estudios Peruanos.

Albó, Xavier. 1979. ¿Khitipxtansa? ¿Quiénes somos? Identidad localista, étnica y clasista en los Aymaras de hoy. América Indígena 34(3): 477–528.

Albro, Robert. 2006. Actualidades: Bolivia's "Evo phenomenon": From identity to what? Journal of Latin American Anthropology 11(2): 408–428.

———. 2001. Fictive feasting: Mixing and parsing Bolivian popular sentiment. Anthropology and Humanism 25(2): 142–157.

Allen, Catherine. 2002 [1988]. The Hold Life Has: Coca and Cultural Identity in an Andean Community. 2nd ed. Washington, D.C.: Smithsonian Institution Press.

———. 1983. Of bear-men and he-men: Bear metaphors and male self-perception in a Peruvian community. Latin American Indian Literatures 7(1): 38–51.

Alonso, Ana María. 1994. Politics of space, time and substance: State formation, nationalism and ethnicity. Annual Review of Anthropology 23: 379–405.

Anderson, Benedict. 1983. Imagined Communities: Reflections on the Origin and Spread of Nationalism. London: Verso.

Andreas, Peter, and Kenneth E. Sharpe. 1992. Cocaine politics in the Andes. Current History 91(562): 74–79.

Anzaldúa, Gloria, ed. 1990. Making Face, Making Soul: Haciendo Caras. San Francisco: Aunt Lute Foundation.

Appadurai, Arjun. 1992. Putting hierarchy in its place. In Rereading Cultural Anthropology, George Marcus, ed., pp. 191–210. Durham: Duke University Press.

———. 1991. Global ethnoscapes: Notes and queries for a transnational anthropology. In Working in the Present, Richard Fox, ed., pp. 191–210. Santa Fe: School of American Research Press.

———. 1990. Topographies of the self: Praise and emotion in Hindu India. In Language and the Politics of Emotion, Catherine A. Lutz and Lila Abu-Lughod, eds., pp. 92–112. Cambridge: Cambridge University Press.

Appadurai, Arjun, ed. 1986. The Social Life of Things. Cambridge: Cambridge University Press.

Arnold, Denise. 1992. La casa de adobes y piedras del inka: Género, memoria y cosmos en Qaqachaka. In Hacia un orden andina de las cosas: Tres pistas de los Andes meridionales, Denise Arnold, Domingo Jiménez, and Juan de Dios Yapita, eds., pp. 31–108. La Paz, Bolivia: Hisbol/Instituto de Lengua y Cultura Aymara.

Arnold, Denise, ed. 1998. Gente de carne y hueso: Las tramas de parentesco en los

Andes. Vol. 2. Parentesco y género en los Andes. La Paz: Centre for Indigenous America Studies and Exchange/Instituto de Lengua y Cultura Aymara.

―――. 1997. Más allá del silencio: Las fronteras de género en los Andes. Vol. 1. Parentesco y género en los Andes. La Paz, Bolivia: Centre for Indigenous America Studies and Exchange/Instituto de Lengua y Cultura Aymara.

Arnold, Denise, and Juan de Dios Yapita. 1997. La lucha por la dote en un ayllu andino. *In* Más allá del silencio: Fronteras de género en los Andes, Vol. 1, Denise Arnold, ed., pp. 109–173. La Paz: Centre for Indigenous America Studies and Exchange/Instituto de Lengua y Cultura Aymara.

―――. 1996. Los caminos de género en Qaqachaka: Saberes femeninos y discursos textuales alternativos en los Andes. *In* Ser mujer indígena, chola, o birlocha en la Bolivia postcolonial de los años 90, Silvia Rivera Cusicanqui, ed., pp. 303–392. La Paz: Hisbol/Instituto de Lengua y Cultura Aymara.

Astvaldsson, Astvaldur. 1998. Las cabezas que hablan: Autoridad, género y parentesco en una comunidad andina. *In* Gente de carne y hueso: Las tramas de parentesco en los Andes, Vol. 2, Parentesco y género en los Andes, Denise Arnold, ed., pp. 227–261. La Paz: Centre for Indigenous America Studies and Exchange/Instituto de Lengua y Cultura Aymara.

Bakhtin, Mikhail M. 1981. The Dialogic Imagination. Michael Holquist and C. Emerson, eds. and trans. Austin: University of Texas Press.

―――. 1968. Rabelais and His World. Cambridge, MA: MIT Press.

Bamberg, Michael. 2006. Stories: Big or small—why do we care? Special Issue: Narrative—State of the Art. Narrative Inquiry 16(1): 139–147.

Barragán, Rossana. 1997. Miradas indiscretas a la patria potestad: Articulación social y conflictos de género en la ciudad de La Paz, Siglos XVII–XIX. *In* Más allá del silencio: Fronteras de género en los Andes, Vol. 1, Denise Arnold, ed., pp. 407–454. La Paz: Centre for Indigenous America Studies and Exchange/Instituto de Lengua y Cultura Aymara.

Bastien, Joseph. 1978. Mountain of the Condor: Metaphor and Ritual in an Andean Ayllu. American Ethnological Society, Monograph no. 64. St. Paul, MN: West Publishing Company.

Bauman, Richard, and Charles Briggs. 1990. Poetics and performance as critical perspectives on language and social life. Annual Review of Anthropology 19: 59–88.

Behar, Ruth. 1995. Rage and redemption: Reading the life story of a Mexican marketing woman. *In* The Dialogic Emergence of Culture, Dennis Tedlock and Bruce Mannheim, eds., pp. 148–178. Urbana and Chicago: University of Illinois Press.

Benjamin, Walter. 1992 [1923]. The task of the translator. H. Zohn, trans. *In* Theories of Translation: An Anthology of Essays from Dryden to Derrida, Rainer Schulte and John Biguenet, eds., pp. 71–82. Berkeley: University of California Press.

Bertonio, Ludovico. 1956 [1612]. Vocabulario de la lengua Aymara. La Paz: Don Bosco.

Besnier, Niko. 1993. Reported speech and affect on Nukulaelae Atoll. *In* Responsibility and Evidence in Oral Discourse, Jane H. Hill and Judith T. Irvine, eds., pp. 161–181. Cambridge: Cambridge University Press.

———. 1990. Language and affect. Annual Review of Anthropology 19: 419–451.

———. 1989. Information withholding as a manipulative and collusive strategy in Nukulaelae gossip. Language in Society 18: 315–341.

Bigenho, Michelle. 2002. Sounding Indigenous: Authenticity in Bolivian Music Performance. New York: Palgrave.

Blackwood, Evelyn. 2005. Wedding bell blues: Marriage, missing men, and matrifocal follies. American Ethnologist 32(1): 3–19.

———. 2000. Webs of Power: Women, Kin, and Community in a Sumatran Village. Lanham, MD: Rowman and Littlefield Publishers, Inc.

Blunt, Alison, and Gillian Rose, eds. 1994. Writing Women and Space: Colonial and Postcolonial Geographies. New York: Guilford Press.

Bolin, Inge. 2006. Growing Up in a Culture of Respect: Child Rearing in Highland Peru. Austin: University of Texas Press.

———. 1998. Rituals of Respect: The Secret of Survival in the High Peruvian Andes. Austin: University of Texas Press.

Bolton, Ralph. 1981. Susto, hostility, and hypoglycemia. Ethnology 20: 261–276.

———. 1977. The Qolla marriage process. *In* Andean Kinship and Marriage, Ralph Bolton and Enrique Mayer, eds., pp. 217–239. Washington, D.C.: American Anthropological Association.

Bolton, Ralph, and Charlene Bolton. 1975. Conflictos en la familia andina. Cusco: Centro de Estudios Andinos.

Bolton, Ralph, and Enrique Mayer, eds. 1977. Andean Kinship and Marriage. Washington, D.C.: American Anthropological Association.

Borneman, John. 1996. Until death do us part: Marriage/death in anthropological discourse. American Ethnologist 23(2): 215–235.

———. 1992. Belonging in Two Berlins: Kin, State, Nation. Cambridge: Cambridge University Press.

Bourdieu, Pierre. 1990a. The Logic of Practice. Richard Nice, trans. Stanford, CA: Stanford University Press.

———. 1990b. The scholastic point of view. Loïc J. D. Wacquant, trans. Cultural Anthropology 5(4): 380–391.

———. 1984. Distinction: A Social Critique of the Judgement of Taste. Richard Nice, trans. Cambridge, MA: Harvard University Press.

————. 1977 [1972]. Outline of a Theory of Practice. Richard Nice, trans. Cambridge: Cambridge University Press.

————. 1976. Marriage strategies as strategies of social reproduction. *In* Family and Society, Robert Forster and Orest Ranum, eds., pp. 117–144. Baltimore: Johns Hopkins University Press.

Bourque, Nicole. 1994. Savages and angels: The spiritual, social, and physical development of individuals and households in Andean life-cycle festivals. Ethnos 60(1–2): 99–114.

Bourque, Susan, and Barbara Kay Warren. 1981. Women of the Andes: Patriarchy and Social Change in Two Peruvian Towns. Ann Arbor: University of Michigan Press.

Bouysse-Cassagne, Thérèse. 1986. Urco and uma: Aymara concepts of space. *In* Anthropological History of Andean Polities, John Murra, Nathan Wachtel, and Jacques Revel, eds., pp. 201–227. New York: Cambridge University Press.

Bouysse-Cassagne, Thérèse, and Olivia Harris. 1987. Pacha: En torno al pensamiento aymara. *In* Tres reflexiones sobre el pensamiento andino, Thérèse Bouysse-Cassagne, Olivia Harris, Tristan Platt, and Vernonica Cereceda, eds., pp. 11–59. La Paz: HISBOL.

Brenneis, Donald. 1990. Shared and solitary sentiments: The discourse of friendship, play and anger in Bhatgaon. *In* Language and the Politics of Emotion, Catherine Lutz and Lila Abu-Lughod, eds., pp. 113–125. Cambridge: Cambridge University Press.

————. 1987. Performing passions: Aesthetics and politics in an occasionally egalitarian community. American Ethnologist 14: 236–250.

————. 1982. Grog and gossip in Bhatgaon: Style and substance in Fiji Indian conversation. American Ethnologist 11: 487–506.

Briggs, Charles. 1986. Learning How to Ask: A Sociolinguistic Appraisal of the Role of the Interview in Social Science Research. New York: Cambridge University Press.

Brubaker, Rogers, and Frederick Cooper. 2000. Beyond "identity." Theory and Society 29(1): 1–47.

Buchler, Ira R., and Henry A. Selby. 1968. Kinship and Social Organization: An Introduction to Theory and Method. New York: Macmillan Company.

Bucholtz, Mary, A. C. Liang, and Laurel Sutton. 1999. Reinventing Identities: The Gendered Self in Discourse. New York: Oxford University Press.

Buechler, Hans, and Judith-Maria Buechler. 1996. The World of Sofía Velásquez: The Autobiography of a Bolivian Market Vendor. New York: Columbia University Press.

Butler, Judith. 1993. Bodies That Matter: On the Discursive Limits of Sex. New York: Routledge.

————. 1990. Gender Trouble: Feminism and the Subversion of Identity. New York: Routledge.

Canessa, Andrew. 2005a. The Indian within, the Indian without: Citizenship, race, and sex in a Bolivian hamlet. *In* Natives Making Nation: Gender, Indigeneity, and the State in the Andes, Andrew Canessa, ed., pp. 130–155. Tucson: University of Arizona Press.

————. 2004. Reproducing racism: Schooling and race in highland Bolivia. Race, Ethnicity and Education 7(2): 185–204.

————. 2000. Fear and loathing on the Kharisiri trail: Alterity and identity in the Andes. Journal of the Royal Anthropological Institute 6(4): 705–720.

Canessa, Andrew, ed. 2005b. Natives Making Nation: Gender, Indigeneity, and the State in the Andes. Tucson: University of Arizona Press.

Cardoso, Ruth C. L. 1984. Creating kinship: The fostering of children in favela families in Brazil. *In* Kinship Ideology and Practice in Latin America, Raymond T. Smith, ed., Elizabeth Hansen, trans., pp. 196–203. Chapel Hill: University of North Carolina Press.

Carroll, Vern, ed. 1970. Adoption in Eastern Oceania. Honolulu: University of Hawaii Press.

Carsten, Janet. 2004. After Kinship. Cambridge: Cambridge University Press.

————. 1995. The substance of kinship and the heat of the hearth: Feeding, personhood, and relatedness among Malays in Pulau Lagkawi. American Ethnologist 22: 223–241.

Carsten, Janet, ed. 2000. Cultures of Relatedness: New Approaches to the Study of Kinship. Cambridge: Cambridge University Press.

Carter, William E. 1977. Trial marriage in the Andes? *In* Andean Kinship and Marriage, Ralph Bolton and Enrique Mayer, eds., pp. 177–216. Washington, D.C.: American Anthropological Association.

————. 1968. Secular reinforcement in Aymara death ritual. American Anthropologist 70: 238–263.

Cereceda, Verónica. 1978. Mundo Quechua. Cochabamba, Bolivia: Editorial Serrano.

Certeau, Michel de. 1984. The Practice of Everyday Life. Steven Rendall, trans. Berkeley and Los Angeles: University of California Press.

Christian, Barbara. 1987. The race for theory. Cultural Critique 6: 51–63.

Christiansen, Tanja. 2004. Disobedience, Slander, Seduction, and Assault: Women and Men in Cajamarca, Peru, 1862–1900. Austin: University of Texas Press.

Classen, Constance. 1993. Inca Cosmology and the Human Body. Salt Lake City: University of Utah Press.

Clifford, James. 1983. On ethnographic authority. Representations 1(2): 118–146.

Clifford, James, and George Marcus, eds. 1986. Writing Culture: The Poetics and Politics of Ethnography. Berkeley: University of California Press.

Collier, Jane Fishburne. 1988. Marriage and Inequality in Classless Societies. Stanford: Stanford University Press.

Collier, Jane, and Sylvia Yanagisako, eds. 1987. Gender and Kinship: Essays toward a Unified Analysis. Stanford: Stanford University Press.

Collins, Jane. 1988. Unseasonal Migrations: The Effects of Rural Labor Scarcity in Peru. Princeton, NJ: Princeton University Press.

———. 1986. The household and relations of production in southern Peru. Comparative Studies in Society and History 28(4): 651–671.

———. 1983. Translation traditions and the organization of productive activity: The case of Aymara affinal kinship terms. Proceedings—Southern Anthropological Society 16(1): 11–21.

Collins, Patricia Hill. 2004. Black Sexual Politics: African Americans, Gender, and the New Racism. New York: Routledge.

———. 1990. Black Feminist Thought: Knowledge, Consciousness, and the Politics of Empowerment. New York: Routledge.

Colloredo-Mansfeld, Rudi. 1999. The Native Leisure Class: Consumption and Cultural Creativity in the Andes. Chicago: University of Chicago Press.

Comaroff, John. 1987. Sui genderis: Feminism, kinship theory, and structural domains. In Gender and Kinship: Essays Toward a Unified Analysis, Jane F. Collier and Sylvia Yanagisako, eds., pp. 53–85. Stanford: Stanford University Press.

Connolly, William E. 1987. Politics and Ambiguity. Madison: University of Wisconsin Press.

Coronil, Fernando. 1996. Beyond orientalism: Towards non-imperial geohistorical categories. Cultural Anthropology 11(1): 51–87.

Crain, Mary. 1996. The gendering of ethnicity in the Ecuadorian Andes: Native women's self-fashioning in the urban marketplace. In Machos, Mistresses, and Madonnas: Contesting the Power of Latin American Gender Imagery, Marit Melhuus and Kristi Anne Stølen, eds., pp. 134–183. London and New York: Verso Press.

———. 1991. Poetics and politics in the Ecuadorian Andes: Women's narratives of death and devil possession. American Ethnologist 18(1): 67–89.

Crandon-Malamud, Libbet. 1991. From the Fat of Our Souls: Social Change, Political Process, and Medical Pluralism in Bolivia. Berkeley: University of California Press.

Csordas, Thomas. 1990. Embodiment as a paradigm for anthropology. Ethos 18: 5–47.

Csordas, Thomas, ed. 1994. Embodiment and Experience: The Existential Ground of Culture and the Self. New York: Cambridge University Press.

Cusihuamán Gutiérrez, Antonio. 1976. Gramática Quechua: Cuzco-Collao. Lima: Instituto de Estudios Peruanos.

Daniel, E. Valentine. 1997. Mood, moment, and mind. *In* Violence and Subjectivity, Veena Das, Arthur Kleinman, Mamphela Ramphele, and Pamela Reynolds, eds., pp. 333–366. Berkeley: University of California Press.

———. 1996. Charred Lullabies: Chapters in an Anthropography of Violence. Princeton, NJ: Princeton University Press.

Dávila, Amanda, ed. 1996. Legislación andina y violencia contra la mujer (Legislación del seminario andino "Legislación y Violencia" Cochabamba 1995). La Paz: Vicepresidencia de la República de Bolivia y Ministerio de Desarrollo Humano.

Daza, Jaime. 1983. The Cultural Context of Courtship and Betrothal in a Quechua Community of Cochabamba, Bolivia. Dissertation. University of California, Los Angeles.

DeBernardi, Jean. 1995. Tasting the water. *In* The Dialogic Emergence of Culture, Dennis Tedlock and Bruce Mannheim, eds., pp. 179–197. Urbana: University of Illinois Press.

Dedenbach-Salazar Sáenz, Sabine. 1997. Point of view and evidentiality in the Huarochirí texts (Peru, 17th century). *In* Creating Contexts in Andean Cultures, Rosaleen Howard-Malverde, ed., pp. 149–167. Oxford: Oxford University Press.

Degregori, Carlos Ivan. 1989. Introducción. *In* Amor brujo: Imagen y cultura del amor en los Andes, Luis Millones and Mary Louise Pratt, eds., pp. 9–12. Lima, Peru: Instituto de Estudios Peruanos.

de la Cadena, Marisol. 2000. Indigenous Mestizos: The Politics of Race and Culture in Cuzco, Peru, 1919–1991. Durham, NC: Duke University Press.

———. 1997. Matrimonio y etnicidad en comunidades andinas (Chitapampa, Cusco). *In* Más allá del silencio: Fronteras de género en los Andes, Vol. 1, Denise Arnold, ed., pp. 123–149. La Paz: Centre for Indigenous America Studies and Exchange/Instituto de Lengua y Cultura Aymara.

———. 1995. "Women are more Indian": Ethnicity and gender in a community near Cuzco. *In* Ethnicity, Markets, and Migration in the Andes: At the Crossroads of History and Anthropology, Brooke Larson and Olivia Harris, eds., pp. 329–348. Durham, NC: Duke University Press.

———. 1991. "Las mujeres son más indias": Etnicidad y género en una comunidad del Cusco. Revista Andina 9(1): 7–29.

Desjarlais, Robert. 1996. Presence. *In* The Performance of Healing, Carol Laderman and Marina Roseman, eds., pp. 143–164. New York: Routledge.

———. 1992. Body and Emotion: The Aesthetics of Illness and Healing in the Nepal Himalayas. Philadelphia: University of Pennsylvania Press.

di Leonardo, Micaela, ed. 1991. Gender at the Crossroads of Knowledge: Feminist Anthropology in the Postmodern Era. Berkeley: University of California Press.

Dore, Elizabeth, and Maxine Molyneux, eds. 2000. Hidden Histories of Gender and the State in Latin America. Durham, NC: Duke University Press.

Duranti, Alessandro. 1994. From Grammar to Politics: Linguistic Anthropology in a Western Samoan Village. Berkeley: University of California Press.

Duranti, Alessandro, and Charles Goodwin, eds. 1992. Rethinking Context: Language as an Interactive Phenomenon. New York: Cambridge University Press.

Duvoils, Pierre. 1973. Huari y llacuaz: Una relación prehispánica de oposición y complementariedad. Revista del Museo Nacional (Lima) 39: 153–191.

Earls, John. 1971. The structure of modern Andean social categories. Journal of the Steward Anthropological Society 3(1): 69–106.

———. 1969. The organisation of power in Quechua mythology. Journal of the Steward Anthropological Society 1(1): 63–82.

Earls, John, and Irene Silverblatt. 1976. La realidad física y social en la cosmología andina. Proceedings of the 42nd International Congress of Americanists 4: 299–325.

Eckert, Penelope. 1993. Cooperative competition in adolescent "girl talk." In Gender and Conversational Interaction, Deborah Tannen, ed., pp. 32–61. New York: Oxford University Press.

Eckert, Penelope, and Sally McConnell-Ginet. 1995. Constructing meaning, constructing selves: Snapshots of language, gender and class from Belten High. In Gender Articulated: Language and the Socially Constructed Self, Kira Hall and Mary Bucholtz, eds., pp. 469–507. New York: Routledge.

Eng, David L. 2003. Transnational adoption and queer diasporas. Social Text 21(3): 1–37.

Equipo Pastoral de la Zona Centro de la Diócesis de Potosí. 1989. Diusninchej Kuska Chasqanta Ama Runa T'aqachunchu. Sucre: Impreso en Talleres Gráficos Qori Llama.

Evans-Pritchard, E. E. 1951. Kinship and Marriage among the Nuer. Oxford, UK: Clarendon Press.

Fabian, Johannes. 1983. Time and the Other: How Anthropology Makes Its Object. New York: Columbia University Press.

Feld, Steven, and Keith Basso, eds. 1996. Senses of Place. Santa Fe, NM: School of American Research Press.

Femenías, Blenda. 2005. Gender and the Boundaries of Dress. Austin: University of Texas Press.

Ferraro, E. 2004. Owing and being in debt: A contribution from the Northern Andes of Ecuador. Social Anthropology 12(1): 77–94.

Flores Galindo, Alberto. 1988. Buscando un Inca: Identidad y utopía en los Andes. Lima: Instituto de Apoyo Agrario.

Fortes, Meyer. 1969. Kinship and the Social Order: The Legacy of Lewis Henry Morgan. Chicago: University of Chicago Press.

Foucault, Michel. 1978. The History of Sexuality. Vol. 1. An Introduction. Robert Hurley, trans. London: Allen Lane.

————. 1972. The Archaeology of Knowledge. A. M. Sheridan, trans. New York: Harper Colophon.

Fox, Richard G., ed. 1991. Recapturing Anthropology: Working in the Present. Santa Fe, NM: School of American Research Press.

Franklin, Sarah, and Susan McKinnon, eds. 2001. Relative Values: Reconfiguring Kinship Studies. Durham, NC: Duke University Press.

Freeman, Mark. 2006. Life "on holiday"?: In defense of big stories. Special Issue: Narrative—State of the Art. Narrative Inquiry 16(1): 131–138.

Fricke, Tom. 2006. Imagining Yhebe: Of friendship and the field. Special Issue: The Documentary Imagination, Part Two. Tom Fricke and Keith Taylor, eds. Michigan Quarterly Review 45(1) (Spring): 197–217. Ann Arbor: University of Michigan Press.

————. 1997. Marriage change as moral change: Culture, virtue and demographic transition. In The Continuing Demographic Transition, Gavin W. Jones, Robert M. Douglas, John C. Caldwell, and Rennie M. D'Souza, eds., pp. 183–212. Oxford: Oxford University Press.

Gal, Susan. 1995. Language, gender and power: An anthropological review. In Gender Articulated: Language and the Socially Constructed Self, Kira Hall and Mary Bucholtz, eds., pp. 169–182. New York: Routledge.

García, María Elena. 2000. Ethnographic responsibility and the anthropological endeavor: Beyond identity discourse. Anthropological Quarterly 73(2): 89–101.

García Argañarás, Fernando. 1997. The drug war at the supply end: The case of Bolivia. Latin American Perspectives 24(5): 59–80.

Geertz, Clifford. 1973. The Interpretation of Cultures. New York: Basic Books.

Geertz, Hildred. 1959. The vocabulary of emotion: A study of Javanese socialization processes. Psychiatry 22: 225–236.

Gelles, Paul H. 1995. Equilibrium and extraction: Dual organization in the Andes. American Ethnologist 22(4): 710–742.

Gellner, Ernest. 1987 [1973]. The Concept of Kinship and Other Essays. London: Basil Blackwell.

Georgakopoulou, Alexandra. 2006. Thinking big with small stories in narrative and identity analysis. Special Issue: Narrative—State of the Art. Narrative Inquiry 16(1): 122–130.

Gill, Lesley. 1997. Creating citizens, making men: The military and masculinity in Bolivia. Cultural Anthropology 12(4): 527–550.

———. 1994. Precarious Dependencies: Gender, Class, and Domestic Service in Bolivia. New York: Columbia University Press.

Ginzburg, Carlo. 1989. Clues: Roots of an evidential paradigm. *In* Clues, Myths, and the Historical Method, John Tedeschi and Anne C. Tedeschi, trans., pp. 96–125. Baltimore: Johns Hopkins University Press.

Glenn, Evelyn Nakano, Grace Chang, and Linda Rennie Forcey, eds. 1994. Mothering: Ideology, Experience and Agency. New York: Routledge.

Godoy, Ricardo A. 1986. The fiscal role of the Andean ayllu. Man 21(4): 723–741.

Godoy, Ricardo, and Mario DeFranco. 1992. High inflation and Bolivian agriculture. Journal of Latin American Studies 24: 617–637.

Goffman, Erving. 1981. Forms of Talk. Philadelphia: University of Pennsylvania Press.

Goldstein, Daniel M. 2004. The Spectacular City: Violence and Performance in Urban Bolivia. Durham, NC: Duke University Press.

Goodale, Mark. 2006. Reclaiming modernity: Indigenous cosmopolitanism and the coming of the second revolution in Bolivia. American Ethnologist 33(4): 634–649.

Goodwin, Marjorie. 1990. He-Said-She-Said: Talk as Social Organization among Black Children. Bloomington: University of Indiana Press.

Goodwin, Marjorie H., and Charles Goodwin. 2001. Emotion within situated activity. *In* Linguistic Anthropology: A Reader, Alessandro Duranti, ed., pp. 239–257. Malden, MA: Blackwell.

Gordon, Linda. 1988. Heroes of their Own Lives: The Politics and History of Family Violence, Boston 1880–1960. New York: Viking.

Gose, Peter. 1994. Deathly Waters and Hungry Mountains: Agrarian Ritual and Class Formation in an Andean Town. Toronto: University of Toronto Press.

———. 1986. Sacrifice and the commodity form in the Andes. Man 21: 296–310.

Gow, Peter. 1991. Of Mixed Blood: Kinship and History in Peruvian Amazonia. New York: Oxford University Press.

———. 1989. The perverse child: Desire in a Native Amazonian subsistence economy. Man 24: 567–582.

Grosz, Elizabeth. 1994. Volatile Bodies: Toward a Corporeal Feminism. Bloomington and Indianapolis: Indiana University Press.

Guaman Poma de Ayala, Felipe. 1987 [1615]. El primer nueva crónica y buen gobierno (1583–1615). John V. Murra, Rolena Adorno, and Juan Urioste, eds. Madrid: Historia 16.

Guillet, David. 1992. Covering Ground: Communal Water Management and the State in the Peruvian Highlands. Ann Arbor: University of Michigan Press.

Gutiérrez, Ramón A. 1991. When Jesus Came the Corn Mothers Went Away: Marriage, Sexuality, and Power in New Mexico, 1500–1846. Stanford: Stanford University Press.

Gutmann, Matthew. 1996. The Meanings of Macho: Being a Man in Mexico City. Berkeley: University of California Press.

Hall, Kira, and Mary Bucholtz, eds. 1995. Gender Articulated: Language and the Socially Constructed Self. New York: Routledge.

Hamilton, Sarah. 1998. The Two-Headed Household: Gender and Rural Development in the Ecuadorian Andes. Pittsburgh: University of Pittsburgh Press.

Hanks, William. 1996. Language and Communicative Practice. Boulder, CO: Westview Press.

———. 1990. Referential Practice: Language and Lived Space among the Maya. Chicago: University of Chicago Press.

Haraway, Donna. 1991. Simians, Cyborgs, and Women: The Reinvention of Nature. New York: Routledge.

Harris, Olivia. 1995. The sources and meanings of money: Beyond the market paradigm in an Ayllu of Northern Potosí. In Ethnicity, Markets, and Migration in the Andes: At the Crossroads of History and Anthropology, Brooke Larson and Olivia Harris, eds., pp. 297–328. Durham, NC: Duke University Press.

———. 1994. Condor and bull: The ambiguities of masculinity in Northern Potosí. In Sex and Violence: Issues in Representation and Experience, Penelope Harvey and Peter Gow, eds., pp. 40–65. New York: Routledge.

———. 1989. Money and the morality of exchange: The sources and meanings of money in Northern Potosí, Bolivia. In Money and the Morality of Exchange, J. Parry and Maurice Bloch, eds., pp. 232–268. Cambridge: Cambridge University Press.

———. 1986. From asymmetry to triangle: Symbolic transformations in Northern Potosí. In Anthropological History of Andean Polities. John Murra, Nathan Wachtel, and Jacques Revel, eds., pp. 260–280. New York: Cambridge University Press.

———. 1985. Ecological duality and the role of the center: Northern Potosí. In Andean Ecology and Civilization, S. Masuda, I. Shimada, and C. Morris, eds., pp. 311–335. Tokyo: University of Tokyo Press.

———. 1982. The dead and the devils among the Bolivian Laymi. In Death and the Regeneration of Life, Maurice Bloch and Jonathan Parry, eds., pp. 45–73. New York: Cambridge University Press.

———. 1981. Households as natural units. In Of Marriage and the Market: Women's Subordination in International Perspective, Kate Young, Carol Wolkowitz, and Roslyn McCullagh, eds., pp. 49–68. London: CSE Books.

———. 1980. The power of signs: Gender, culture and the wild in the Bolivian

Andes. *In* Nature, Culture and Gender, Carol MacCormack and Marilyn Strathern, eds., pp. 70–94. Cambridge: Cambridge University Press.

———. 1978. Complementarity and conflict: An Andean view of women and men. *In* Sex and Age as Principles of Social Differentiation, J. S. La Fontaine, ed., pp. 21–40. Association of Social Anthropologists Monograph 17. London: Academic Press.

Harrison, Regina. 1989. Signs, Songs, and Memory in the Andes: Translating Quechua Language and Culture. Austin: University of Texas Press.

Harvey, Penelope. 1998. Los "hechos naturales" de parentesco y género en un contexto andino. *In* Gente de carne y hueso: Las tramas de parentesco en los Andes, Denise Y. Arnold, ed., pp. 69–82. La Paz: Centre for Indigenous America Studies and Exchange/Instituto de Lengua y Cultura Aymara.

———. 1994. Domestic Violence in the Andes. *In* Sex and Violence: Issues in Representation and Experience, pp. 66–89. New York: Routledge.

———. 1993. Género, comunidad y confrontación: Relaciones de poder en la embriaguez en Ocongate, Perú. *In* Borrachera y memoria: La experiencia de lo sagrado en los Andes, Thierry Saignes, ed., pp. 113–138. La Paz: HISBOL/IFEA.

———. 1991. Drunken speech and the construction of meaning: Bilingual competence in the Southern Andes. Language in Society 20: 1–36.

Harvey, Penelope, and Peter Gow, eds. 1994. Sex and Violence: Issues in Representation and Experience. New York: Routledge.

Heise, Lori. 1995. Violence, sexuality, and women's lives. *In* Conceiving Sexuality: Approaches to Sex Research in a Postmodern World, Richard Parker and John Gagnon, eds., pp. 109–134. New York: Routledge Press.

Herrero, Joaquín, S.J., and Federico Sánchez de Lozada. 1983. Diccionario quechua-español/Español-quechua. Cochabamba: Editorial C.E.F.

Hill, Jane. 1995. The voices of Don Gabriel: Responsibility and self in a modern Mexicano narrative. *In* The Dialogic Emergence of Culture, Dennis Tedlock and Bruce Mannheim, eds., pp. 97–147. Urbana: University of Illinois Press.

Hines, Caitlin. 1999. Rebaking the pie: The woman as dessert metaphor. *In* Reinventing Identities: The Gendered Self in Discourse, Mary Bucholtz, A. C. Liang, and Laurel A. Sutton, eds., pp. 145–162. New York: Oxford University Press.

Hirsch, Jennifer. 2003. A Courtship after Marriage: Sexuality and Love in Mexican Transnational Families. Berkeley: University of California Press.

Hirsch, Susan F. 1998. Pronouncing and Persevering: Gender and the Discourses of Disputing in an African Islamic Court. Chicago: University of Chicago Press.

Hopkins, Diane. 1982. Juego de enemigos. Allpanchis 20: 167–188.

Howard-Malverde, Rosaleen. 1995. Pachamama is a Spanish word: Linguistic tension

between Aymara, Quechua, and Spanish in Northern Potosí (Bolivia). Anthropological Linguistics 37(2): 141–168.

————. 1990. The Speaking of History: "Willapaakushayki" or Quechua Ways of
Telling the Past. London: Institute of Latin American Studies Research Papers.

————. 1989. Storytelling strategies in Quechua narrative performance. Journal of
Latin American Lore 15: 3–71.

————. 1988. Talking about the past: Tense and testimonials in Quechua narrative
discourse. Amerindia 13: 125–155.

Howard-Malverde, Rosaleen, ed. 1997. Creating Context in Andean Cultures. New
York: Oxford University Press.

Howell, Signe. 2001. Self-conscious kinship: Some contested values in Norwegian
transnational adoption. In Relative Values: Reconfiguring Kinship Studies, Sarah
Franklin and Susan McKinnon, eds., pp. 203–223. Durham: Duke University
Press.

Hünefeldt, Christine. 2000. Liberalism in the Bedroom: Quarreling Spouses in
Nineteenth-Century Lima. University Park: Pennsylvania State University Press.

————. 1997. Las cambiantes del conflicto matrimonial en Lima durante el siglo 19
y su significado social. In Más allá del silencio: Fronteras de género en los Andes,
Vol. 1, Denise Arnold, ed., pp. 387–406. La Paz: Centre for Indigenous America
Studies and Exchange/Instituto de Lengua y Cultura Aymara.

Hymes, Dell H. 1981. "In Vain I Tried to Tell You": Essays in Native American Eth-
nopoetics. Philadelphia: University of Pennsylvania Press.

————. 1980. Particle, pause and pattern in American Indian narrative verse. American Indian Culture and Research Journal 4(4): 7–51.

Irvine, Judith. 1996. Shadow conversations: The indeterminacy of participant roles.
In Natural Histories of Discourse, Michael Silverstein and Greg Urban, eds., pp.
131–159. Chicago: University of Chicago Press.

————. 1990. Registering affect: Heteroglossia in the linguistic expression of emotion. In Language and the Politics of Emotion, Catherine A. Lutz and Lila Abu-
Lughod, eds., pp. 126–161. New York: Cambridge University Press.

————. 1982. Language and affect: Some cross-cultural issues. In Contemporary Perceptions of Language: Interdisciplinary Dimensions, Heidi Byrnes, ed., pp. 31–47.
Washington, D.C.: Georgetown University Press.

Isbell, Billie Jean. 1997. De inmaduro a duro: Simbólico femenino y los esquemas
andinos de género. In Más allá del silencio: Las fronteras de género en los Andes,
Denise Arnold, ed., pp. 253–300. La Paz, Bolivia: Centre for Indigenous America
Studies and Exchange/Instituto de Lengua y Cultura Aymara.

————. 1978. To Defend Ourselves: Ecology and Ritual in an Andean Village. Austin:
University of Texas Press.

———. 1977. Those who love me: An analysis of Andean kinship and reciprocity within a ritual context. *In* Andean Kinship and Marriage, Ralph Bolton and Enrique Mayer, eds., pp. 81–105. Washington, D.C.: American Anthropological Association.

Isbell, Billie Jean, and Fredy Amilcar Roncalla Fernández. 1977. The ontogenesis of metaphor: Riddle games among Quechua speakers seen as cognitive discovery procedures. Journal of Latin American Lore 3(1): 19–49.

Island, David, and Patrick Letellier. 1991. Men Who Beat the Men Who Love Them. Binghamton, NY: Harrington Park Press.

Jacobs-Huey, Lanita. 2002. The natives are gazing and talking back: Reviewing the problematics of positionality, voice, and accountability among "native" anthropologists. American Anthropologist 104(3): 791–804.

Jankowiak, William R., and Edward Fischer. 1992. A cross-cultural perspective on romantic love. Ethnology 31(2): 149–155.

Jeffery, Patricia, and Roger Jeffery. 1996. Don't Marry Me to a Ploughman!: Women's Everyday Lives in Rural North India. Boulder: Westview Press.

Jelin, Elizabeth. 1991. Family, Household, and Gender Relations in Latin America. London: Kegan Paul and United Nations Educational, Scientific and Cultural Organization.

Johnson, Lyman, and Sonya Lipsett-Rivera, eds. 1998. The Faces of Honor: Sex, Shame, and Violence in Colonial Latin America. Albuquerque: University of New Mexico Press.

Josselin de Jong, J. P. E. 1952. Lévi-Strauss' Theory on Kinship and Marriage. Museum voor Volkekunde, Nedelelingen 10. Leiden: E. J. Brill.

Kendall, Christopher, and Wayne Martino, eds. 2006. Gendered Outcasts and Sexual Outlaws: Sexual Oppression and Gender Hierarchies in Queer Men's Lives. New York: Harrington Park Press.

Klein, Herbert. 2003. A Concise History of Bolivia. New York: Oxford University Press.

———. 1993. Haciendas and "Ayllus": Rural Society in the Bolivian Andes in the Eighteenth and Nineteenth Centuries. Stanford, CA: Stanford University Press.

Kristeva, Julia. 1993. The speaking subject is not innocent. *In* Freedom and Interpretation, Barbara Johnson, ed., pp. 147–174. New York: Basic Books.

———. 1980. Desire in Language. Leon Roudiez, trans. New York: Columbia University Press.

Kulick, Don. 1998. Travestí: Sex, Gender, and Culture among Brazilian Transgendered Prostitutes. Chicago: University of Chicago Press.

Lagos, Maria L. 1994. Autonomy and Power: The Dynamics of Class and Culture in Rural Bolivia. Philadelphia: University of Pennsylvania Press.

―――. 1993. "We have to learn to ask": Hegemony, diverse experiences, and antagonistic meanings in Bolivia. American Ethnologist 20(1): 52–71.

Lakoff, Robin Tolmach. 1995. Cries and whispers: The shattering of the silence. In Gender Articulated: Language and the Socially Constructed Self, Kira Hall and Mary Bucholtz, eds., pp. 25–50. New York: Routledge.

Lamphere, Louise. 2005. Replacing heteronormative views of kinship and marriage. American Ethnologist 32(1): 34–36.

Lancaster, Roger N. 1992. Life Is Hard: Machismo, Danger, and the Intimacy of Power in Nicaragua. Berkeley and Los Angeles: University of California Press.

Langer, Erick D. 1989. Economic Change and Rural Resistance in Southern Bolivia, 1880–1930. Stanford, CA: Stanford University Press.

Lara, Jesús. 1991. Diccionario qheshwa-castellano, castellano-qheshwa. 3rd ed. La Paz: Editorial Los Amigos del Libro.

Larson, Brooke, and Olivia Harris, eds. 1995. Ethnicity, Markets, and Migration in the Andes: At the Crossroads of History and Anthropology. Durham, NC: Duke University Press.

Lavrin, Asunción, ed. 1989. Sexuality and Marriage in Colonial Latin America. Lincoln: University of Nebraska Press.

Leach, Edmund. 1977 [1954]. Political Systems of Highland Burma: A Study of Kachin Social Structure. London: Athlone Press.

―――. 1968. Rethinking Anthropology. London: Athlone Press.

Leinaweaver, Jessaca. 2007. On moving children: The social implications of Andean child circulation. American Ethnologist 34(1): 163–180.

―――. 2005a. Accompanying and overcoming: Subsistence and sustenance in an Andean City. Michigan Discussions in Anthropology 15: 150–182.

―――. 2005b. Familiar Ways: Child Circulation in Andean Peru. Ph.D. dissertation. University of Michigan.

Léons, Madeline Barbara, and Harry Sanabria, eds. 1997. Coca, Cocaine, and the Bolivian Reality. Albany: State University of New York Press.

Letellier, Patrick. 1994. Gay and bisexual male domestic violence victimization: Challenges to feminist theory and response to violence. Violence and Victims 9(2): 95–106.

Lévi-Strauss, Claude. 1969 [1949]. Elementary Structures of Kinship. J. H. Bell and I. R. von Sturmer, trans. Boston: Beacon Press.

―――. 1963. Structural Anthropology. Claire Jacobson and Brooke Grundfest Schoepf, trans. New York: Basic Books.

―――. 1956. The family. In Man, Culture, and Society, H. L. Shapiro, ed., pp. 333–357. New York: Oxford University Press.

————. 1955. The structural study of myth. Journal of American Folklore 67: 428–444.

Levy, R. I. 1984. Emotion, knowing, and culture. *In* Culture Theory: Essays on Mind, Self, and Emotion, R. A. Shweder and R. A. LeVine, eds., pp. 214–237. New York: Cambridge University Press.

Liffman, Paul. 1977. Vampires of the Andes. Michigan Discussions in Anthropology 2: 205–226.

Limón, José. 1989. Carne, *carnales,* and the carnivalesque: Bakhtinian *batos,* disorder and narrative discourse. American Ethnologist 16: 471–486.

Lira, Jorge A. 1944. Diccionario kkéchuwa-español. Tucumán, Argentina: Universidad Nacional de Tucumán.

Livia, Anna, and Kira Hall, eds. 1997. Queerly Phrased: Language, Gender, and Sexuality. New York: Oxford University Press.

Lobel, Kerry, ed. 1986. Naming the Violence: Speaking Out about Lesbian Battering. Seattle: Seal Press.

Lutz, Catherine. 1988. Unnatural Emotions: Everyday Sentiments in a Micronesian Atoll and Their Challenge to Western Theory. Chicago: University of Chicago Press.

————. 1982. The domain of emotion words on Ifaluk. American Ethnologist 9: 113–128.

Lutz, Catherine, and Lila Abu-Lughod, eds. 1990. Language and the Politics of Emotion. New York: Cambridge University Press.

Lutz, Catherine, and Geoffrey White. 1986. The anthropology of emotions. Annual Review of Anthropology 15: 405–436.

Luykx, Aurolyn. 1999. The Citizen Factory: Schooling and Cultural Production in Bolivia. Albany: State University of New York Press.

Lyon, Margot L. 1995. Missing emotion: The limitations of cultural constructionism in the study of emotion. Cultural Anthropology 10: 244–263.

MacCormack, Carol, and Marilyn Strathern, eds. 1980. Nature, Culture, and Gender. Cambridge: Cambridge University Press.

MacCormack, Sabine. 1991. Religion in the Andes: Vision and Imagination in Early Colonial Peru. Princeton: Princeton University Press.

MacLeod, Arlene Elowe. 1992. Hegemonic relations and gender resistance: The new veiling as accommodating protest in Cairo. Signs 17(3): 533–557.

Mageo, Jeannette Marie. 1998. Theorizing Self in Samoa: Emotions, Genders, and Sexualities. Ann Arbor: University of Michigan Press.

Malinowski, Bronislaw. 1963 [1913]. The Family among the Australian Aborigines: A Sociological Study. New York: Schocken Books.

Mangan, Jane. 2005. Trading Roles: Gender, Ethnicity, and the Urban Economy in Colonial Potosí. Durham: Duke University Press.

Mannheim, Bruce. 1998a. A nation surrounded. *In* Native Traditions in the Post-conquest World, Elizabeth Boone and Tom Cummins, eds., pp. 381–418. Washington, D.C.: Dumbarton Oaks.

———. 1998b. "Time, not the syllables, must be counted": Quechua parallelism, word meaning, and cultural analysis. *In* Linguistic Form and Social Action. Michigan Discussions in Anthropology 13: 245–287

———. 1992. The Inka language in the colonial world. Colonial Latin American Review 1(1–2): 77–108.

———. 1991a. After dreaming: Image and interpretation in Southern Peruvian Quechua. Etnofoor 4(2): 43–79.

———. 1991b. The Language of the Inka since the European Invasion. Austin: University of Texas Press.

———. 1986. Popular song and popular grammar: Poetry and metalanguage. Word 37(1–2): 45–73.

Mannheim, Bruce, and Dennis Tedlock. 1995. Introduction. *In* The Dialogic Emergence of Culture, Dennis Tedlock and Bruce Mannheim, eds., pp. 1–32. Urbana: University of Illinois Press.

Mannheim, Bruce, and Krista Van Vleet. 1998. The dialogics of Southern Quechua narrative. American Anthropologist 100(2): 326–346.

Martin, Emily. 1991. Egg and the sperm: How science has constructed a romance based on stereotypical women's roles. Signs: Journal of Women in Culture and Society 16(3): 485–501.

———. 1987. The Woman in the Body: A Cultural Analysis of Reproduction. Boston: Beacon Press.

Martinez-Alier, Verena. 1989 [1974]. Marriage, Class and Colour in Nineteenth-Century Cuba: A Study of Racial Attitudes and Sexual Values in a Slave Society. Ann Arbor: University of Michigan Press.

Massey, Doreen. 1994. Space, Place, and Gender. Minneapolis: University of Minnesota Press.

Mauss, Marcel. 1979 [1934]. Sociology and Psychology: Essays. London: Routledge and Kegan Paul. Reprinted from 1950 Sociologie et anthropologie, Parts 3–6. Paris: Presses Universitaires de France.

———. 1969 [1925]. The Gift: Forms and Functions of Exchange in Archaic Societies. Ian Cunnison, trans. New York: W. W. Norton.

———. 1935. The techniques of the body. Economy and Society 2: 70–88.

Mayer, Enrique. 2002. The Articulated Peasant: Household Economies in the Andes. Boulder, CO: Westview Press.

————. 1984. A tribute to the household: Domestic economy and the *encomienda* in colonial Peru. *In* Kinship Ideology and Practice in Latin America, Raymond Smith, ed., pp. 85–117. Chapel Hill: University of North Carolina Press.

————. 1977. Beyond the nuclear family. *In* Andean Kinship and Marriage, Ralph Bolton and Enrique Mayer, eds., pp. 60–80. Washington, D.C.: American Anthropological Association.

McDermott, R. P., and Henry Tylbor. 1995. On the necessity of collusion in conversation. *In* The Dialogic Emergence of Culture, Dennis Tedlock and Bruce Mannheim, eds., pp. 218–236. Urbana: University of Illinois Press.

McDowell, John H. 1974. Aspects of verbal art in Bolivian Quechua. Folklore Annual 6: 68–81.

Merry, Sally Engle. 2006. Human Rights and Gender Violence: Translating International Law into Local Justice. Chicago: University of Chicago Press.

Millones, Luis, and Mary Pratt. 1989. Amor brujo: Imagen y cultura del amor en los Andes. Lima: Instituto de Estudios Peruanos.

Ministerio de Desarrollo Humano, Secretaría Nacional de Asuntos Étnicos de Género y Generacionales, Subsecretaría de Asuntos de Género. 1996a. Ley 1674 contra la violencia en là familia o doméstica. La Paz: Ministerio de Desarrollo Humano.

————. 1996b. Más que madres. La Paz, Bolivia: Ministerio de Desarrollo Humano.

Modell, Judith. 2001. Open adoption: Extending families, exchanging facts. *In* New Directions in Anthropological Kinship, Linda Stone, ed., pp. 246–263. Lanham: Rowman and Littlefield Publishers.

————. 1994. Kinship with Strangers: Adoption and Interpretations of Kinship in American Culture. Berkeley: University of California Press.

————. 1986. In search: The purported biological basis of parenthood. American Ethnologist 13: 646–661.

Mohanty, Chandra Talpade. 1984. Under western eyes: Feminist scholarship and colonial discourses. Boundary 2 12(3)/13(1): 333–358.

Montoya, Rosario, Lessie Jo Frazier, and Janise Hurtig, eds. 2002. Gender's Place: Feminist Anthropologies of Latin America. New York: Palgrave Macmillan.

Morató Peña, Luis, and Luis Morató Lara. 1993. Quechua boliviano trilingüe: Curso intermedio. Cochabamba, Bolivia: Universidad Mayor de San Simón/Instituto de Idiomas "Tawantisuyu."

Morgan, Lynn M. 1997. Imagining the unborn in the Ecuadorian Andes. Feminist Studies 23(2): 323–350.

Morote Best, Efraín. 1952. El degollador (Nakaq). Tradición 11: 67–91.

Morris, Rosalind. 1995. All made up: Performance theory and the new anthropology of sex and gender. Annual Review of Anthropology 24: 567–592.

Morrison, Andrew R., and María Loreto Biehl, eds. 1999. Too Close to Home: Domestic Violence in the Americas. Washington, D.C.: Inter-American Development Bank.

Mróz, Marcin. 1992. Los runa y los wiraqucha: La ideología social andina en la tradición oral quechua. Warsaw: Centro de Estudios Latinoamericanos, Universidad de Varsovia.

Myers, Fred. 1979. Emotions and the Self: A Theory of Personhood and Political Order among Pintupi Aborigines. Ethos 7: 343–370.

Narayan, Kirin. 1993. How native is a "native" anthropologist? American Anthropologist 95(3): 671–686.

Nash, June. 1993 [1979]. We Eat the Mines and the Mines Eat Us: Dependency and Exploitation in Bolivian Tin Mines. New York: Columbia University Press.

———. 1992. Interpreting social movements: Bolivian resistance to economic conditions imposed by the International Monetary Fund American Ethnologist 19(2): 275–293.

Nuckolls, Janis B. 1996. Sounds Like Life: Sound-Symbolic Grammar, Performance, and Cognition in Pastaza Quechua. Oxford: Oxford University Press.

Ochs, Elinor. 1979. Transcription as theory. In Developmental Pragmatics, Elinor Ochs and B. B. Schieffelin, eds., pp. 43–72. New York: Academic Press.

Ochs, Elinor, and Lisa Capps. 2001. Living Narratives: Creating Lives in Everyday Storytelling. Cambridge, MA: Harvard University Press.

———. 1996. Narrating the self. Annual Review of Anthropology 25(1): 19–43.

Olivera, Oscar. 2004. Cochabamba!: Water War in Bolivia. Cambridge, MA: South End Press.

Ortner, Sherry, and Harriet Whitehead, eds. 1981. Sexual Meanings: The Cultural Construction of Gender and Sexuality. New York: Cambridge University Press.

Ossio, Juan M. 1992. Parentesco, reciprocidad, y jerarquía en los Andes: Una aproximación a la organización social de la comunidad de Andamarca. Lima: Pontificia Universidad Católica de Perú.

———. 1984. Cultural continuity, structure, and context: Some peculiarities of the Andean compadrazgo. In Kinship Ideology and Practice in Latin America, Raymond T. Smith, ed., pp. 118–146. Chapel Hill: University of North Carolina Press.

Overing, Joanna, and Alan Passes. 2000. The Anthropology of Love and Anger: The Aesthetics of Conviviality in Native Amazonia. New York: Routledge.

Paerregaard, Karsten. 1997. Linking Separate Worlds: Urban Migrants and Rural Lives in Peru. Oxford/New York: Berg.

Parker, Richard. 1999. Beneath the Equator: Cultures of Desire, Male Homosexuality, and Emerging Gay Communities in Brazil. New York: Routledge.

———. 1991. Bodies, Pleasures and Passions. New York: Beacon Press.

Parker, Richard, and John Gagnon, eds. 1995. Conceiving Sexuality: Approaches to Sex Research in a Postmodern World. New York: Routledge.

Parry, J., and M. Bloch, eds. 1989. Money and the Morality of Exchange. Cambridge/ New York: Cambridge University Press.

Paulson, Susan. 1996. Familias que no "conyugan" e identidades que no conjugan. In Ser mujer indígena, chola birlocha en la Bolivia postcolonial de los años 90, Silvia Rivera Cusicanqui, ed., pp. 85–161. La Paz: Subsecretaría de Asuntos de Género.

Peletz, Michael G. 2001. Ambivalence in kinship since the 1940s. In Relative Values: Reconfiguring Kinship Studies, Sarah Franklin and Susan McKinnon, eds., pp. 413–444. Durham, NC: Duke University Press.

———. 1995. Kinship studies in late twentieth-century anthropology. Annual Review of Anthropology 24: 343–372.

Platt, Tristan. 1987. Entre ch'axwa y muxsa, para una historia del pensamiento político aymara. In Tres Reflexiones sobre el pensamiento andino, pp. 61–132. La Paz: HISBOL.

———. 1986 [1978]. Mirrors and maize: The concept of yanantin among the Macha of Bolivia. In Anthropological History of Andean Polities, John Murra, Nathan Wachtel, and Jacques Revel, eds., pp. 228–259. New York: Cambridge University Press.

———. 1982. The role of the Andean ayllu in the reproduction of the petty commodity regime in Northern Potosí (Bolivia). In Ecology and Exchange in the Andes, David Lehmann, ed., pp. 27–69. New York: Cambridge University Press.

———. 1978. Mapas coloniales de la Provincia de Chayanta: Dos visiones conflictivas de un solo paisaje. In Estudios bolivianos en homenaje a Gunnar Mendoza, Martha U. de Aguierre and Gunnar Mendoza L., eds., pp. 101–118. La Paz: n.p.

Polanyi, Livia. 1989. Telling the American Story: A Structural and Cultural Analysis of Conversational Storytelling. Cambridge, MA: MIT Press.

Pollock, Della. 2006. Memory, remembering, and histories of change: A performance praxis. In The Sage Handbook of Performance Studies, D. Soyini Madison and Judith Hamera, eds., pp. 87–105. Thousand Oaks, CA: Sage.

———. 1999. Telling Bodies, Performing Birth. New York: Columbia University Press.

Postero, Nancy. 2005. Indigenous responses to neoliberalism: A look at the Bolivian uprising of 2003. PoLAR: Political and Legal Anthropology Review 28(1): 73–92.

Price, Richard. 1965. Trial marriage in the Andes. Ethnology 4(3): 310–322.

Radcliffe, Sarah, and Sallie Westwood. 1997. Remaking the Nation. New York: Routledge.

Ragoné, Heléna. 1994. Surrogate Motherhood: Conception in the Heart. Boulder, CO: Westview Press.

Ragoné, Heléna, and France Winddance Twine, eds. 2000. Ideologies and Technologies of Motherhood: Race, Class, Sexuality, Nationalism. New York: Routledge.

Raheja, Gloria, and Ann G. Gold. 1994. Listen to the Heron's Words: Reimagining Gender and Kinship in North India. Berkeley: University of California Press.

Rappaport, Joanne. 1994. Cumbe Reborn: An Andean Ethnography of History. Chicago: University of Chicago Press.

Rasnake, Roger. 1988. Domination and Cultural Resistance: Authority and Power among an Andean People. Durham, NC: Duke University Press.

Rebhun, L. A. 1999. The Heart Is Unknown Country: Love in the Changing Economy of Northeast Brazil. Palo Alto: Stanford University Press.

Reddy, William M. 2001. The Navigation of Feeling: A Framework for the History of Emotions. New York: Cambridge University Press.

Reiter, Rayna. 1975. Toward an Anthropology of Women. New York: Monthly Review Press.

Remy, María Isabel. 1991. Los discursos sobre la violencia en los Andes: Algunas reflexiones a propósito del Chiaraje. In Poder y violencia en los Andes, Henrique Urbano and Mirko Lauer, eds., pp. 261–275. Cusco, Perú: Centro de Estudios Regionales Andinos, Bartolomé de las Casas.

Ricoeur, Paul. 1981. Hermeneutics and the Human Sciences. Cambridge: Cambridge University Press.

Rivera Cusicanqui, Silvia, ed. 1996. Ser mujer indígena, chola o birlocha en la Bolivia postcolonial de los años 90. La Paz: Subsecretaría de Asuntos de Género.

———. 1993. Anthropology and society in the Andes: Themes and issues. Critique of Anthropology 13(1): 77–96.

Robertson, Jennifer. 2002. Reflexivity redux: A pithy polemic on "positionality." Anthropology Quarterly 75(4): 785–792.

Rosaldo, Michelle. 1984. Toward an anthropology of self and feeling. In Culture Theory: Essays on Mind, Self and Emotion, Richard A. Shweder and Robert A. LeVine, eds., pp. 137–157. New York: Cambridge University Press.

———. 1980a. Knowledge and Passion: Ilongot Notions of Self and Social Life. New York: Cambridge University Press.

———. 1980b. The use and abuse of anthropology: Reflections on feminism and cross-cultural understanding. Signs 5(3): 389–417.

Rosaldo, Renato. 1989. Culture and Truth: The Remaking of Social Analysis. Boston: Beacon Press.

———. 1984. Grief and a headhunter's rage: On the cultural force of emotions. In Text, Play, and Story: The Construction and Reconstruction of Self and Society, E. Bruner, ed., pp. 178–195. Washington, D.C.: American Ethnological Society.

Roseberry, William. 1989. Anthropologies and Histories. New Brunswick, NJ: Rutgers University Press.

Rösing, Ina. 1997. Los diez géneros de Amarete, Bolivia. *In* Más allá del silencio: Fronteras de género en los Andes, Vol. 1, Denise Arnold, ed., pp. 77–92. La Paz: Centre for Indigenous America Studies and Exchange/Instituto de Lengua y Cultura Aymara.

Rubin, Gayle. 1975. The traffic in women: Notes on the "political economy" of sex. *In* Toward an Anthropology of Women, Rayna R. Reiter, ed., pp. 157–210. New York: Monthly Review Press.

Saignes, Thierry, ed. 1993. Borrachera y memoria: La experiencia de lo sagrado en los Andes. La Paz: HISBOL/IFEA.

Sallnow, Michael J. 1989. Precious metals in the Andean moral economy. *In* Money and the Morality of Exchange, J. Parry and M. Bloch, eds., pp. 209–231. Cambridge: Cambridge University Press.

———. 1987. Pilgrims of the Andes: Regional Cults in Cusco. Washington, D.C.: Smithsonian Institution Press.

Salman, Tony, and Annelies Zoomers, eds. 2003. Imaging the Andes: Shifting Margins of a Marginal World. Amsterdam: Aksant.

Salomon, Frank. 1997. "Conjunto de nacimiento" y "línea de esperma" en el manuscrito quechua de Huarochirí (ca. 1608). *In* Más allá del silencio: Las fronteras de género en los Andes, Vol. 1, Denise Y. Arnold, ed., pp. 301–322. La Paz: Centre for Indigenous America Studies and Exchange/Instituto de Lengua y Cultura Aymara.

Salomon, Frank, and George L. Urioste, trans. 1991. The Huarochirí Manuscript: A Testament of Ancient and Colonial Andean Religion. Austin: University of Texas Press.

Sanabria, Harry. 1993. The Coca Boom and Rural Social Change in Bolivia. Ann Arbor: University of Michigan Press.

Sánchez Parga, Jorge. 1990. ¿Por qué golpearla? Quito, Ecuador: Centro Andino de Acción Popular.

Sanjek, Roger, ed. 1990. Fieldnotes: The Makings of Anthropology. Ithaca, NY: Cornell University Press.

Scheffler, Harold W. 1991. Sexism and naturalism in the study of kinship. *In* Gender at the Crossroads of Knowledge: Feminist Anthropology in the Postmodern Era, Micaela di Leonardo, ed., pp. 361–382. Berkeley: University of California Press.

Scheper-Hughes, Nancy. 1992. Death without Weeping: The Violence of Everyday Life in Brazil. Berkeley: University of California Press.

Schneider, David. 1984. A Critique of the Study of Kinship. Ann Arbor: University of Michigan Press.

————. 1972. What is kinship all about? *In* Kinship Studies in the Morgan Centennial Year, Priscilla Reining, ed., pp. 32–63. Washington, D.C.: Anthropological Society of Washington.

————. 1968. American Kinship: A Cultural Account. Englewood Cliffs, NJ: Prentice Hall.

Scott, James C. 1990. Domination and the Arts of Resistance: Hidden Transcripts. New Haven: Yale University Press.

Seligmann, Linda J. 1993. Between worlds of exchange: Ethnicity among Peruvian market women. Cultural Anthropology 8(2): 187–213.

Silverblatt, Irene. 1988. Imperial dilemmas, the politics of kinship, and Inca reconstructions of history. Comparative Studies in Society and History 30(1): 83–102.

————. 1987. Moon, Sun, and Witches: Gender Ideologies and Class in Inca and Colonial Peru. Princeton, NJ: Princeton University Press.

Smith, Raymond T., ed. 1984. Kinship Ideology and Practice in Latin America. Chapel Hill: University of North Carolina Press.

Solá, Donald, and Antonio Cusihuamán Gutiérrez. 1978. The Structure of Cusco Quechua. Mimeographed. Cornell University.

Spedding, Alison. 1998. Contra-afinidad: Algunos comentarios sobre el compadrazgo andino. *In* Gente de carne y hueso: Las tramas de parentesco en los Andes, Vol. 2, Parentesco y género en los Andes, Denise Y. Arnold, ed., 115–137. La Paz: Centre for Indigenous America Studies and Exchange/Instituto de Lengua y Cultura Aymara.

————. 1997a. "Esa mujer no necesita hombre": En contra de la "dualidad andina"— imágenes de género en Los Yungas de La Paz. *In* Más allá del silencio: Fronteras de género en los Andes, Vol. 1, Denise Arnold, ed., pp. 325–343. La Paz: Centre for Indigenous America Studies and Exchange/Instituto de Lengua y Cultura Aymara.

————. 1997b. Investigaciones sobre género en Bolivia: Un comentario crítico. *In* Más allá del silencio: Fronteras de género en los Andes, Vol. 1, Denise Arnold, ed., pp. 53–74. La Paz: Centre for Indigenous America Studies and Exchange/Instituto de Lengua y Cultura Aymara.

Spivak, Gayatri Chakravorty. 1988. In Other Worlds: Essays in Cultural Politics. New York: Routledge.

————. 1985. Can the subaltern speak?: Speculations on widow-sacrifice. Wedge 7/8: 120–130.

Stack, Carol B. 1997 [1974]. All Our Kin. New York: Basic Books.

Starn, Orin. 1999. Nightwatch: The Politics of Protest in the Andes. Durham, NC: Duke University Press.

————. 1994. Rethinking the politics of anthropology: The case of the Andes. Current Anthropology 35(1): 13–38.

————. 1991. Missing the revolution: Anthropologists and the war in Peru. Cultural Anthropology 6(1): 63–91.

Steedman, Carolyn Kay. 1994. Landscape for a Good Woman: A Story of Two Lives. New Brunswick, NJ: Rutgers University Press.

Stephenson, Marcia. 1999. Gender and Modernity in Andean Bolivia. Austin: University of Texas Press.

Stern, Steve, ed. 1987. Resistance, Rebellion, and Consciousness in the Andean Peasant World, 18th to 20th Centuries. Madison: University of Wisconsin Press.

Stobart, Henry, and Rosaleen Howard, eds. 2002. Knowledge and Learning in the Andes: Ethnographic Perspectives. Liverpool: Liverpool University Press.

Stoler, Ann Laura. 1991. Carnal knowledge and imperial power: Gender, race, and morality in colonial Asia. In Gender at the Crossroads of Knowledge: Feminist Anthropology in a Postmodern Era, Micaela de Leonardo, ed., pp. 51–101. Berkeley: University of California Press.

Strathern, Andrew. 1996. Body Thoughts. Ann Arbor: University of Michigan Press.

Strathern, Marilyn. 1991. After Nature: English Kinship in the Late Twentieth Century. Cambridge: Cambridge University Press.

Suleri, Sara. 1992. Woman skin deep: Feminism and the postcolonial condition. Critical Inquiry 18: 756–769.

Szeminski, Jan. 1987. Why kill the Spaniard?: New perspectives on Andean insurrectionary ideology in the 18th century. In Resistance, Rebellion, and Consciousness in the Andean Peasant World, 18th to 20th Centuries, Steve J. Stern, ed., pp. 166–192. Madison: University of Wisconsin Press.

Tapias, Maria. 2006a. "Always ready and always clean?": Competing discourses of breast-feeding, infant illness and the politics of mother-blame in Bolivia. Body and Society 12(2): 83–108.

————. 2006b. Emotions and the intergenerational embodiment of social suffering in rural Bolivia. Medical Anthropological Quarterly 20(3): 399–415.

Taussig, Michael. 1987. Shamanism, Colonialism, and the Wild Man: A Study in Terror and Healing. Chicago and London: University of Chicago Press.

————. 1980. The Devil and Commodity Fetishism in South America. Chapel Hill: University of North Carolina Press.

Tedlock, Barbara. 1991. From participant observation to the observation of participation: The emergence of narrative ethnography. Journal of Anthropological Research 47(1): 69–94.

Tedlock, Dennis. 1995. Interpretation, participation, and the role of narrative in dialogical anthropology. *In* The Dialogic Emergence of Culture, Dennis Tedlock and Bruce Mannheim, eds., pp. 253–287. Urbana: University of Illinois Press.

———. 1990. From voice and ear to hand and eye. Journal of American Folklore 103: 133–156.

———. 1983. The Spoken Word and the Work of Interpretation. Philadelphia: University of Pennsylvania Press.

Tedlock, Dennis, and Bruce Mannheim, eds. 1995. The Dialogic Emergence of Culture. Urbana: University of Illinois Press.

Thornton, Arland. 2001. The developmental paradigm, reading history sideways, and family change. Demography 38(4): 449–466.

Trawick, Margaret. 1990. Notes on Love in a Tamil Family. Berkeley: University of California Press.

Trouillot, Michel-Rolph. 1991. Anthropology and the savage slot: The poetics and politics of otherness. *In* Recapturing Anthropology: Working in the Present, Richard G. Fox, ed., pp. 17–44. Santa Fe, NM: School of American Research Press.

Turner, Bryan. 1984. The Body and Society: Explorations in Social Theory. Oxford: Blackwell.

Turner, Victor. 1986. The Anthropology of Performance. New York: PAJ Publications.

———. 1969. The Ritual Process: Structure and Anti-Structure. Chicago: Aldine Publication Company.

Urban, Greg. 1991. A Discourse-Centered Approach to Culture. Austin: University of Texas Press.

———. 1984. Speech about speech in speech about action. Journal of American Folklore 97: 310–328.

Urbano, Henrique, ed. 1993. Mito y simbolismo en los Andes. Cusco, Peru: Centro de Estudios Regionales Andinos: "Bartolomé de las Casas."

Urton, Gary. 1985. Animal metaphors and the life cycle in an Andean community. *In* Animal Myths and Metaphors in South America, Gary Urton, ed., pp. 251–284. Salt Lake City: University of Utah Press.

Valderrama, Ricardo, and Carmen Escalante. 1998. Matrimonio en las comunidades quechuas andinas. *In* Gente de carne y hueso: Las tramos de parentesco en los Andes, vol. 2, Parentesco y género en los Andes, Vol. 2, Denise Y. Arnold, ed., pp. 291–322. La Paz: Centre for Indigenous America Studies and Exchange/Instituto de Lengua y Cultura Aymara.

———. 1997. Ser mujer: *Warmi kay*—La mujer en la cultura andina. *In* Más allá del silencio: Fronteras de género en los Andes, Vol. 1, Denise Arnold, ed., pp. 153–170. La Paz: Centre for Indigenous America Studies and Exchange/Instituto de Lengua y Cultura Aymara.

Van Vleet, Krista E. 2003a. Adolescent ambiguities and the negotiation of belonging in the Andes. Ethnology 42(4): 349–363.

———. 2003b. Partial theories: On gossip, envy and ethnography in the Andes. Ethnography 4(4): 491–519.

———. 2002. The intimacies of power: Rethinking violence and kinship in the Andes. American Ethnologist 29(3): 567–601.

———. 1999. "Now My Daughter Is Alone": Performing Kinship and Embodying Affect in Marriage Practices among Native Andeans in Bolivia. Ph.D. dissertation. Department of Anthropology, University of Michigan.

Wade, Peter. 1997. Race and Ethnicity in Latin America. London: Pluto Press.

Weismantel, Mary. 2001. Cholas and Pishtacos: Stories of Race and Sex in the Andes. Chicago: University of Chicago Press.

———. 1997. White cannibals: Fantasies of racial violence in the Andes. Identities 4(1): 9–44.

———. 1995. Making kin: Kinship theory and Zumbagua adoptions. American Ethnologist 22(4): 685–709.

———. 1988. Food, Gender, and Poverty in the Ecuadorian Andes. Philadelphia: University of Pennsylvania Press.

Weston, Kath. 2001. Kinship, controversy, and the sharing of substance: The race/class politics of blood transfusion. *In* Relative Values: Reconfiguring Kinship Studies, Sarah Franklin and Susan McKinnon, eds., pp. 147–174. Durham, NC: Duke University Press.

———. 1991. Families We Choose: Lesbians, Gays, Kinship. New York: Columbia University Press.

White, Hayden. 1987. The Content of the Form: Narrative Discourse and Historical Representation. Baltimore, MD: Johns Hopkins University Press.

White, Luise. 2000. Speaking with Vampires: Rumor and History in Colonial Africa. Berkeley: University of California Press.

Wikan, Unni. 1990. Managing Turbulent Hearts: A Balinese Formula for Living. Chicago: University of Chicago Press.

Williams, Raymond. 1977. Marxism and Literature. Oxford: Oxford University Press.

———. 1961. The Long Revolution. New York: Columbia University Press.

Wilson, Fiona. 1984. Marriage, property, and the position of women in the Peruvian Central Andes. *In* Kinship Ideology and Practice in Latin America, Raymond T. Smith, ed., pp. 297–325. Chapel Hill: University of North Carolina Press.

Woolard, Kathryn. 1992. Language ideology: Issues and approaches. Pragmatics 2: 235–249.

Yanagisako, Sylvia, and Jane Collier. 1987. Toward a unified analysis of gender and kinship. *In* Gender and Kinship: Essays toward a Unified Analysis, Jane F. Collier and Sylvia J. Yanagisako, eds., pp. 14–50. Stanford: Stanford University Press.

Yanagisako, Sylvia, and Carol Delany, eds. 1995. Naturalizing Power: Essays in Feminist Cultural Analysis. New York: Routledge.

Yuval-Davis, Nira. 1997. Gender and Nation. London: Sage.

Zavella, Patricia. 1997. "Playing with fire": The gendered construction of Chicana/Mexicana sexuality. *In* The Gender/Sexuality Reader: Culture, History, Political Economy, Roger Lancaster and Micaela di Leonardo, eds., pp. 392–408. New York: Routledge.

Zuidema, R. Tom. 1990. Inca Civilization in Cuzco. Jean-Jacques Decoster, trans. Austin: University of Texas Press.

———. 1989. The moieties of Cuzco. *In* The Attraction of Opposites, David Maybury-Lewis and Uri Almagor, eds., pp. 255–275. Ann Arbor: University of Michigan Press.

———. 1978. Shafttombs and the Inca empire. Journal of the Steward Anthropological Society 9: 133–178.

———. 1964. The Ceque System of Cuzco: The Social Organization of the Capital of the Inca. Leiden: E. J. Brill.

Zuidema, R. Tom, and Ulpiano Quispe. 1968. "A visit to God": The account and interpretation of a religious experience in the Peruvian community of Choque Huarcaya. Bijdragen Tot de Taal-, Land-, en Volkenkunde 124: 22–39.

Zuidema, R. Tom, and Gary Urton. 1976. La constelación de la llama en los Andes peruanos. Allpanchis 9: 59–119.